T4-AHV-644

VANCOUVER ISLAND

Land of Contrasts

DISCARDED
& BALMORAL
MAN.
CANADA

DISCARDED

GB
132
B7V3

VANCOUVER ISLAND

Land of Contrasts

edited by

CHARLES N. FORWARD

Western Geographical Series Volume 17

Department of Geography, University of Victoria
Victoria, British Columbia
Canada

1979   University of Victoria

Western Geographical Series, Volume 17

editorial address

Harold D. Foster, Ph.D.
Department of Geography
University of Victoria
Victoria, British Columbia
Canada

Publication of the Western Geographical Series has been generously supported by the Leon and Thea Koerner Foundation, the Social Science Federation of Canada, the National Centre for Atmospheric Research, the International Geographical Union Congress, the University of Victoria and the National Research Council of Canada.

Copyright 1979, University of Victoria

VANCOUVER ISLAND
(Western geographical series; v. 17 ISSN 0315-2022)
Bibliography: p.
ISBN 0-919838-07-3
1. Vancouver Island—Description and travel.   2. Physical geography—British Columbia—Vancouver Island. I. Forward, Charles N. II. University of Victoria (B.C.). Dept. of Geography. III. Series.
FC3844.4.V35   917.11'34'02   C79-091020-9   F1089.V3V35

ALL RIGHTS RESERVED

This book is protected by copyright.
No part of it may be duplicated or reproduced
in any manner without written permission.

ACKNOWLEDGEMENTS

This volume has been published with the financial assistance of the Natural Sciences and Engineering Research Council of Canada. Its production is designed to commemorate the hosting, by the University of Victoria, of the May 28-May 31, 1979 Annual Meeting of the Canadian Association of Geographers.

Many staff and faculty members have assisted in the production of this volume. Initial manuscript drafts were typed by Eleanor Harbord, Linda Williams, Maureen Cummings, Laurel Carr and Renee Stovold. Gilian McDade assisted with proofreading. The cartography is the work of Ole Heggen, Ken Quan and Ian Norie, the latter supervising the work and acting as production manager for the volume. Ian Norie also designed the cover and was responsible for photography. Diane Brazier undertook the demanding tasks of typesetting and layout.

The volume is amply illustrated with photographs provided by many individuals and organizations. These are acknowledged in the text. Special mention must be made of the permission granted by P and R Enterprises allowing the republication of a portion of their copyrighted 'Space Photomap of Vancouver Island and the Lower Mainland.' Readers wishing to purchase complete copies of this publication can do so from P and R Enterprise, c/o 1340 Wain Road, R.R. 1, Sidney, B.C., V8L 4R9.

The assistance of all these individuals is very gratefully acknowledged.

University of Victoria   Harold D. Foster
Victoria, B.C.   Series Editor
January, 1979

PREFACE

One of the great traditions of geography is the regional or area study method of achieving an overall appreciation of the character and function of a region. Vancouver Island is a well defined region for study because the water barriers around an island create sharp and satisfying boundaries. The concept of the book was firmly rooted in the regional tradition and the goal was to produce a comprehensive geography of Vancouver Island. Such regional studies of parts of Canada, hopefully, will fill a gap in the geographic literature by providing building blocks for a greater, in-depth understanding of Canada as a whole.

Admittedly, not all of the authors conceived of their work as furthering the regional tradition, but, together, the systematic, individualistic contributions injected into a conventional, regional study mold constitute a comprehensive view of the region. A further benefit of the individualistic approach within each chapter is the diversity of viewpoints that results. This may seem like a rationalization or justification for the production of a multi-authored work, but without a team effort this study could not have been produced.

In a sense it was a labour of love. When it became known that the University of Victoria would host the Annual Meeting of the Canadian Association of Geographers for the first time in 1979 the idea arose that the Department of Geography should produce a comprehensive work on Vancouver Island in honour of the occasion. Pride in their Island homeland and the wish to convey to others the nature of this somewhat remote and little known Island motivated the members of the Department to undertake original research and contribute chapters to the joint effort embarked upon. To a considerable extent, the division of labour was according to academic fields of interest and attests to the diversity of expertise that the Department contains, running the gamut of physical, economic and cultural geographic specialties.

The book is divided into five distinct parts and the major topics are organized in a traditional, regional study framework. The stage is set with a consideration of settlement and population characteristics. In the second part the physical environment is portrayed, followed in part three by studies of the natural resource industries. The fourth part is focused on utilities and their resource bases, including water, energy and transportation. Among the many economic and cultural topics that might be considered in portraying the secondary, tertiary, recreational, behavioural and social dimensions, a few have been selected and grouped in part five, namely, manufacturing, parks, tourism and urban social patterns. A photographic essay illustrating many elements of the Island's character complements the text.

The book is a contemporary geographic work in that all of the topics are dealt with in the present context, but many of the chapters contain historical sections that explain how the present environment evolved. In addition, many of the authors venture glances into the future and some suggest courses of action that should be taken, although the book was not designed as a policy statement. Its main purpose is to acquaint the reader with the rich diversity of Vancouver Island in terms of its form, function and character, and as an important region of Canada.

Charles N. Forward

Department of Geography
University of Victoria
Victoria, British Columbia

A Note on Metrication

Although Canada is in the process of converting to the metric system, figures are quoted in both metric and English measurements, except in the chapter on climate where dual notations would clutter the text excessively. This was done as a concession to readers in the United States where the English system is still in use, and to those who have not yet become fully familiar with the metric system.

PLATE 1   Victoria: capital city.   *I.H. Norie Photo* ▶

TABLE OF CONTENTS

LIST OF TABLES

LIST OF FIGURES

LIST OF PLATES

Plates

PLATE 2   Building Mosaic (by I.H. Norie).   *B.C. Government Photos* ▶

PLATE 3   A Victorian celebration.   *Jim Ryan Photo* ▶

THE PEOPLE

INTRODUCTION

Vancouver Island is a land of many contrasts. It was on its south-eastern coastal plain that European settlement first developed beyond the stage of the isolated fur trading post. Yet, this most historic cultural landscape in British Columbia abuts the wilderness frontier that still constitutes the greater part of the Island. Even metropolitan Victoria, its largest city, is little more than a tiny bridgehead of urbanization at the southern tip. Its abbreviated rural settlement exists as a few strings and patches along the coasts, instead of the robust development that surrounds most Canadian cities. As a result, Victoria is practically bereft of a tributary area, and ranks near the bottom of the list of major Canadian cities as a wholesaling centre. This lack of an extensive agricultural hinterland, however, bestows the great virtue of a scenic mountainous terrain within easy reach of the urban dwellers for their enjoyment and recreation. Many other contrasts exist as well, mostly related to this basic duality or to the notable physical environmental variations that abound.

The Indian occupance of Vancouver Island and the intrusion of European explorers, followed by settlers, are the introductory topics of Chapter 1 on settlement and population. The growth of population and the major factors responsible are traced through more than a century since colonial times. A brief consideration of the present urban hierarchy and demographic structure provides a background for the more detailed investigation of ethnic groups in Chapter 2. A systematic approach is employed, each ethnic group being considered separately, in order to trace its role and distinctiveness through time. Although the Island's population today is more than two-thirds of British origin, there is a rich mixture of other groups, many of whom have retained their identity and make a valued contribution to cultural diversity.

PLATE 4 Playing the game. *B.C. Archives Photo* ▶

1

1 SETTLEMENT AND POPULATION

Colin J.B. Wood

The cultural geography of Vancouver Island is comprised of several distinct and colourful strands, with the settlement of the land being, perhaps, the strongest thread in the fabric of human occupance. In this chapter a description will be undertaken of the main elements of the Indian and European settlement patterns, together with a brief note on the Island's demography. In this way, it is hoped that the reader will obtain an understanding of the Island's personality and its origins.

INDIAN SETTLEMENT

While the archaeological record is still incomplete, it is clear that the Indian people have occupied Vancouver Island for several thousand years.[1] During this period a tribal, village society evolved whose economy was based on fishing, collecting and hunting. The prolific marine and forest resources found along the coasts enabled a thriving primitive culture to flourish.[2] Rich in oral tradition and artistic expression, two main linguistic families developed and continue to exist, Salishan and Wakashan, the latter having distinct subdivisions of Nootka and Kwakiutl. Further sub-categorization according to language and dialect is also possible (Figure 1,1). Each language group is comprised of smaller tribal bodies which are identified with a particular location and territory.[3] For example, the Cowichan people are Coastal Salish and originally dwelt in seven villages in the Cowichan River area (Figure 1,1).

Traditionally, villages were comprised of several stoutly constructed cedar longhouses and usually were situated in sheltered coves or a short distance up-river from the sea. The prevalence of internecine warfare meant that defence was an element in site selection. During the hunting season each tribe would migrate through a well defined territory. In the

3

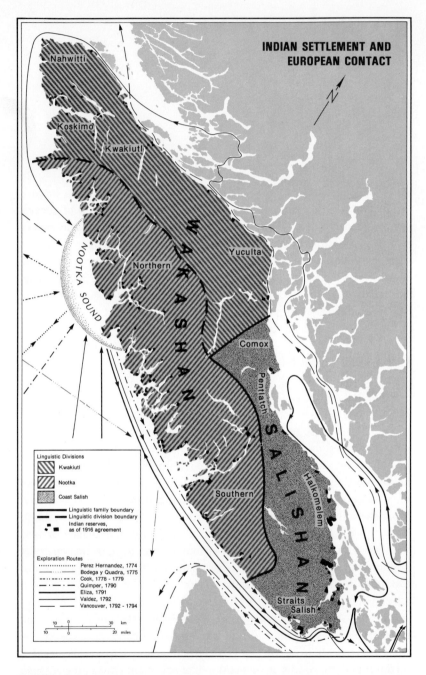

FIGURE 1,1 Indian Reserves, linguistic divisions and European exploration routes by sea.

early nineteenth century the population was probably about 15,000.[4] It is clear that the Indian people lived in equilibrium and harmony with the physical environment and made little impact upon it.

EUROPEAN SETTLEMENT

Spanish, Russian, French, British and American explorers and traders began penetrating the waters of the northeast Pacific in the eighteenth century (Figure 1,1). The Spanish established a small garrison at Nootka Sound in 1789. However, Britain gradually ousted the other contenders from the region through the activities of its trading companies, the Royal Navy's presence, and negotiation and threat in Europe.[5] George Vancouver's circumnavigation and hydrographic survey of the Island between 1792 and 1794 provided the information for increased British penetration and left his name as a legacy. The diversity of Spanish and British place names with which the Island and its waters abound are a permanent record of this exploratory period.

Dissatisfaction with Fort Vancouver in Oregon led the Hudson's Bay Company to search for a Pacific base more accessible to the ocean in the late 1830's. This became a reality in 1843 when:

> ...early in the spring of the year, the Hudson's Bay
> Company first effected a settlement in Vancouver
> Island. They landed about forty men under charge
> of Mr. Finlayson, and in a very short time con-
> structed a picket enclosure...they landed at Vic-
> toria, called then by the Natives, Tsomus, from the
> name of the tribe which lives there.[7]

The wisdom of this move was reinforced by the effects of the Oregon Boundary Treaty of 1846 which prompted the Hudson's Bay Company to withdraw from the lower Columbia region of Oregon Territory when the boundary between American and British claims was finally determined.[8] With the foundation of Victoria, the trader's arrival was one of the seeds which would germinate and eventually flourish as British Columbia. In 1849 the Colony of Vancouver Island was proclaimed; New Caledonia, the mainland, was renamed British Columbia in 1858 and the two colonies united in 1866, joining Canada in 1871.

The European population grew slowly, partly due to the relatively high price of land, and partly to its isolation. The Hudson's Bay Company

5

which effectively controlled the Colony until 1859 established a price of one pound per acre, at a time when free or nominally priced land was available in many other frontier regions.[9] In contrast, the Indian population declined, decimated by alcohol and European diseases introduced in the early 1860's; it was a downward trend which would not be reversed until the 1940's. Settlement clustered around Victoria in the 1850's, as company farms were established to serve the fort with fresh food.[10] A particular attraction of this region for the first settlers was the open, park-like oak woodlands, with their rich black soil. The discovery of coal farther north along the east coast induced the Company to set up two small settlements at Fort Rupert in 1849 and Nanaimo in 1851 to exploit this resource. The first site never really developed, owing to the poor quality and limited extent of coal, whereas Nanaimo grew to be the major coal producer of the west coast of North America during the nineteenth and early twentieth centuries.[11] It had the advantage, moreover, of a strategic, mid-Island position opposite the mouth of the Fraser River, while Fort Rupert was isolated.

The discovery of gold on the mainland along the Fraser River and coal on the Island led to the first significant increase in population in the 1860's, even though much of it was transient in nature. Some of those disappointed in the gold fields turned to farming and coal mining and joined the growing trickle of settlers carving out homesteads on the narrow eastern lowlands of the Island, now that the Company no longer controlled development.

Two other foci of settlement were established at this time, the Duncan area of the Cowichan River valley[12] and the Courtenay-Comox region (Figure 2,1).[13] Both valleys seemed attractive and fertile to the incoming settlers: they offered open, park-like land, a major asset in an age when land clearing relied mainly on human muscle and animal power. Although the forest was an obstacle to the pioneer farmer, its sheer quantity and high quality stimulated the growth of lumber mills at points accessible to tidewater, such as Port Alberni (1861) and Chemainus (1862), which became nuclei for further urban growth.

In direct contrast to the eastern lowlands, the wetter, more rugged and exposed west and north coasts attracted few settlers other than traders, missionaries, and fishermen engaged in sealing and whaling operations. Where some settlement was possible, as in the San Juan Valley, pioneering did not develop until the 1880's. Even those land grants were abandoned within a few decades, mainly due to isolation. A major settlement of Scottish crofters was purposed but never materialized, although the dream survives in the name, Port Renfrew.[14]

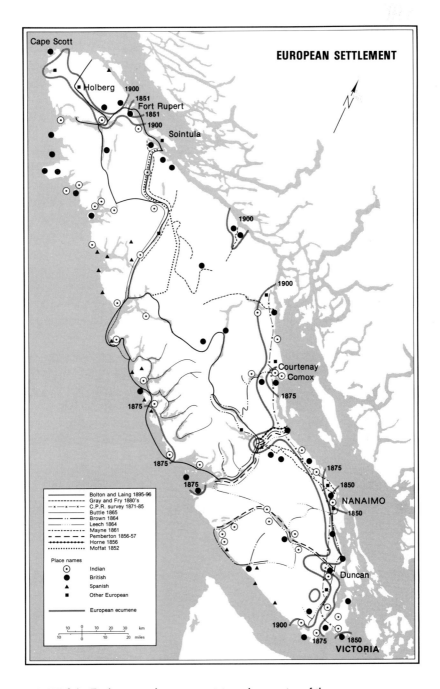

EUROPEAN SETTLEMENT

Cape Scott

Holberg 1900
          1851
          Fort Rupert
          1851
          1900
          Sointula

1900

1900

1900

Courtenay
Comox

1875

1875

1875

1875

1875

1875   1850

NANAIMO
    1850

Duncan

1900   1875   1850
                VICTORIA

Bolton and Laing 1895-96
Gray and Fry 1880's
C.P.R. survey 1871-85
Buttle 1865
Brown 1864
Leech 1864
Mayne 1861
Pemberton 1856-57
Horne 1856
Moffat 1852

Place names
⊙ Indian
● British
▲ Spanish
■ Other European

— European ecumene

10   0   10   20   30 km
10   0   10   20 miles

FIGURE 2.1 Exploration, place name origin and expansion of the ecumene.

7

In the north, some attempts at occupation were made before the turn of the century and, unlike the predominantly British tone of the south, small communities of French Canadians and Scandinavians were the first arrivals. French Canadians settled in the Salmon River area north of Campbell River during the depression of the 1890's.[15] Norwegians pioneered at Quatsino in 1891 and Danish people established farms in the Cape Scott and Holberg Inlet areas in 1897, but the majority of the latter group eventually abandoned their settlements in the face of an adverse climate and the deprivations associated with isolation.[16] At Sointula, a Finnish group, many of whom had worked in the Vancouver Island coal mines, set up a utopian, cooperative community in 1901, but many had left the Island by 1905 (Figure 2,1).[17]

As a result, the ecumene, historically, was mainly restricted to the eastern and southern parts of the Island (Figure 2,1). There, the construction of the Esquimalt and Nanaimo Railway in 1886 provided the infrastructure for expansion of the lumber and mining industries. The reservation of land for the railway prevented further settlement for a decade, although this did not deter squatters. With the limited agricultural potential and slow but steady expansion of forestry, mining, and urban settlement, the population of the Island at the turn of the century stood at about 51,000, with nearly ninety percent concentrated in the Victoria-Nanaimo region (Table 1,1).[18]

Two significant features of European settlement warrant special attention. First, there was little opposition from the indigenous Indian people who were generally friendly, perhaps overawed by the occasional show of Imperial colonial power, and undoubtedly weakened by the smallpox epidemics of the 1860's. Their predominantly coastal way of life did not conflict unduly with the incoming pioneer farmers, lumber developers and mine operators. Moreover, the Hudson's Bay Company entered into a series of treaties to transfer to the Europeans Indian rights to land and resources, a process which seemed reasonably fair at the time, but in modern terms seems to have been an autocratic take-over.[19] By 1861 a land title and Indian reserve system was established, although some land surveys of the eastern part of the Island had been carried out in the late 1850's. During the following decades, Indian claims to land were dismissed or ignored, a sordid aspect of the European settlement which, like the railway land grant, has risen again to confront the provincial and federal governments of today. Remnants of the Indian occupance survive as the ''native archipelago'' of 180 reservations, comprising 0.3 percent of the total land area, and in numerous Indian place names

8

TABLE 1,1 Population Growth, Vancouver Island and British Columbia, 1881-1976

Year	Vancouver Island	British Columbia
1881	17,292	49,459
1891	37,744	98,173
1901	50,888	178,657
1911	81,241	392,480
1921	108,792	524,582
1931	120,933	694,263
1941	150,407	817,861
1951	215,003	1,165,210
1961	290,835	1,629,082
1971	381,292	2,184,621
1976	441,417	2,466,608

SOURCE: *Census of Canada*, 1881-1976.

(Figure 1,1). Second, a high proportion of the settlers in the nineteenth century were from Britain, many of whom had made the trip "around the Horn". They were attracted by the strong similarity in climate to the "old country" and the protection afforded them in a quiet backwater of the Empire. The relatively short period of settlement, slightly more than five generations, together with the isolation from mainland Canada has somewhat perpetuated the British flavour of the Island.[21] This has been reinforced recently by the canny eye of the tourism promoter and a continued preference for the region by British immigrants.

The period 1901-1921 saw the Island's population more than double from about 50,000 to over 100,000. Immigration continued, as the lumber and mining industries developed. Nanaimo expanded and new mines were opened at Cumberland, Ladysmith and Union Bay, their pits disgorging over 2,000,000 tons of coal annually. Travelling through the region today it is difficult to visualize the great hive of coal mining activity which existed from the mid-nineteenth century until the late 1930's. Cumberland had six pits in production at one time and Nanaimo ten, but by the 1930's the best seams of coal were exhausted.[22] While Cumberland suffered a decline in population which would last for three decades, Nanaimo has been able to benefit from its role as a port and from the general growth of the lumber industry in the mid-island region. Boom conditions also existed at Crofton at the turn of the century where one of the smelters for the copper-zinc mines of the Duncan area was situated.[23]

The evolution of the main threads of the Island's cultural landscape up to World War I can be illustrated by using the Duncan area as an example (Figure 3,1). The missionaries, explorers and surveyors intruded upon the original Indian base, followed by three waves of resource developers: farmers, lumbermen and miners. The railways brought improved transportation, facilitating resource development, and the townsite of Duncan became established as the regional centre.[24]

The pace of population growth between 1921 and 1941 slowed appreciably (Table 2,1). Little suitable land remained for extensive agricultural settlement and the exhaustion of the best coal deposits meant that further development could be linked only with the expansion of the forest products, hardrock mining and fishing industries. The potential for tourism was gradually becoming apparent, as road communications improved, and so also was the attraction of the region as a retirement area.[25]

The postwar period saw a new surge of growth, with population nearly doubling between 1941 and 1961 to a total of 291,000. This has been associated with a continued rise in activity in the forest products industry, with new or expanded mills at Port Alberni, Crofton, Campbell River and Gold River (Figure 4,1). The government has become more actively involved in the development and management of the growing provincial economy. Thus, the administrative and agency functions have expanded, with Victoria, as the provincial capital, being the main beneficiary of this change. Population growth rates during the present century illustrate well the crest and trough elements of natural resource development cycles. Yet, clearly, the Island has lagged behind the Province as a whole in rate of growth, except during the most recent period (Table 2,1). Recent elements of growth, which in turn have stimulated it further, have been highway and hydro-electric power construction, modernization of the ferry system and the expansion of military bases. Rising

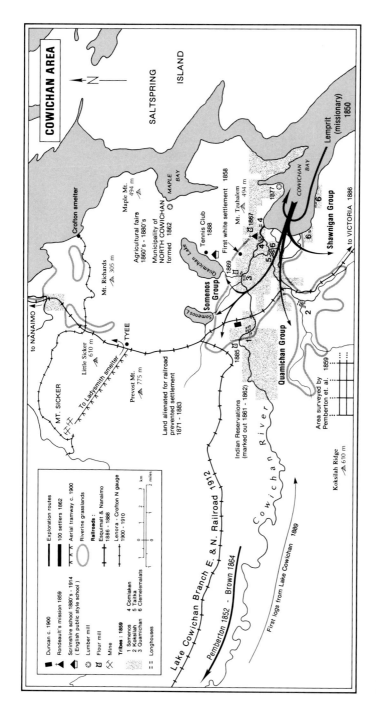

FIGURE 3.1 Settlement in the lower Cowichan region.

11

TABLE 2,1 Percentage Change in Population,
Vancouver Island and British Columbia

	1901-1921	1921-1941	1941-1961	1961-1976
Vancouver Island	100	38	87	52
British Columbia	190	56	99	51

incomes and greater leisure time, coupled with the Island's physical attractions, have boosted the tourist and retirement sectors of the service industries.

Despite the century of occupance, the population is still concentrated along the southeastern lowland, the original entry point for European settlers (Figures 2,1 and 4,1). The west and north are very sparsely populated, aside from a scatter of resource-oriented towns. This ribbon of humanity is remarkably thin in places; squeezed between sea and mountain, areas of high population density often have abrupt transitions from subdivision split levels to wilderness mountains, forests and rushing streams.

Yet, the small total population and limited extent of ecumene must not detract from the appreciable impact of the European settlement on the environment. In contrast to the Indian settlement's harmony with nature the keynote of European contact and occupation has been, and continues to be, resource exploitation and depletion: only recently has it become resource conservation.[26]

URBAN HIERARCHY

Today, the majority of the Island's population lives in Victoria, Duncan, Nanaimo, Port Alberni, Courtenay, Campbell River and numerous small towns and villages (Figure 4,1). Most of the urban settlements owed their origins and early growth to resource extraction or processing. During the present century, those centres which possessed both locational accessibility, as ports or railway stations, and more than one resource extraction activity continued to grow, acquired central place functions and made the successful transition from single resource,

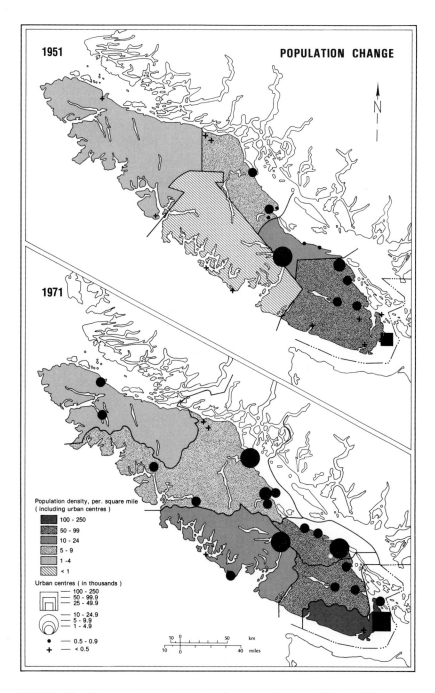

FIGURE 4,1 Urban population and density by census division, 1951 and 1971.

13

TABLE 3,1 Ratios of Males to Females

Year	1911	1921	1931	1941	1951	1961	1971
Ratio	183	123	121	no data	107	103	97

company towns. Others stagnated or became ghost towns, for example, Leechtown and Cumberland.

Victoria had an early lead as a port and administrative centre within the urban system of the Pacific coast region, but with a smaller and less productive hinterland it was soon overtaken by Vancouver and Seattle.[27] Had the capital of the Province been established permanently on the mainland, as nearly happened, Victoria might have remained a small garrison town and retirement centre. Although it is the provincial capital and the Island's metropolis, providing nearly all of the high order urban functions, it suffers from a continual trickle of industry relocating in Vancouver. Nanaimo is the only other place which approaches a city level functional unit. Slightly smaller, Port Alberni lacks Nanaimo's regional focus. Duncan and Courtenay have city incorporations, but in functional terms they are really small towns.[28] The switch in importance from coastal steamer and railway to road transportation and improved ferry systems is reflected in the growth of commercial and light industrial premises along, and oriented to, the main Island Highway.

DEMOGRAPHY

The development of the Island's settlement pattern has been parallelled by the evolution of its demographic structure from a male dominated resource frontier to a family based urban society (Table 3,1). This difference between the past and present persists in areal terms today: the north and west (Mt. Waddington and Alberni Clayoquot census divisions) have a younger population with a higher male ratio than that of the Capital Region Division which has a high proportion of retired people and females (Figure 5,1). This is a reflection of different economic opportunities for the sexes, the attraction of the southeast's environment for senior citizens and the greater longevity of females. Other elements of the human geography of the Island have a noticeable relationship with its

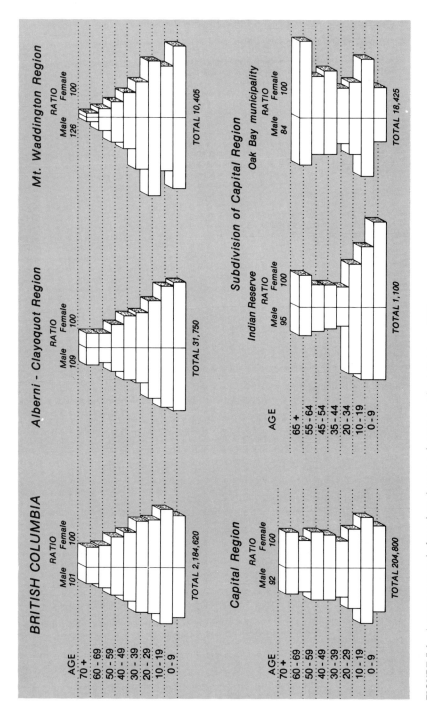

FIGURE 5,1 Age-sex pyramids for selected census divisions and subdivisions, 1971.

15

TABLE 4,1 Common Causes of Death,
Rate per 100,000 Population, 1966-1974

Cause	British Columbia	City of Vancouver	City of Victoria
Lungneoplasm	49.3	52.3	52.0
Motor Accidents	30.0	22.0	26.6
Suicide	15.0	21.5	21.3
Cirrhosis of Liver	11.6	18.5	12.3
Homicide	3.6	4.8	2.3

SOURCE: British Columbia, *Annual Report*. Victoria: Ministry of Health, 1966-1974.

demographic base. For example, the political geography of the Island correlates with the regional variations in demography, economic activity and income. The north and west tend to vote socialist (New Democratic Party) and the southeast, conservative (Progressive Conservative, Social Credit and Liberal). A closer scrutiny of the Capital Region's figures shows that marked differences in demography can occur at the local level. The Municipality of Oak Bay's genteel image and quiet boulevards are magnets for the retired. At the other extreme, the Indian reservations are dominated by young families (Figure 5,1). Population projections forecast that the Island's population will both continue to increase and to age slowly.[29]

An indication of the quality of life enjoyed by a community is given by the rates per 100,000 population of common causes of death.[30] Due to the small sample sizes involved, only a comparison between the cities of Vancouver and Victoria has any real meaning and, even then, any interpretation must be treated with caution (Table 4,1). Curiously, although the rates of causes of death from violence and heavy drinking are significantly higher for Vancouver, suicide rates are identical, and, clearly, driving conditions and/or drivers are poorer in Victoria. Rates for both cities reflect the problems associated with urban living, yet the figures hint that life in Victoria is definitely more tranquil.

CONCLUSION

The European colonization of Vancouver Island has been recent, rapid and concentrated in the southeast, and is in marked contrast to the Indian settlement which evolved along the coasts over a period of several millennia. Waves of resource development and exploitation have generated its settlement and urban growth. Yet, elements of the native culture have survived and, mingling with that of the Europeans, have contributed to the evolution of the regional personality and contemporary human landscape of the Island. This mixture is seen and heard daily in several ways: in the use of Indian, Spanish and English place names; in much of the Island's architecture, where interesting hybrids of American ranch style post and beam, incorporating traditional native building materials, rub shoulders with English tudor; in regional dress, where Cowichan knitwear, a variation on traditional British knitwear incorporating bold Indian designs, is a popular apparel; and in regional dialect, where the pronunciation of many words is different from that of mainland British Columbia and Canada. Whether or not these elements of the region's personality will survive depends on the willingness with which the Islanders accept the pressures of conformity from taste-makers and governments.

REFERENCES

1. CARLSON, R.L. "Archaeology in British Columbia," *B.C. Studies*, 6, (Fall 1970).

2. JENNESS, D. *Indians of Canada*. Ottawa: National Museum of Canada, Bulletin No. 65, Anthropology Ser. No. 15, 5th ed., 1960, pp. 327-350.

3. DUFF, W. *The Indian History of British Columbia*. Victoria: Provincial Museum, Anthropology in B.C., Memoir No. 5, Vol. 1, 1964.

4. *Ibid.*, p. 41.

5. ORMSBY, M.A. *British Columbia: A History*. Toronto: MacMillan, 1971, pp. 16-18. The rivalry between Spain and Britain which led to several incidents along the coast was resolved peacefully by the Nootka Convention, thus permitting further British penetration.

6. *Ibid.*, p. 89.

7. GRANT, W.C. as quoted by HAZLITT, W.C. *British Columbia and Vancouver Island [1858]*. New York: Johnson Reprint Corporation, 1966, p. 157.

8. ORMSBY, M.A., *op. cit.*, p. 93. Fort Victoria became the Hudson's Bay Company western headquarters in 1849. The Island was leased to the Company for ten years for a fee of seven shillings per year.

9.   *Ibid.*, pp. 96-101. There was tremendous argument in London and Victoria over the method of land settlement for the Colony. Through the high price of land, the intention was to set up an English-style squirearchy system.

10.   *Ibid.*, p. 102.

11.   For further information on the development of coal mining *see* JOHNSON, P.M. *A Short History of Nanaimo.* Nanaimo: Evergreen Press, 1958, 55 pp.

12.   DUNCAN, K. *History of Cowichan.* (no date, no place of publication).

13.   HUGHES, B. *History of the Comox Valley.* Nanaimo: Everygreen Press, 1962, p. 11.

14.   GODMAN, J. *Pioneer Days of Port Renfrew.* Victoria: Solitaire Publications, 1973, p. 11.

15.   DUNCAN, F. *The Sayward-Kelsey Bay Saga.* Courtenay: Argus Publications, 1958.

16.   PETERSON, L.R. *The Cape Scott Story.* Vancouver: Mitchell Press, 1974, p. 20.

17.   KOLEHMAINEN, J.I. "Harmony Island," *B.C. Historical Quarterly*, Vol. V (1941), pp. 111-160.

18.   *Census of Canada*, 1901.

19. Government land policy in British Columbia differed from that in the rest of Canada in that the existence of native land entitlement was ignored or denied. See DUFF, W. *op. cit.*, pp. 65-71 and DUFF, W. "The Fort Victoria Treaties," *B.C. Studies*, 3, (1969), pp. 3-57. However, both areas were similar in not following a policy of extermination — a method favoured in many parts of the nineteenth century world, including North America.

20. Canada, *Schedule of Indian Reserves and Settlements*. Ottawa: Department of Indian and Northern Affairs, 1972.

21. For example, the Duncan area had an influx of British immigrants of the tweed and deerstalker variety, as reported in JACKMAN, S.W. *Vancouver Island*. Newton Abbot, Devon: David and Charles, 1972, pp. 46-49. Numerous pamphlets were published to encourage British immigration, for example, *B.C. as a Field for Emigration and Investment*. Victoria: Wolfenden 1891.

22. Vancouver Island had its share of nineteenth century industrial magnates in the Dunsmuir family which owned and developed coal mines and, hence, had an appreciable effect on the rate and direction of settlement. See ORMSBY, M.A., *op. cit.*, p. 306.

23. DUNCAN, K., *op. cit.*, p. 7.

24. FORWARD, C.N. *Land Use of the Victoria Area, B.C.* Ottawa: Department of Energy, Mines and Resources, Geographical Paper No. 43, 1969, p. 9.

25. A government map of 1925, "British Columbia," published by the Department of Lands and Forests, Victoria, shows that the Province had hopes for resources development in practically all parts of the Island. Most of these hopes were unrealistic, due to isolation. Recreation and tourism are stressed as major attractions.

26. See, for example, HAIG-BROWN, R. *Measure of the Year*. Toronto: Collins, 1950, pp. 226-234.

27. FORWARD, C.N., *op. cit.*, p. 9.

28. FORRESTER, E.A.M. "The Urban Hierarchy of Central Vancouver Island," *B.C. Geographical Series*, 24 (1977), pp. 121-135.

29. "Projected School Enrollments in B.C." *Education Today*, 4, No. 6, (1978).

30. British Columbia, *Annual Report*. Victoria: Ministry of Health, 1966-1974.

PLATE 5 Cultural diversity. *B.C. Government Photos* ▶

22

2 ETHNIC GROUPS

Chuen-yan David Lai

One of the major problems in the study of Vancouver Island's ethnicity is the scarcity of information. There are no data, for example, on the Island's various ethnic groups with respect to their age and sex composition, education levels, occupations, birth and death rates, and many other demographic elements. The population returns for Vancouver Island before 1881 classified its residents according to four racial groups, namely, native Indians, White, Chinese and Coloured (mostly American Blacks). When the province of British Columbia was included in the national census in 1881 the population of Vancouver Island was first reported by ethnic group.[1] Succeeding censuses provide the basic documentation for the study of ethnic groups. Population growth, distribution and changing characteristics of the major ethnic groups are the principal themes of this chapter.

EUROPEANS

When the Colony of Vancouver Island was established in 1849, nearly all of the early European immigrants were of British origin because the colony was set up primarily as a bulwark of the British Empire on the Pacific coast of North America. It was not until the onset of the gold rush in 1858 that other peoples surged into the Colony. These new immigrants included many German, French, other European and non-Caucasian people. The British have always been the most numerous group, whereas all other European groups remained small minorities. In 1971, the German, French, Dutch, Norwegian, Ukrainian, Swedish and Italian groups constituted about eighty percent of European minorities. The remaining twenty percent included other European groups, such as Polish, Hungarian, Finnish, Russian, Belgian, and Austrian.

British

The census of 1881 revealed that nearly half of the Island's population was of British origin (Table 1,2). After the turn of the century, the British increased in number so greatly that by 1941 they constituted over seventy-seven percent of the Island's population (Table 2,2). Their proportion has been decreasing since the end of World War II because of the influx of other Europeans, and by 1971 it was down to sixty-nine percent (Table 3,2 and Figure 1,2). Nevertheless, in 1971 English was the mother tongue of nearly ninety percent of the Island's population and was the language most often spoken at home by ninety-seven percent.[2]

Among those of British origin, the English are by far the most numerous, constituting about two-thirds of the total (Table 4,2). Before World War II, about one-third of the English resided in the city of Victoria and their pattern of life and customs represented the social norm to which peoples of other ethnic groups were expected to conform. Victoria prided itself on its English character. With a strong will to preserve their heritage, other peoples of the British Isles established their own associations. For example, the St. Andrew's, Caledonian, Burns and Highland societies, Sons of Scotland, and the *An Comun Gaidhealach* were formed to protect the Scottish heritage, while the Welsh established the St. David's, Welsh and Cambrian societies to promote friendship among their fellow clansmen and to preserve their group ethnicity.[3]

German

The Germans now form the largest European minority, though as recently as 1941 they were exceeded in number by the Scandinavians and French. During the Fraser gold rush a number of Germans came to British Columbia. Many of them were professional men, small businessmen, shopkeepers or artisans, and they settled in Victoria and other Island centres where they were readily integrated into the majority English-speaking community.[4] After the outbreak of World War I some of the older German people who had not been naturalized and still spoke German were pestered. A riot broke out in Victoria on May 8, 1915 after the sinking of the *Lusitania*.[5] The crowd wrecked the Kaiserhof Hotel, German Club, German Consulate, Lenz and Leiser Company, and other businesses whose proprietors had German names (Figure 2,2). Largely because of the anti-German atmosphere during the war, many Germans left the Island. In 1911, for example, the German population in Victoria and Nanaimo was 619 and 498, respectively, but by 1921 it had been

24

TABLE 1,2   Population of Vancouver Island by Ethnic Group, 1881

Ethnic Group	Population	Percentage
British*	8,538	49.4
Native Indian	5,647	32.7
Chinese	980	5.7
German	446	2.6
French	298	1.7
Africans	236	1.4
Scandinavian	87	0.5
Italian	71	0.4
Spanish and Portuguese	72	0.4
Dutch	43	0.2
Swiss	21	0.1
Russian	19	0.1
Jewish	11	0.1
Other	119	0.7
Unknown	704	4.0
Total	17,292	100.0

*Including English (4,780), Scottish (2,114), Irish (1,410) and Welsh (234).

SOURCE: *Census of Canada*, 1881.

reduced to 362 in Victoria and 97 in Nanaimo.[6] Not until the second half of the 1920's was there any significant German migration to the Island and by World War II they numbered little more than 2,000 (Table 2,2). Prejudice against them in that war was minimal because many of them

TABLE 2,2 Population of Vancouver Island by Ethnic Group, 1941

Ethnic Group	Population	Percentage
British	116,092	77.2
German	2,132	1.4
French	2,925	1.9
Scandinavian	5,552	3.7
Dutch	1,152	0.8
Ukrainian	673	0.4
Italian	1,448	1.0
Other European*	5,904	3.9
Chinese	5,653	3.8
Japanese	3,154	2.1
Other Asiatic	610	0.4
Native Indian and Eskimo	4,556	3.0
Other	556	0.4
Total	150,407	100.0

*Including Finnish (1,237), Russian (867), Polish (791), Belgian (457), Austrian (444), Czech and Slovak (352), Jewish (193), Hungarian (179), Romanian (144) and other Europeans (1,240).

SOURCE: *Census of Canada*, 1941.

volunteered for service against the Nazis.[7] Following the war a wave of German immigration led to a rapid increase in their population (Figure 3,2. They became more widely distributed on the Island as their numbers grew, in contrast with their strong concentration in Victoria and vicinity before the war. They were assimilated quickly and by 1971 only nine percent reported that they spoke German most often at home.

TABLE 3,2 Population of Vancouver Island by Ethnic Group, 1971

Ethnic Group		Population	Percentage
British		258,605	69.0
German		21,565	5.8
French		15,705	4.2
Scandinavian		17,780	4.7
Norwegian	7,755		
Swedish	5,130		
Danish	3,820		
Icelandic	1,075		
Dutch		10,060	2.7
Ukrainian		6,110	1.6
Italian		4,840	1.3
Other European*		13,180	3.5
Chinese		5,070	1.4
Japanese		435	0.1
East Indian		3,850	1.0
Other Asiatic		250	0.1
Native Indian		7,225	1.9
Eskimo		30	-
Other		10,035	2.7
Total		374,740**	100.0

*Including Polish (3,905), Hungarian (1,955), Finnish (1,895), Russian (1,370), Austrian (1,230), Belgian (930), Czech (855), Jewish (750), Slovak (140) and other European (150)

**This figure is less than the published census total in Table 1,1 because of random rounding of the ethnic group data for confidentiality by the Data Dissemination Division of Statistics Canada.

SOURCE: *Census of Canada*, 1971.

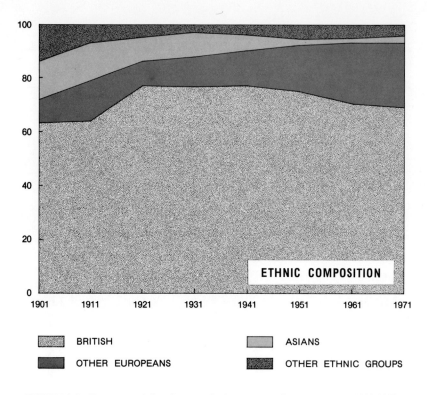

100

80

60

40

20

ETHNIC COMPOSITION

0

1901   1911   1921   1931   1941   1951   1961   1971

BRITISH   ASIANS

OTHER EUROPEANS   OTHER ETHNIC GROUPS

FIGURE 1,2 Proportional distribution of ethnic groups by percentage, 1901-1971.

French

The French, one of the two founding peoples in Canada, were overtaken by the Germans numerically after the 1950's, but their number
increased fivefold from 1941 to 1971 (Tables 2,2 and 3,2). They became so completely assimilated into the predominant English society
that the French ethnic presence was not obvious, although a few traces
may be cited. In Victoria, at one time, there was a French language
parish, and in Port Alberni there was a bilingual parish and a *Caisses
Populaire*, a credit union originating in Quebec.[8] According to the 1971
census, about one-third of the French on the Island regarded French
as their mother tongue, but only 8.6 percent of them spoke it most
often at home.

28

TABLE 4.2 Ethnic Subdivisions of the British Population, 1911, 1941 and 1971

Ethnic Group	1911		1941		1971	
	Population	Percentage	Population	Percentage	Population	Percentage
English	33,925	62	74,239	64	175,675	68
Scottish	14,209	26	26,592	23	50,505	20
Irish	5,597	10	12,448	11	28,890	11
Other*	1,280	2	2,813	2	3,535	1
	55,111	100	116,092	100	258,605	100

*Including Welsh and Manx.

SOURCES: *Census of Canada*, 1911, 1941 and 1971.

29

FIGURE 2,2
German-owned
business premises
after the
May, 1915 riot.

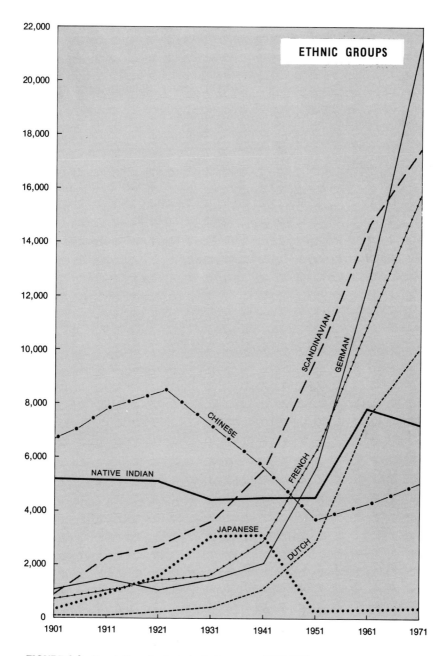

FIGURE 3,2 Population of selected ethnic groups, 1901-1971.

31

Scandinavian

The Scandinavian peoples, namely, the Norwegians, Swedes, Danes and Icelanders, were among the earliest settlers of Vancouver Island.[9] Most of them originally were engaged in farming, fishing, lumbering and mining in the rural areas, and some had attempted to establish permanent settlements on the isolated northwestern coast of the Island. In 1895, the Nova Cooperative Society of Minneapolis established a Norwegian colony of about 200 people near Quatsino Narrows where the land was timbered with hemlock and balsam and the Sound abounded in salmon, halibut, herring, cod and other kinds of fish.[10] Two years later Danish settlers from Enumclaw, Washington set up a colony at Cape Scott where the development of dairy farming, stock raising, and deep sea fisheries was deemed possible.[11] In 1898, the Danish colony had about ninety members.[12] After the turn of the century, many Scandinavians left the rural areas for the cities where they became engaged in various trades. Their population continued to increase and, benefiting from postwar immigration, reached nearly 18,000 by 1971, of which about forty-six percent were Norwegians and twenty-nine percent Swedes (Tables 2,2 and 3,2).

Dutch

The Dutch were readily assimilated into the British culture, partly because most of them had studied English at school and partly because their population was at first minimal. In 1921 there were only 366 Dutch on the Island, over one-third of them residing in Victoria, another third in Nanaimo and the rest mostly in Comox.[13] Throughout the 1930's and 1940's, Dutch immigration continued, owing to population pressure in the Netherlands (Table 3,2). However, the Dutch Empire was the main receiving area of emigrants until it collapsed after World War II. Overcrowding and postwar economic difficulties in the Netherlands forced the Dutch government to encourage emigration. Canada, whose troops had liberated the country from the Germans, was a favoured country for large scale Dutch emigration, by mutual agreement of the Dutch and Canadian governments.[14] Within three decades, from 1941 to 1971, the Dutch population on the Island grew nearly tenfold (Tables 2,2 and 3,2).

Ukrainian

The Ukrainian people were not classified as a separate ethnic group before World War I. In the 1901 and 1911 censuses, those who immigrated to Canada from the Austro-Hungarian Empire were described as "Austro-Hungarians," and those from the Russian Empire as "Russians." After the collapse of these empires the Ukrainians were listed separately, numbering 77 in 1921. During the 1930's, many Ukrainians came from the Prairies and their numbers reached nearly 700 by 1941 (Table 2,2). After World War II, the Ukrainian population increased rapidly, owing to renewed migration from the Prairies and substantial immigration (Table 3,2). Predominantly rural in 1941, the Ukrainian population has become largely urban in residence.

Italian

The Italian community on the Island numbered about 1,400 in 1911 and remained at this level until after World War II (Table 2,2). After the rise of Fascism in Italy there were few male Italian emigrants. Young women coming out to marry Italian men in British Columbia were the main immigrants during the late 1920's and early 1930's.[15] Italian emigration eventually was halted by Mussolini in the 1930's. However, the Italian population more than tripled in the postwar period, with heavy inflows of new immigrants (Tables 2,2 and 3,2).

NATIVE INDIANS

During the colonial period the number of Indians on Vancouver Island was not accurately estimated because of their mobility. Following the arrival of the Europeans the Indian population declined rapidly, mainly because they had no immunity against the introduced diseases, of which smallpox was the worst. The most severe smallpox epidemic, which started in Victoria in April, 1862, spread rapidly up the Island and onto the mainland.[16] When the epidemic was over it had claimed the lives of about 20,000 Indians, or one-third of British Columbia's total.[17] Other diseases, including measles, whooping cough and scarlet fever, took their toll as well, and the native population, which was estimated at about 10,000 in 1865, continued to decline.[18] The census of 1881 reported only 5,600 Indians on the Island. Until the 1950's the native population fluctuated around 5,000, but in recent decades the Indians have increased to more than 7,000, mainly owing to a decrease in their death rate (Tables 2,2 and 3,2).

33

The Indian bands can be classified into three major linguistic groups (Figure 1,1).[19] The largest group, by population, is the Coast Salish, who occupy the entire southeastern portion of Vancouver Island and speak dialects belonging to the Salishan linguistic family.[20] The others are the Nootka, who inhabit the west coast from River Jordan north to Brooks Peninsula, and the Kwakiutl who occupy the northeastern part of the Island south to Cape Mudge. Many of the coastal Indians still depend on fishing, especially for salmon, halibut, cod, and herring, and on the gathering of clams and edible seaweed for their livelihood. They excel in woodworking and are known for their arts and crafts.[21]

The distribution of the Indian population has changed considerably in recent years (Figure 4,2). Traditionally, the Indians lived in villages on their reserves. Even in 1941 only sixteen of the 4,556 Indians on the Island were classified as "urban". This pattern changed rapidly as many Indians left their villages to obtain employment and live elsewhere. In 1971, over fifty-five percent of the native Indians lived outside their reserves and were engaged in various occupations.

ASIANS

British Columbia, historically, has contained a major share of Canada's Asian peoples, mainly because it is the part of the country situated closest to Asia. On Vancouver Island, Asians have formed part of the population since colonial times, the principal groups being the Chinese, Japanese and East Indian. Before World War II, the Chinese and Japanese together accounted for over ninety percent of the Asia total, with East Indians and a few Southeast Asians making up the remainder. By 1971 it was the Chinese and East Indians who constituted over ninety percent of the Island's Asian population, whereas the Japanese had been reduced to only five percent.

Chinese

In June, 1858, the first group of Chinese arrived in Victoria where they equipped themselves as gold seekers and left as soon as possible for the Fraser Valley.[22] However, a few merchants, artisans and craftsmen stayed behind in Victoria where they formed the nucleus of a Chinese community (Figure 5,2).[23] When the coal mining industry was developed at Nanaimo, many Chinese moved there and sought employment in the

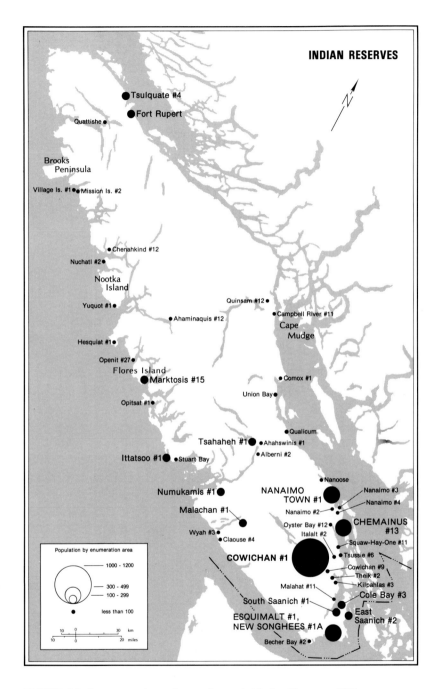

FIGURE 4,2 Location and population of occupied Indian Reserves, 1971.

mines, while others set up businesses in mining districts. The Royal Commission on Chinese Immigration reported that in 1884 the Chinese people numbered 1,767 in Victoria, 685 in Wellington, 169 in Nanaimo, 69 in Wellington District, and 47 in Departure Bay, amounting to 2,736 on Vancouver Island.[24]

The Chinese, at first, were free to enter Canada because they were desperately needed as cheap labourers. As they increased in number they began to compete with white workers for jobs. The anti-Chinese feeling simmering in the 1870's became intense in the early 1880's when thousands of Chinese labourers were recruited by railway contractors for the construction of the Canadian Pacific Railway on the mainland and the Esquimalt and Nanaimo Railway on the Island.

Because of the growing outcry of the white workers in British Columbia against the immigration of Chinese labourers, the Canadian government passed legislation in 1885 imposing a head tax of fifty dollars on each Chinese of the labouring class entering Canada.[25] The tax was raised to 100 dollars in 1900 and to 500 dollars in 1903.[26] Despite this heavy tax, a large number of Chinese continued to emigrate to Canada, mainly because of dire poverty and political unrest at home. Between 1905 and 1911, a total of 9,100 Chinese immigrants paid their head tax and entered Canada.[27] According to the 1911 census, there were 7,800 Chinese on Vancouver Island, as much as one-fifth of the British population at that time and higher than that of any other ethnic group (Figure 3,2). Having failed to restrict Chinese immigration by means of a head tax, the government eventually passed the Chinese Immigration Act in 1923, by which people of Chinese origin or descent were not permitted to enter Canada, with a few exceptions. Entry was confined to students, diplomatic attaches, Chinese children born in Canada and "merchants" who were defined according to whatever regulations the Minister of Immigration and Colonization might prescribe.[28] Under this Act, Chinese domiciled or even those born in Canada were not permitted to bring in their wives and children.

The Chinese population declined after the passing of the 1923 Act which was not repealed until 1947.[29] Since then, Chinese immigrants have come to Canada in increasing numbers, but most have gone to large cities, such as Vancouver, Edmonton, Toronto and Montreal, and only a few have come to Vancouver Island. By 1971, the Chinese population on the Island had risen to a level close to what it was in 1941 (Tables 2,2 and 3,2, and Figure 3,2). Today about sixty-five percent of the Chinese live in metropolitan Victoria and twenty percent in Port Alberni, Nanaimo and

FIGURE 5,2
A Chinese merchant's family in Victoria, late nineteenth century.

FIGURE 6,2
The Victoria Rifle Corps organized in 1861 by American Blacks.

Duncan. All the Chinatowns except Victoria's have disappeared, and even there no more than 200 Chinese still live in Chinatown, most being scattered throughout the metropolitan area.

Japanese

The Japanese did not arrive in sizeable numbers until the 1890's when the Canadian Pacific and Japan Mail lines started their regular trans-Pacific services between Japan and Vancouver.[30] Most of the Japanese immigrants were fishermen or farmers, but some were contract workers. In the 1890's, for example, about 200 Japanese arrived by contract to work in the Union Mine at Cumberland.[31] Since most of the Japanese immigrants were single men, in 1906 they began to arrange for brides to be sent from Japan through the exchange of photographs. As a result, a total of 11,565 Japanese, including many "picture brides," entered Canada between 1906 and 1908, and most of them settled on the Pacific coast.[32]

Because of the growing opposition in British Columbia to Japanese immigration, the Canadian government signed a "gentlemen's agreement" with Japan in 1908, under which Japan agreed to limit by a passport system the emigration to Canada of Japanese subjects of the labouring class to a number not exceeding 400 annually, while Canada would admit the Japanese residents, their wives and children, domestic servants or agricultural labourers engaged by residents, and labourers introduced under contracts by the Dominion government.[33] Unlike the virtual prohibition of Chinese immigration after 1923, this agreement permitted limited Japanese entry, and the number of Japanese on Vancouver Island increased from 981 in 1911 to 3,154 in 1941 (Table 2,2 and Figure 3,2).

The Japanese suffered a complete upheaval in 1942 when they were evacuated from the protected area which was defined as British Columbia west of the coastal mountains.[34] The British Columbia Security Commission undertook the removal of all people of Japanese origin from the protected area to New Denver, Greenwood and road camps in the interior of British Columbia or to the sugar beet fields in Alberta and Manitoba.[35] The process of evacuation was carried out quickly and throughout the war years there were virtually no Japanese within 100 miles of the coast. On Vancouver Island, only thirteen Japanese were permitted to remain. Most of these were married to non-Japanese or were veterans who fought with the Canadian Army during World War I.[36] A survey

THE
UNIVERSITY OF WINNIPEG
PORTAGE & BALMORAL
WINNIPEG. MAN.
CANADA

conducted after the war revealed that eighty percent of the evacuated Japanese did not want to return to their old homes, fifteen percent had no preference and only five percent wanted to move back to the Pacific Coast.[37] Also, the reestablishment of the Japanese was delayed because the wartime restrictions were not lifted until 1949. Relatively few returned to Vancouver Island and even by 1971 the Japanese numbered fewer than 500 (Table 3,2). Whereas most of the prewar Japanese were fishermen and farmers and widely distributed on the Island, the present small community is mainly urban, about one-quarter of them living in metropolitan Victoria.

East Indians

The East Indians came to British Columbia somewhat later than the Chinese and Japanese. Sikhs from the Punjab and some natives of northern Indian, who were working in Burma, Straits Settlement, Hong Kong and China, discovered that wages were much higher in British Columbia and began to cross the Pacific in 1904.[38] Within four years about 5,000, mostly Sikhs, had arrived in the Province.[39] The anti-Oriental agitators were influential in persuading the government to include the "Hindus" with the Japanese and Chinese immigrants, despite the fact that they were British subjects.[40] The Canadian government issued an Order in Council in 1908, declaring its right "to prohibit the landing in Canada of any specified class of immigrants who have come to Canada otherwise than by a continuous journey from the country of which they are natives or citizens on through tickets purchased in that country."[41] The Order also required East Indians to possess 200 dollars on entry to Canada.[42] Since most of the potential East Indian immigrants did not possess that much money, and at that time there were no direct steamship connections between India and Canada. East Indians were practically prohibited from coming to Canada. The official explanation to the British government for the exclusion of these British subjects was said to be based on the grounds of "humanity."

> The native of India is not a person suited to this country (Canada), that, accustomed as many of them are to the conditions of a tropical climate, and possessing manners and customs so unlike those of our own people, their inability to readily adapt themselves to surroundings entirely different could not do other than entail an amount of privation and suf-

39

fering which renders a discontinuance of such immigration most desirable in the interests of the Indians themselves.[43]

Because of the "continuous journey" regulation, East Indian immigration practically ceased after 1908 and in 1911 there were only 307 "Hindus" on Vancouver Island.[44] Subsequently, the "Hindu" population was so small that it was included under the heading of "Other Asians." Not until 1930 were the married East Indians permitted to bring in their wives and unmarried children under the age of eighteen. The postwar influx of East Indians was substantial, especially after 1967 when the Indians, like other nationals, were permitted to enter Canada according to the point system. By 1971, their population on the Island stood at 3,850, of whom about seventy-two percent resided in metropolitan Victoria, Port Alberni and Lake Cowichan.

AMERICAN BLACKS

American Blacks are not an important ethnic group on Vancouver Island today, but were of historical significance because they were the major non-Caucasian group, other than the Chinese, during the 1860's. Most of them came to British Columbia from California during the 1858 gold rush to seek freedom and equal treatment rather than gold. The Californian government had passed various discriminatory laws against them and Governor Douglas assured them that, "if they should come and settle in Victoria, they shall have all the rights and privileges and protection of the laws of the country."[45] The first group to arrive, including farmers, carpenters, hairdressers, and tailors, obtained employment in Victoria or on surrounding farms, while some set up their own businesses. By 1860 there were over 1,000 Blacks on Vancouver Island. They were the only non-white immigrants who had taken the trouble to become naturalized as British subjects and wanted to be assimilated into the white community. Victoria then was described by these early Black immigrants as "a God-sent land for the coloured people," but it did not take them long to discover that Victoria was by no means a sanctuary for non-white peoples.[46] They encountered various forms of debarment and segregation in hotels, inns, whisky shops, the opera house and even in the churches.[47] Having been denied membership in the Victoria fire brigade and police force, they organized the Victoria Pioneer Rifle Corps in 1861, the first volunteer militia in the city[48] (Figure 6,2). After the American Civil War, most of the Blacks returned to the United States, partly because slavery had been abolished and partly because prejudice against them in British Columbia was increasing. By 1870 only 365 Blacks remained on the Island and they have not been reported as a separate ethnic group in succeeding Canadian censuses.[49]

CONCLUSION

Throughout the first half of the twentieth century over seventy-seven percent of the Island's population was of British origin. The Chinese formed the largest ethnic minority, followed by the Scandinavian, Japanese and native Indian groups, as the next most numerous. Unlike the urban-oriented Chinese, the Japanese resided in the coastal and rural areas and were engaged in fishing and farming. Because of the growing anti-Oriental sentiment in British Columbia, Japanese immigration was restricted after 1908 and the Chinese were excluded after 1923. The effects were most pronounced on the Chinese population which declined rapidly. Most of the European minorities grew slowly, although the Scandinavians increased at a higher rate than the others, while the Germans experienced a dip in population induced by World War I.

After World War II, the ethnic composition of Vancouver Island underwent a drastic change. The postwar influx of peoples from Europe greatly altered the population, reducing the British to about sixty-nine percent of the total. Most of the Japanese who had been evacuated from the Island did not return after the war and the present Japanese population is negligible. On the other hand, the East Indian population which was very small before the war has increased rapidly during the past two decades. The Chinese population which had been declining since the 1920's began to rise gradually after the 1947 repeal of the Chinese Immigration Act. No longer the largest ethnic minority, the Chinese also do not confine themselves within Victoria's Chinatown, which is the only Chinatown still surviving on Vancouver Island.

REFERENCES

1. "Ethnic group" refers to ethnic or cultural background traced through the father's side. Language spoken by the person or by his paternal ancestor on first coming to North America was a guide to the determination of ethnic or cultural group in some cases. For further information see the *Dictionary of the 1971 Census Terms*. Ottawa: Statistics Canada, 1972, p. 6.

2. Unless stated otherwise all 1971 statistics were obtained from the Data Dissemination Division of Statistics Canada, as very limited data were published for Vancouver Island.

3. NORRIS, J. (ed.) *Strangers Entertained: A History of the Ethnic Groups of British Columbia*. Vancouver: British Columbia Centennial '71 Committee, 1971, pp. 78-80; and GIBBON, J.M. *Canadian Mosaic*. Toronto: McClelland and Stewart, 1938.

4. NORRIS, J. (ed.), *op. cit.*, p. 99.

5. "Rioters Wreck City Premises," *Colonist*, May 9, 1915, p. 2; and "Crowds Do Much Damage in City," *Victoria Times*, May 10, 1915, pp. I and II.

6. Canada, *Census of Canada*, 1911 and 1921.

7. "Island Germans Pro-Canadian," *Victoria Times*, September 12, 1939, p. 2.

8. NORRIS, J. (ed.), *op. cit.*, p. 89.

9. This definition of the Scandinavian peoples is used in the *Census of Canada*.

10. British Columbia, "Crown Land Surveys for 1895," *Sessional Papers, 1896*. Victoria: British Columbia Legislative Assembly, 1895, p. 835; British Columbia, *Sessional Papers, 1897*. Victoria: British Columbia Legislative Assembly, 1897, pp. 765-776; "Another Colony," *Colonist*, April 2, 1895, p. 1; and "The Scandinavian Colony," *Colonist*, January 10, 1896, p. 2.

11. British Columbia, *Sessional Papers, 1897, op. cit.*, pp. 776-780; British Columbia, *Sessional Papers, 1898*. Victoria: British Columbia Legislative Assembly, 1898, pp. 731-733; and "To Settle the Land," *Colonist*, March 11, 1878, p. 8.

12. British Columbia, *Sessional Papers, 1899*. Victoria: British Columbia Legislative Assembly, 1899, p. 1,321.

13. Canada, *Census of Canada*, 1921.

14. NORRIS, J. (ed.), *op. cit.*, p. 94.

15. "Italians Start Registration, Victoria Follows City's Lead," *Province*, June 12, 1940, p. 5.

16. *Colonist*, 1872. April 26, p. 3; April 8, p. 2; April 30, p. 3; May 8, p. 2; June 5, p. 3; June 19, p. 3; June 21, p. 3; July 7, p. 3; July 11, p. 3; July 22, p. 3; August 7, p. 3; and November 24, p. 3.

17. DUFF, W. *The Indian History of British Columbia: The Impact of the White Man*. Victoria: Provincial Museum, 1964, p. 43.

18. Great Britain, *Blue Books of Statistics [Vancouver Island], 1863-1865*. London: Public Record Office, 1865, pp. 224-225.

19. An Indian band or local tribe is the most fundamental unit which occupies one or a number of village sites and has its own territory. A regional group is a cluster of bands or local tribes living in a well defined area and sharing a common dialect. For further information see Canada, *Indian of British Columbia*. Ottawa: Indian Affairs Branch, 1965.

20. BORDEN, C.E. "Distribution, Culture and Origin of the Indigenous Population of B.C.", *Transactions of the Seventh British Columbia Natural Resources Conference*. Victoria: British Columbia Natural Resources Conference, 1954, pp. 186-196.

21. For further information see Drucker, P. *Cultures of the North Pacific Coast*. San Francisco: Chandler Publishing, 1965.

22. *Victoria Gazette*, June 30, 1858, p. 3.

23. LAI, CHUEN-YAN, "Socio-economic Structures and Viability of Chinatown," in FORWARD, C.N. (ed.) *Residential and Neighbourhood Studies in Victoria*. Victoria: University of Victoria, Department of Geography, Western Geographical Series, Vol. 5, Chap. 3, 1973, p. 102.

24. Canada, *Report and Evidence*. Ottawa: Royal Commission on Chinese Immigration, 1885, p. 363.

25. Canada, "An Act to Restrict and Regulate Chinese Immigration into Canada," *Statutes of Canada, 1885*. Ottawa: Queen's Printer, 1885, Chap. 71, p. 208.

26. Canada, "An Act Respecting and Restricting Chinese Immigration," *Statutes of Canada, 1900*. Ottawa: Queen's Printer, 1900, Chap. 32, p. 216; Canada, "An Act Respecting and Restricting Chinese Immigration," *Statutes of Canada, 1903*. Ottawa: King's Printer, 1903, Chap. 8, p. 106.

27. Canada, *Canada Year Book 1915*, p. 116.

28. Canada, "An Act Respecting Chinese Immigration," *Statutes of Canada, 1923*. Ottawa: King's Printer, 1923, Chap. 38, pp. 303-304; and Canada, "An Act Respecting Chinese Immigration," *Revised Statutes of Canada, 1927*. Ottawa: King's Printer, 1927, Vol. II, Chap. 95, pp. 2,123-2,124.

29. Canada, "An Act to Amend the Immigration Act and to Repeal the Chinese Immigration Act," *Statutes of Canada, 1947*. Ottawa: King's Printer, 1947, Chap. 19, p. 109.

30. NORRIS, J. (ed.), *op. cit.*, p. 220.

31. ADACHI, K. *The Enemy that Never Was: A History of the Japanese Canadians*. Toronto: McClelland and Stewart, 1976, pp. 27-28.

32. Canada, *Canada Year Book*, 1915, p. 117.

33. Canada, *Documents on Canadian External Affairs, 1909-1918*. Ottawa: Department of External Affairs, Vol. 1, 1967.

34. LA VIOLETTE, E.E. "Japanese Evacuation in Canada," *Far Eastern Survey*, II (1942), pp. 163-167. For additional information see "Victoria Japs Start Moving Voluntarily," *Victoria Times*, February 26, 1942, p. 1; "Order Given Japanese to Leave Town," *Colonist*, April 19, 1942, p. 1; "All Japanese Leave Victoria Wednesday," *Victoria Times*, April 20, 1942, p. 1; and "Last of Japanese Leave the Island," *Province*, April 22, 1942, p. 1.

35. Canada, *British Columbia Security Commission Report*. Ottawa: British Columbia Security Commission, 1942.

36. Canada, *Sessional Paper 182[a]*. Ottawa: House of Commons, 19th Parliament, 5th Session, February 28, 1944, pp. 4-5.

37. "Only Small Percentage of Japs Wish to Return to the Coast," *Victoria Times*, January 13, 1948, p. 2.

38. SINGH, S.N. "The Picturesque Immigrant from India's Coral Strand," *Out West*, 30, January-June, 1909, p. 46; and LUGRIN, N.B. "The Far East Comes to Canada," *Victoria Sunday Times Magazine*, September 15, 1951, p. 3.

39. NORRIS, J. (ed.), *op. cit.*, p. 231.

40. Canada, *Documents on Canada's External Affairs, 1909-1918, op. cit.*, p. 664.

41. *Ibid.*, p. 596.

42. *Ibid.*, p. 664.

43. KING, W.L.M. *Report on Mission to England to Confer with the British Authorities on the Subject of Immigration to Canada from the Orient and Immigration from India in particular*. Ottawa: King's Printer, 1908, pp. 7-8.

44. Canada, *Census of Canada*, 1911.

45. "The Colored People on Vancouver Island," *San Francisco Evening Bulletin*, May 7, 1858, p. 3.

46.   "Exodus of Colored People," *San Francisco Evening Bulletin*, April 21, 1858, p. 3.

47.   "Injustice to the Coloured Population," *Colonist*, June 13, 1859, p. 2; "Wouldn't Let Him Drink," *Colonist*, June 26, 1862, p. 3; "Riot at the Theatre," *Colonist*, November 6, 1860, p. 2; "The Theatre Rioters," *Colonist*, November 8, 1860, p. 3; and "Color Phobia in Churches," *The Victoria Gazette*, November 10, 1859, p. 1.

48.   "The Colored Rifles Will Be Sworn In," *Colonist*, July 4, 1861, p. 3; and "African Rifles," *Colonist*, September 20, 1861, p. 3.

49.   Great Britain, *Blue Books of Statistics [Colony of British Columbia]*, 1870, London: Public Record Office, 1870, p. 135.

PLATE 6   The port of Nanaimo.   *I.H. Norie Photo* ▶

PHYSICAL ENVIRONMENT

INTRODUCTION

A mountainous land mantled with evergreens, an embayed and fiorded coastline and a narrow east coastal plain, all enveloped in a cloudy and rainy maritime climate, are salient features of the physical landscape. But generalization must not be allowed to mask the variations, of which there are many. The fundamental contrast between mountain and plain gives rise to obvious physical differences that profoundly affect the settlement pattern and economic activities. In response to the nature of the relief, the character of the air masses and the dynamic behaviour of the atmosphere, there is a marked contrast in precipitation totals between the southeast and other parts of the Island. While Victoria has a relatively low precipitation, some points on the west coast receive nearly ten times as much. Seasonal variations also are pronounced; the dry summer, wet winter conditions in Victoria contrast with the year round wetness of the western and northern regions. Temperature variations in winter juxtapose Canada's mildest, largely snow-free city of Victoria with a white land of deep snows a few kilometres to the northwest. Vegetation differences occur also, in response to environmental variations.

A brief discussion of landforms, drainage and the geomorphological processes that created the present relief introduces Chapter 3. This is followed by a consideration of associated natural hazards, including earthquakes, tsunamis, coastal erosion, mass movement and floods, and their impact on various parts of the Island. The nature of the climate is outlined in Chapter 4 in terms of synoptic features and wind, radiation, temperature, humidity and precipitation phenomena. Instructive comparisons are drawn between climatic features of Vancouver Island and those of other parts of Canada. The pattern of vegetation is the subject of Chapter 5, approached systematically through the concept of biogeoclimatic zones and sub-zones. It is emphasized that the apparent wilderness of today is greatly altered from its pristine condition by extensive logging during a century of forest exploitation.

PLATE 7   Tsunami damage at Alberni.   *Jim Ryan Photo* ▶

49

3 RELIEF, DRAINAGE AND NATURAL HAZARDS

Harold D. Foster

Vancouver Island has an area of some 32,100 square kilometres (12,519 square miles). Situated between latitudes 48°20'–50°40' north and longitudes 123°10'–128°30' west, it is the largest of North America's offshore islands. Predominantly mountainous, its core is composed largely of a heterogeneous group of pre-Cretaceous sedimentary and volcanic rocks, folded about northwesterly trending axes and intruded by numerous granitic batholiths.[1]

These rocks were subjected to extensive Tertiary planation, creating a surface of relatively low relief. Remnants remain, including those in Strathcona Park and the San Juan River Valley (Figure 1,3). Eroded sediments were deposited in the west to form the Oligocene and early Miocene rocks of the Estevan coastal plain.[2]

The Island subsequently was subjected to pre-Pleistocene uplift which stimulated rapid river dissection of this Tertiary erosion surface. Much of the resulting down-cutting was fault-guided and, as a result, the Island's valleys still consist of predominantly north, northeast and northwest trending segments that parallel the regional fault and fracture patterns. Examples include the San Juan and Leech rivers. Several such faults continue to be seismically active.[3] The resulting rugged topography was then, as now, dominated by the Vancouver Island Mountains of the interior. These highlands form part of the Insular Range which includes much of the Queen Charlotte Islands to the north. The highest peaks still remaining are the Golden Hinde, 2,200 metres (7,216 feet), Elkhorn Mountain, 2,194 metres (7,196 feet), Mount Victoria, 2,162 metres (7,091 feet), and Mount Colonel Foster, 2,133 metres (6,996 feet).

In contrast to this mountainous core were the coastal lowlands which still form almost an encircling belt. These are most pronounced in the north and east where the Nahwitti and Nanaimo lowlands are part of a

51

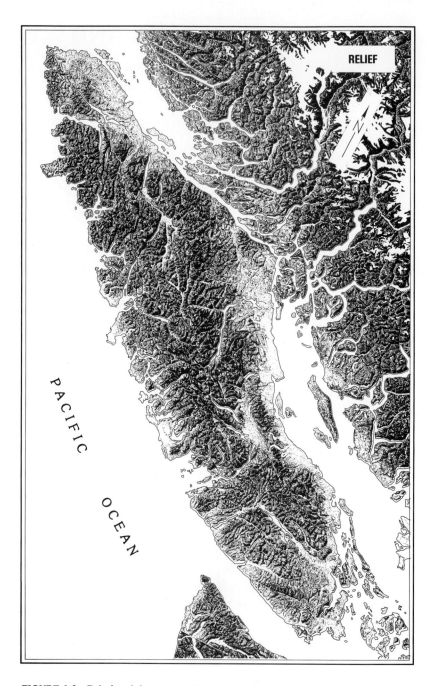

FIGURE 1,3 Relief and drainage pattern.

larger Coastal Trough which stretches from southeastern Alaska to the Puget Depression in Washington (Figure 2,3).[4]

On several occasions this regenerated topography was subjected to extensive Pleistocene glaciation. Although local ice caps developed on the Island itself, much of the ice originated on the British Columbia mainland. On at least two occasions it flowed westward onto the Island from an ice shed situated east of the Coast Mountains.[5] As a result of these frequent glaciations, Vancouver Island now is marked by a wide range of striking erosional and depositional features. Of particular significance are the frequently occurring cirques, U-shaped valleys and fjords. The pre-existing, fault-guided drainage pattern was extensively ice modified, particularly by the creation of deep, elongated fjords, such as the Alberni valley and Nootka and Barkley sounds. In addition, the coastal plains, and to a lesser extent the interior mountain valleys, are mantled by large deposits of till and other sediments, both glacio-fluvial and glacio-marine.

Because of the generally high relief and westerly circulation of the atmosphere, Vancouver Island receives ample, if seasonal, precipitation. Great differences do occur, however, annual totals ranging from over 3.8 metres (12.5 feet) in the western flanks of the Vancouver Island Mountains to less than .8 metres (2.6 feet) in the southeast of the Nanaimo Lowland.[6] In higher locations much of the precipitation falls as snow, the mean annual snowfall being over 2.5 metres (8.2 feet) in the highlands east of Zeballos.[7] Despite relatively high summer temperatures, rugged mountains and heavy precipitation support 219 small, alpine glaciers and glacierets at elevations from 670 to 2,073 metres (2,198 to 6,799 feet) above sea level. This perennial ice and snow, however, covers only some 27.6 square kilometres (10.8 square miles), almost half of which occurs in Strathcona Provincial Park.[8] Much of the Island's precipitation returns to the Pacific Ocean through a series of rapid flowing, deeply incised, relatively short rivers. Several of these, such as the Nanaimo River (Figure 3,3) and the Campbell River (Figure 4,3) are monitored by the Inland Waters Directorate, Environment Canada.[9] Discharge is seasonal, with peaks reflecting heavy autumn and winter precipitation. Fairly extensive ground water also occurs in aquifers formed by fractured volcanics, sedimentary rocks and Pleistocene sands and gravels.[10]

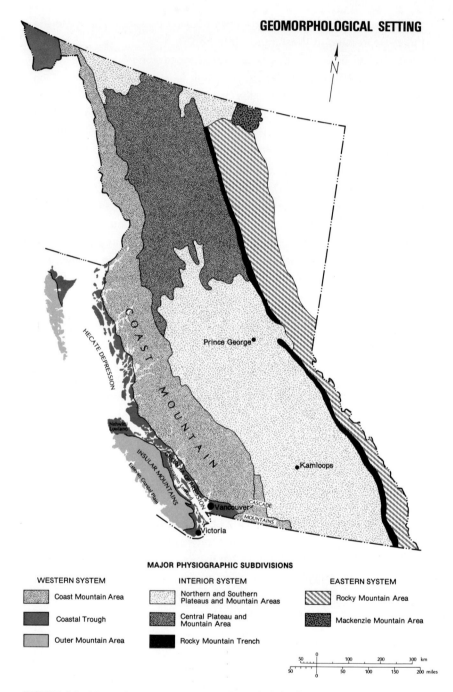

MAJOR PHYSIOGRAPHIC SUBDIVISIONS

WESTERN SYSTEM	INTERIOR SYSTEM	EASTERN SYSTEM
Coast Mountain Area	Northern and Southern Plateaus and Mountain Areas	Rocky Mountain Area
Coastal Trough	Central Plateau and Mountain Area	Mackenzie Mountain Area
Outer Mountain Area	Rocky Mountain Trench	

FIGURE 2,3 Major physiographic regions of British Columbia.

54

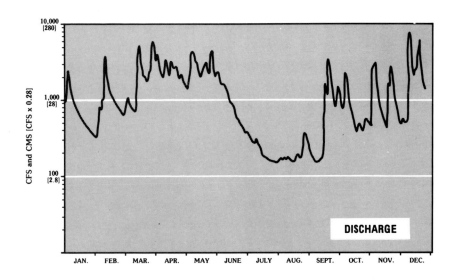

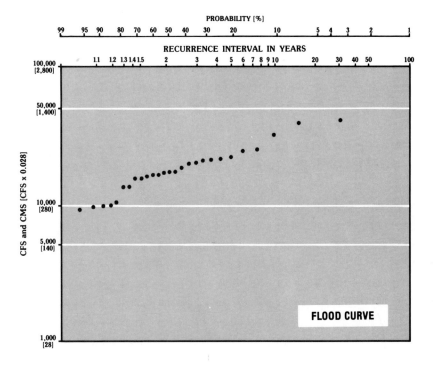

FIGURE 3,3   Nanaimo River discharge hydrograph for 1965 and flood probability curve.

55

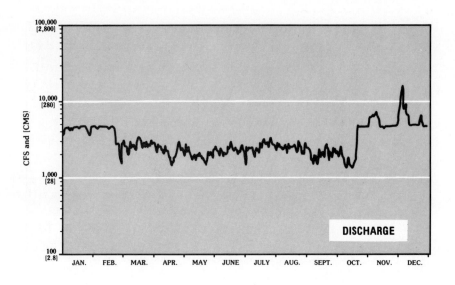

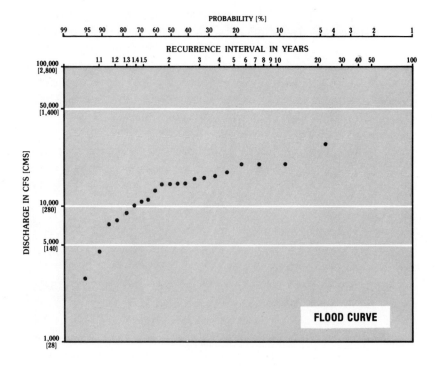

FIGURE 4,3   Campbell River discharge hydrograph for 1965 and flood probability curve.

ASSOCIATED HAZARDS

As may be seen from the illustrations presented in several of the other chapters in this volume, the geology, geomorphology and hydrology of Vancouver Island provide numerous resource opportunities. However, the active seismisity, heavy precipitation, steep, glaciated slopes and faulted or unstable rocks and sediments are associated also with a wide variety of natural hazards. It is on these that the remainder of this chapter is focused.

Earthquakes

Earthquakes are relatively common on Vancouver Island. From the earliest recorded seismic event which occured in 1841, the west coast of British Columbia has experienced one great earthquake (Richter magnitude 8.0) and five major earthquakes (Richter magnitude 7.0-7.9). In the city of Victoria alone over 100 seismic events have been felt since record-keeping began.[11] Experience has shown that the degree of damage caused by such earthquakes is a reflection of several variables, mainly the distance from the epicentre, the type of sediment upon which building has taken place and the nature of the structure involved.

In an attempt to influence planners to adjust to variations in earthquake risk, the author and students from the University of Victoria have undertaken seismic microzonations of several municipalities. Such maps reflect the fact that the highest seismic risk sites are those where fill has been extensively used in shoreline reclamation or where pre-development marshy ground occurs, underlain by deep surficial sediments, with a high water table. The lowest Modified Mercalli intensity values experienced during earthquakes, and hence the least damage, normally occurs on outcrops or where sediments, less than three metres (9.84 feet) thick, rest directly on bedrock. Intermediate in risk are areas of deeper Pleistocene deposits, generally consisting of inter-bedded horizons of till, glaciofluvial sands and gravels, and marine sediments.[12]

The seismic microzonation of Victoria has been published in an earlier volume of this series.[13] The map was prepared from sewer excavation records, borehole data, information from building sites, and field work to identify sediment type and depth. It has also proved possible, by conducting land use surveys and constructing a mean damage ratio matrix based on experience elsewhere, to produce anticipated earthquake damage simulations for events of differing magnitude in the City of

Victoria. This information is of value to developers, town planners and disaster mitigation officials. An earthquake microzonation of the Municipality of Esquimalt has been prepared recently (Figure 5,3).[14]

Tsunamis

Vancouver Island is influenced also by seismic events which occur hundreds, if not thousands of kilometres, from its shores. On ten occasions since the establishment of the Tofino tide gauge some sixty years ago tsunamis have been recorded.[15] These are trains of seismically triggered sea waves, most frequently generated by submarine dip-slip faulting, which are capable of causing extensive damage in low-lying coastal areas. Although occurring in other oceans, tsunamis have been recorded most frequently within the Pacific basin where, between 1900-1970, 138 were reported, thirty-four of which were locally destructive, while nine also caused damage at great distances from their sources. Tsunami waves usually measure 160 kilometres (99 miles) or more from crest to crest and may travel at speeds greater than 960 kilometres (595 miles) per hour in the deepest regions of the open ocean, traversing the Pacific in twenty to twenty-five hours. Although often having amplitudes of less than thirty centimetres (one foot) in deep water, on entering shallow water along a coast they are slowed to less than sixty-four kilometres (forty miles) per hour, much of their energy being converted to wave heights of up to ten metres (thirty-three feet) or greater.

The largest wave experienced on Vancouver Island during this century was the 1964 Alaskan tsunami which caused widespread damage to many coastal settlements. Destruction was extensive along the west coast. At Winter Harbour booming ground piles were demolished and a twelve metre (thirty-eight foot) tender was beached. At Amai Inlet, ten buildings were damaged and the radio-telephone system was rendered inoperative. Seismic sea waves caused destruction estimated at 150,000 dollars at Zeballos, where they surged up the main street, causing extensive flooding in homes and stores. Thirty houses were moved off their foundations. The village of Hot Springs Cove also suffered extensive damage, sixteen of its eighteen homes being swept into the inlet. The wharf was structurally impaired and fuel lines connecting it to nearby storage tanks were broken. Destruction was estimated at 100,000 dollars.

The greatest impact occurred at Port Alberni where the first wave arrived without any official warning. Including the damage to the MacMillan Bloedel plants, estimates of the total losses have reached as high

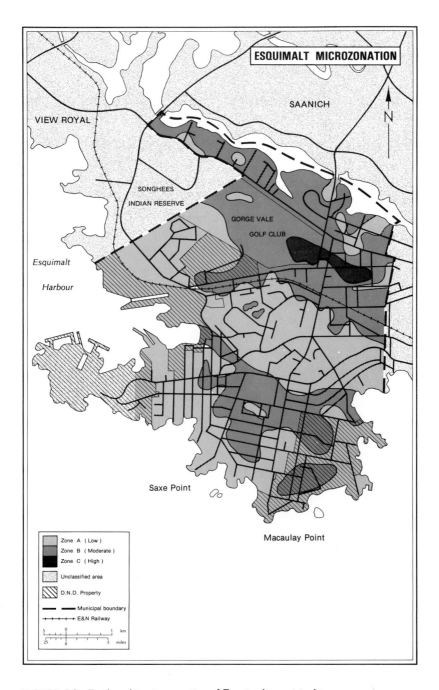

FIGURE 5,3 Earthquake microzonation of Esquimalt municipality.

59

as 10,000,000 dollars. Houses were displaced up to 300 metres (984 feet) and logs moving at speeds in excess of thirty-two kilometres (twenty miles) per hour were driven into buildings. As a result, fifty-eight properties were completely destroyed and 320 dwellings suffered damage.[16]

Since only tsunamis generated at great distances from Vancouver Island's west coast have as yet been recorded, there is no basis for predicting the potential impact of any locally created seismic sea waves. However, a knowledge of the location of major submarine structures and the epicentres of earthquakes in the northeastern Pacific for the period 1954-1963 permits some conjecture (Figure 6,3).[17] If tsunamigenic earth movements were to occur along either the southern portion of the Queen Charlotte Islands Fault or the Blanco Fracture Zone, the parallel alignment of these structures and the west coast of Vancouver Island suggests that wave energy might be preferentially directed against this stretch of British Columbia's coastline. Fortunately, although seismically active, the motion of these faults is predominantly strike-slip, but the possibility that tsunamigenic dip-slip motion may take place cannot be entirely discounted. Since these structures are less than 485 kilometres (300 miles) offshore, such tsunamigenic movement would be potentially far more damaging to coastal settlements on Vancouver Island than any so far recorded.

The government of British Columbia is well aware of the tsunami threat. Currently, it operates a seismic sea wave warning system that is an integral part of the Pacific-wide network controlled by the International Tsunami Information Center in Honolulu, Hawaii. There is considerable variation in anticipated risk at coastal settlements (Table 1,3).[18]

Coastal Erosion

In contrast to most of the tsunami related damage which occurs on the west coast of Vancouver Island, coastal erosion losses are predominantly experienced in the east. Even along the Nahwitti and Nanaimo lowlands. rates of cliff recession vary markedly. These depend upon two distinct groups of variables, termed passive and active factors. Passive factors, such as geology, topography and coastal orientation, and to a lesser extent vegetation, do not alter rapidly through time, but are nevertheless important, since they control the nature of the cliff against which wave energy is expended. Active factors, such as sea state, wave spectrum, wind direction and force, storm path, and heigh of the tide, alter quickly.

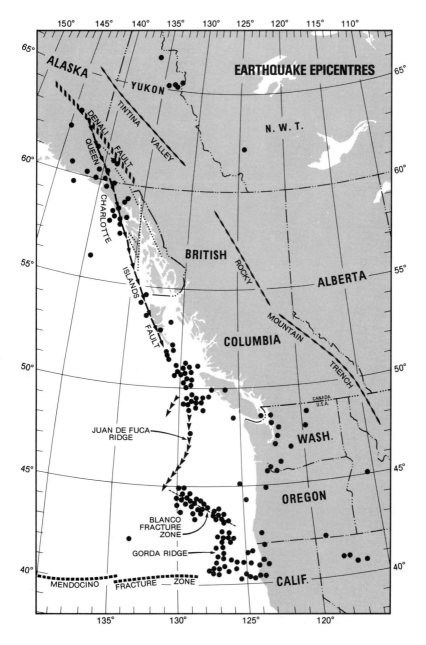

FIGURE 6,3 Submarine structures and epicentres of major earthquakes.

61

TABLE 1,3   Tsunami-Endangered Vancouver Island Settlements

Settlement	Population 1971**	Risk; High, Medium And Low	Communications†	Responsible RCMP Detachment
Ahousat	—	H	RT,R	Tofino
*Alert Bay	760	M	T	Alert Bay
Bamfield	144	M	T	Port Alberni
Beaver Cove	102	M	T	Port Hardy
Boat Basin	—	H	—	Tofino
Bull Harbour	—	M	T	Port Hardy
Cachelot	—	H	RT	Tahsis
Ceepeecee	—	M	—	Tahsis
Chamiss Bay	—	M	RT	Tahsis
China Creek	—	H	—	Port Alberni
Clayoquot	—	M	T	Tofino
Clo-oose	—	M	T	Lake Cowichan
Coal Harbour	334	L	T	Port Hardy
Ecoole	—	M	—	Port Alberni
Ehatisaht	—	M	—	Port Alberni
Englewood	—	M	T	Port Hardy
Esperanza	45	M	T	Tahsis
Estevan Point	—	M	T	Tofino
Fort Rupert	66	M	T	Port Hardy
Franklin River	187	H	T	Port Alberni
Friendly Cove	—	M	—	Tahsis
*Gold River	1,896	H	T	Gold River
Hecate	—	M	—	Tahsis
Hesquiat	—	M	—	Tahsis
Holberg	333	L	T	Port Hardy
Hot Springs Cove	—	H	T	Tofino
Jeune Landing	—	H	T	Port Alice
Kakawis	—	M	T	Tofino
Kildonan	—	H	T,R	Port Alberni

Settlement	Population 1971**	Risk; High, Medium And Low	Communications†	Responsible RCMP Detachment
Kilpala (Amai Inlet)	—	H	RT	Tahsis
Kyuquot	80	M	T,R	Tahsis
Long Beach	103	M	T	Tofino
Mahatta River	180	H	RT	Port Alice
Nootka	—	M	—	Tahsis
Nuchatlitz	—	H	R	Tahsis
Opitsat	—	M	—	Tofino
*Port Alberni	20,063	H	T	Port Alberni
Port Albion	58	H	T	Ucluelet
*Port Alice	1,507	H	T	Port Alice
Port Eliza (Queens Cove)	—	M	RT,R	Tahsis
*Port Hardy	534	M	T	Port Hardy
*Port McNeill	934	M	T	Port Hardy
Port Renfrew	362	M	T	Sooke
Port Tahsis	—	H	—	Tahsis
Quatsino	51	L	T	Port Alice
San Josef Bay	—	H	T	Port Hardy
Sarita River	—	M	T	Port Alberni
Sointula	575	M	T	Alert Bay
*Tahsis	1,351	H	T	Tahsis
Telegraph Cove	45	M	T	Port Hardy
*Tofino	461	M	T	Tofino
*Ucluelet	1,018	H	T	Ucluelet
Winter Harbour	105	H	T	Port Hardy
Yreka	—	H	—	Port Alice
*Zeballos	186	H	T	Tahsis

*Incorporated municipality.
**Population is not shown if under fifty in both 1966 and 1971.
†British Columbia Telephone (T), Radio-telephone (RT), Raven network (R).

Rapid erosion typically takes place where thick Pleistocene sediments are exposed to repeated storm waves which have developed over a long length of fetch. Major losses normally occur during high tides and after periods of heavy rainfall. The disruption of vegetation by human activity exacerbates this process. Under such circumstances shear stress increases, shear strength declines and rotational failure occurs along a concave-upward plane. When this takes place cliff retreat occurs rapidly. This process is being repeated at several locations along the east coast of Vancouver Island and on the Gulf Islands. These include Cowichan Head on the Saanich Peninsula, the Qualicum Beach area, and Komas Bluff on the northeast coast of Denman Island. Similar losses along some parts of the west coast of Vancouver Island are less significant economically because of the relatively sparse settlement.

Although the rates of erosion vary annually, losses in the most active locations appear to be in the order of 1.5 metres (five feet) per year. With the extremely high market value of coastal lots, such erosion is very costly. At Cowichan Head, for example, at least 54,300 square metres (64,943 square yards) have been lost during the past twenty years, which would now be worth, perhaps, almost 3,000,000 dollars. It must be noted, however, that this process of cliff retreat nourishes the sandy beaches so critical to the Island's tourist industry.[19]

Mass Movement

Instability is a common feature of the slopes of the Vancouver Island Mountains. Heavily jointed and faulted sedimentary and igneous rocks, often mantled by pockets of till or glacio-fluvial sediment, are subjected to frequent seismic disturbance. In addition, bedrock slopes commonly have been over-steepened by glacial erosion and are affected by heavy precipitation and associated chemical and physical weathering. Riverine undercutting also is common, as is disturbance by ubiquitous logging operations.

Since the population density in the Island's mountainous interior is extremely low, mass movement rarely poses a major threat to life or property. There is, however, one major exception to this generalization, Port Alice, on the northwest coast. This company town has been subjected to severe mudflows and, indeed, appears to be built on a debris fan. Damage totalling some 800,000 dollars was caused on December 15, 1973 by a mudflow originating at the 700 metre (2,296 foot) level on steep slopes above the town.[20] As a result of this mass movement, one 39,000 dollar home was demolished, nine others were rendered uninhabitable, twenty vehicles were damaged and the town's storm drains and gas lines were rendered inoperable. A further slide occurred in 1975.

Theoretical studies have been conducted since and a scale model of the town and adjacent slopes constructed. Mudflows were reproduced, using bentonite mud with a similar viscosity to the coarse, bouldery gravel actually involved. On the basis of the information obtained, a dyking system was constructed at a cost of 250,000 dollars, designed to protect the town from slides up to 2.5 times the volume of those recently occurring. Future mudflows will be diverted into unsettled areas.[21] It is clear from landforms in the northern part of the Island that such phenomena are relatively common. One is thought to have destroyed an Indian settlement in the area some forty years previously.[22]

Avalanches also are fairly frequent on Vancouver Island. In order to determine the relative seriousness of the avalanche problem in British Columbia as a whole, a hazard index has been established by the provincial Department of Highways Avalanche Task Force. This index illustrates the probability of a vehicle being caught in a snow slide and is based in part on traffic volume, as well as on the magnitude and frequency of avalanches. Little traffic uses the Island's mountainous roads in winter and, as a result, none fall within the high or moderate levels of hazard. The only road which is included in the low avalanche hazard classification is Highway 4 at Sutton Pass, the road which links Port Alberni with the east coast.[23] Many other avalanche areas occur, for example, in Strathcona Park. These generally present little risk, except to occasional skiers and hikers.[24]

Floods

The rivers of Vancouver Island exhibit unusual discharge characteristics. Maximum flows occur during the winter months, as the result of heavy rainfall, rather than during the snow-melt generated, spring freshet period of May to July, as in the vast majority of western Canadian rivers.[25] Flooding, therefore, tends to occur from November to February.

In 1975 Environment Canada announced a national flood hazard mapping program. Some 200 Canadian rural and urban communities threatened by flooding were identified. Five of these, Port Alberni, Campbell River, Courtenay, Duncan and Lake Cowichan, are on Vancouver Island.[26] Together, they have a population in excess of 44,000. Fortunately, Victoria does not have a riverine location. Glacial rock basins within the city are affected occasionally by high water tables, and minor channels, such as Bowker Creek, may overflow after heavy rain, but losses generally are light. Far more damage is likely to be experienced during high stages of Kitsucksus Creek in Port Alberni, the Tsolum River in Courtenay and the Cowichan River in Duncan.[27] In addition, flooding is associated also with inland water bodies, such as Shawnigan and Cowichan lakes where development has taken place close to mean water level.

Some flood hazard maps for Vancouver Island are being produced by the provincial Department of Lands, Forests and Water Resources, Water Investigations Branch. These are designed to show the extent of the anticipated 200 year flood, within which areas development is controlled. Four sheets depicting flood hazards in the southeast of Cowichan Lake have been produced already. Currently being mapped, also, are the White and Salmon rivers near Sayward and low-lying areas near Port Alberni. In addition, work is expected to begin in the relatively near future on the Qualicum, Koksilah, Lower Cowichan and Englishman rivers.

CONCLUSION

Vancouver Island possesses a unique juxtapositioning of mountains, rivers and shorelines which have a major beneficial influence on its resources and aesthetics. Conversely, these elements in the landscape also threaten, because together they create patterns of risk over which the Island's infrastructure has been superimposed. From the preceding brief description of the hazard mapping and risk assessment currently underway it is clear that planners are becoming increasingly more willing to consider such variations in risk in siting new developments. If this trend continues, the benefits of such diversity in relief and drainage may be experienced without the all too frequently associated costs.

REFERENCES

1. HOLLAND, S.S. *Landforms of British Columbia: A Physiographic Outline*. Victoria: British Columbia Department of Mines and Petroleum Resources, Bulletin No. 48, 1964.

2. *Ibid.*, pp. 31-39.

3. WITHAM, K., MILNE, W.G. and SMITH, W.E.T. "The New Seismic Zoning Map for Canada: 1970 Edition," *The Canadian Underwriter*, (June 1970), p. 2.

4. HOLLAND, S.S. *op. cit.*, pp. 34-39.

5. FYLES, J.G., *Surficial Geology of Horne Lake and Parksville Map-Areas, Vancouver Island, British Columbia*. Ottawa: Geological Survey of Canada, Memoir 318, 1963.

6. Canada, *Temperature and Precipitation Tables for British Columbia*. Toronto: Department of Transport, Meteorological Branch, Vol. 1, 1967; and British Columbia Natural Resources Conference, *British Columbia Atlas of Resources*, 1956, Map No. 7.

7. British Columbia, Canada Land Inventory, ARDA, Map No. 18, *Mean Annual Snowfall*.

8. OMMANNEY, C.S.L. "Application of the Canadian Glacier Inventory to Studies of the Static Water Balance. 1. The Glaciers of Vancouver Island." *International Geography*, Vol. 2, 1972, pp. 1,266-1,268.

9. Canada, *Surface Water Data British Columbia 1974*. Ottawa: Environment Canada, Water Survey of Canada, Inland Waters Directorate, 1975.

10. HALSTEAD, E.C. *Hydrogeology of the Coastal Lowland Nanaimo to Victoria, Vancouver Island, Including the Gulf Islands, B.C.* Vancouver: Department of Energy, Mines and Resources, Inland Waters Branch, unpublished manuscript, 1967.

11. For a detailed description of the social impact of some of these earthquakes *see* WUORINEN, V. *A Preliminary Seismic Microzonation of Victoria, British Columbia.* Victoria: University of Victoria, Department of Geography, unpublished M.A. thesis, 1974; and Canada, *Canadian West Coast Earthquakes 1951-1954.* Ottawa: Department of Energy, Mines and Resources, 1967.

12. See SEED, H.D. and IDRISS, I.M. "Influence of Soil Conditions on Ground Motions During Earthquakes," *Journal of the Soil Mechanics and Foundation Division, American Society of Civil Engineers,* 95, (1969); and WUORINEN, V. "Seismic Microzonation of Victoria: A Social Response to Risk," in Foster, H.D. (ed.) *Victoria: Physical Environment and Development.* Victoria: University of Victoria, Department of Geography, Western Geographical Series, Vol. 12, 1976, pp. 185-219.

13. WUORINEN, V., *ibid.*, reference 11, p. 211.

14. FOSTER, H.D. and CAREY, R.F. "The Simulation of Earthquake Damage," in FOSTER, H.D. (ed.), *ibid.*, reference 12, pp. 221-240. The Esquimalt microzonation was prepared by John Horsfield and Clay Saunders as a Geography 377 project.

15. This description of tsunamis and the threat they pose to Vancouver Island is a summary of FOSTER, H.D. and WUORINEN, V. "British Columbia's Tsunami Warning System: An Evaluation," *Syesis,* 9 (1976), pp. 113-122.

16. WHITE, W.R.H. "The Alaska Earthquake — Its Effects in Canada," *Canadian Geographical Journal,* 72 (1966), pp. 210-219.

17. TOVIN, D.G. and SYKES, L.R. "Seismicity and Tectonics of the Northeast Pacific Ocean," *Journal of Geophysical Research,* 73 (1968), pp. 3821-3845.

18. FOSTER, H.D. and WUORINEN, V., *op. cit.*, reference 15.

19. FOSTER, H.D. "Coastal Erosion: A Natural Hazard of the Saanich Peninsula, Vancouver Island," in FOSTER, H.D. (ed.), *ibid.*, reference 12, pp. 131-184.

20. ANDERSEN, J., IZARD, T., STEVENS, J. and TURNER, D. *The Port Alice Mudslide of 1973: A Case Study*. Victoria: University of Victoria, Department of Geography, unpublished paper prepared for Geography 377, 1974.

21. Details of this study and the model were kindly provided by H.W. Nasmith who was personally involved.

22. *Ibid.*

23. British Columbia, *Avalanche Task Force: Report on Findings and Recommendations*. Victoria: Department of Highways, September 1974.

24. IRVINE, B., KELLAS, J., SMITH, D. and WALKER, B. *Strathcona Park Avalanche Inventory*. Victoria: University of Victoria, Department of Geography, unpublished paper prepared for Geography 376, 1976.

25. MACKAY, D.K. "Characteristics of River Discharge and Runoff in Canada," *Geographical Bulletin*, 8, No. 3, (1966), p. 219.

26. Canada, "Federal Flood Damage Reduction," *Emergency Planning Digest*. Ottawa: Environment Canada, 1975, pp. 2-7.

27. See, for example, BELL, L.M. and KALLMAN, R.J. *The Cowichan-Chemainus River Estuaries: Status of Environmental Knowledge to 1975*. Ottawa: Environment Canada, Special Estuary Series No. 4, 1976; BELL, L.M. and KALLMAN, R.J., *The Nanaimo River Estuary: Status of Environmental Knowledge to 1976*. Ottawa: Environment Canada, Special Estuary Series No. 5, 1976; and BELL, L.M. and THOMPSON, J.M. *The Campbell River Estuary: Status of Environmental Knowledge to 1977*. Ottawa: Environment Canada, Special Estuary Series No. 7, 1977. These examine the hydrology of the Campbell, Nanaimo and Cowichan-Chemainus river estuaries.

PLATE 8   The hydrological cycle: precipitation.   *USFS Photo* ▶

4 CLIMATE[1]

Stanton E. Tuller

The purpose of this chapter is to outline the basic patterns of the climate and to draw some comparisons between Vancouver Island and the rest of Canada. The discussion will, of necessity, be very general because a great deal of microclimatic variation occurs, owing to topographic diversity.

Most of the stations operated by the Atmospheric Environment Service which have a long period of record are situated on or near the coast. The majority are concentrated in the southeast between Victoria and Campbell River. A network of temperature and precipitation stations operated by the Resource Analysis Branch of the provincial government during the summers of 1973-1975 has helped to extend station coverage to interior areas. Each station, however, is representative only of its immediate surroundings. For this reason distribution patterns are illustrated with symbols, each indicating the value for a particular station. This system has the benefit of portraying the general pattern of climatic variation over the Island without the inherent inaccuracies of isolines in an area with as much relief and topographic diversity as Vancouver Island.

SYNOPTIC FEATURES

Vancouver Island lies in the zone of the mid-latitude upper air westerlies. Mean flow at 300 and 500 millibars is westerly throughout the year.[2] This upper air flow is faster in winter than in summer (300 millibar windspeeds are about twenty metres per second in January and fourteen in July over the Island),[3] a response to the greater latitudinal gradient of solar radiation and, thus, of temperature and upper air pressure.

Embedded in the westerlies are moving systems of high and low surface pressure. These moving systems are part of nature's mechanism of accomplishing the necessary latitudinal exchanges of energy and angular momentum. The low pressure systems (cyclonic storms) are of primary

71

interest to most people because of their associated precipitation and "inclement" weather.

Low pressure systems over Vancouver Island are more frequent in winter when more are generated in response to the heightened latitudinal energy gradient and when their tracks are farther south than during the summer. Maunder found the weather pattern in the vicinity of Vancouver Island to be dominated by a low pressure system on seventy-six percent of the days in December, 1964 and 1965.[4] December is the usual month of maximum precipitation for most stations on the Island. In contrast, Maunder discovered that high pressure patterns were characteristic of fifty-two percent of the July days, and oceanic lows of only thirty-one percent. Reed plotted the frequency of fronts in 400,000 square kilometre areas. His maps show an approximate frequency of fronts in the Vancouver Island area in winter (December to February) of sixty percent and in summer (June to August) of thirty percent.[5] Reitan found an average of 4.5 cyclonic storm centres passing through the region in January and 1.5 in July.[6]

Areas of winter cyclogenesis in the North Pacific include centres in the western Pacific off the coast of Asia, the Gulf of Alaska, the central North Pacific, and even a secondary one immediately west of Vancouver Island.[7] The Island receives storms from all these sources, many arriving in the occluded stage after a long passage over the Pacific. The major area of cyclogenesis off the coast of Asia remains during the summer, as does a secondary area in the Gulf of Alaska, but most storms go north of Vancouver Island during this season.

The flow of the upper air westerlies is not consistent. A zonal flow in winter brings a steady progression of cyclonic storms to Vancouver Island and produces wet and windy weather. On the other hand, an upper air ridge lying over the west coast forces storms to the north and brings relatively warm, clear conditions. If the ridge is more persistent than usual, an abnormally dry winter is the result, such as those experienced occasionally in recent years. Namias and others have suggested that changes in sea surface temperatures in the North Pacific are associated with variations in the patterns of the upper air long waves and these patterns can persist for extended periods.[8] The importance of the ocean in influencing the climate of Vancouver Island is not confined to the coastal waters.

SURFACE AIR PRESSURE AND WINDS

Winter is marked by surface high pressure over the North American continent and low pressure over the North Pacific, especially the Gulf of Alaska. The continental high is caused by the cold air temperatures. The low over the Pacific is the result of both its relative warmth, which comes from the abundance of stored energy in the water itself, and the passage of numerous cyclonic storms. Surface winds following the winter pressure gradient should be southeasterly in the Vancouver Island area. Local relief often disturbs this theoretical pattern, however, and the passage of storm fronts can lead to a variety of wind directions. Nevertheless, easterly and southerly components are predominant at most stations (Figure 1,4). Wind speeds generally are greater on the west coast of the Island than on the east coast. The highest mean monthly wind speeds occur in December at most stations and in January at many of the remainder. The winter wind speed maximum coincides with the greater frequency of cyclonic storms. Surface air pressure in summer is characterized by low pressure over the warm land. The ocean is relatively cool because of evaporation and its greater heat flux into the subsurface. This results in a higher mean air pressure. The subtropical high pressure cell replaces migratory cyclones as the important dynamic feature in summer. The centre of the subtropical high lies at about 38 degrees north and 150 degrees west during July and the high is oriented along a west southwest-east northeast axis.[9] There is an extension of the high pressure cell northward along the British Columbia coast. Subsidence produces the high pressure in this cell and also a subsidence temperature inversion. The inversion is recorded at Quillayute on the tip of the Olympic Peninsula in Washington sixty-three percent of the time during the June-September period. The mean height of the inversion base is 585 metres.[10]

Northwest winds are the norm over Vancouver Island in summer, as would be expected from the pressure pattern, and wind speeds are lower in the less stormy atmosphere. The month of lowest mean monthly wind speed usually is August or September and average velocities are about sixty-three percent of the highest mean monthly wind speed of winter. Actual values of mean monthly wind speeds vary from 1.6 to 4.7 metres per second for the summer minimum and from 3.8 to 6.6 for the winter maximum.[11] Although differences in anemometer exposure make regional comparisons risky, the mean wind speeds on Vancouver Island are, in general, lower than those of the Prairies or coastal stations in the Maritimes and about the same as those of Southern Ontario and Quebec.

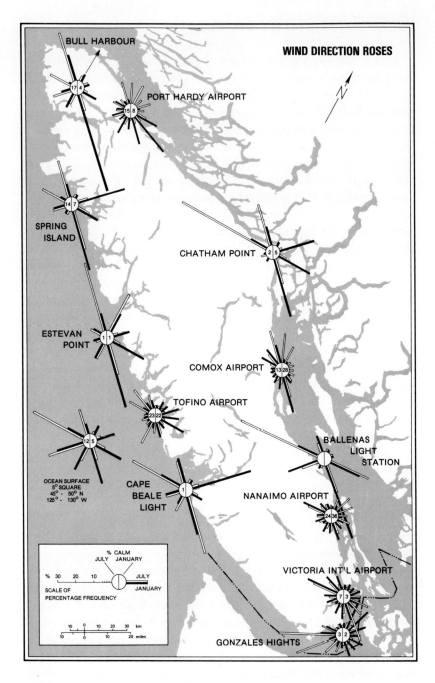

FIGURE 1,4 January and July wind roses.

RADIATION

Total solar radiation reaching the horizontal ground surface is available from actual measurement at Port Hardy and Nanaimo, Departure Bay,[12] but values for other stations must be computed from the mean percentage of possible bright sunshine and the total solar radiation at the top of the atmosphere.[13] Values of net long wave radiation were computed using the method outlined by Sellers.[14] This, along with assumed surface albedos, allowed the approximation of net radiation for three stations which have data for hours of sunshine or measured solar radiation, temperature, humidity and cloud cover (Figure 2,4).

Total solar radiation and hours of bright sunshine decrease from the southeast of the Island to the northwest. The annual hours of bright sunshine in Victoria is less than that recorded in the southern Prairies, but above that at most stations in Ontario, Quebec, and the Atlantic Provinces. Values of both annual sunshine hours and mean daily solar radiation on northwestern Vancouver Island, however, are among the lowest in southern Canada. Winter storms and summer fog are a potent combination in reducing incoming solar radiation.

Solar radiation on the densely populated southeastern coast of the Island is strongly concentrated during the summer when cyclonic storms are few and the subtropical high pressure cell brings clear skies (Figure 2,4 and Table 1,4). The mean cloud cover at Victoria, Gonzales Heights is .79 in January and .36 in July.[15] The percentage of possible bright sunshine is twenty-three in December and seventy in July. In general, solar radiation during the winter anywhere on Vancouver Island is well below that of any other part of southern Canada east of the Coast Mountains. On the other hand, the summer solar radiation on the southeast coast is exceeded only by that of the southern Prairies.

Vancouver Island has a relatively favourable net radiation climate throughout the year. Winter cloudiness and the limited snow cover restrict long wave cooling and reduce surface albedo. The radiation balance is negative only in November, December and January. The winter net radiation deficits on the Island are similar to those of southern Ontario.[16] Summer net radiation is especially high on the southeast coast and decreases to the west and north, as solar radiation is reduced.

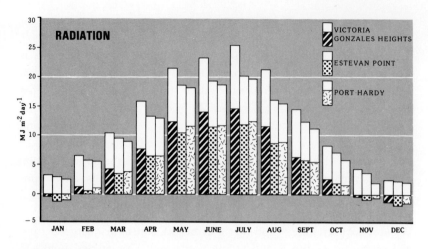

FIGURE 2,4 Mean daily solar and net radiation at selected stations.

TEMPERATURE

The air temperature pattern is strongly influenced by the land and sea distribution. The differing energy budgets of land and sea surfaces make the ocean warmer in winter, when it benefits from energy stored in the water itself; and cooler in summer, when greater evaporation and a higher ground heat flux restrict the amount of energy available to warm the air. The upwelling of cold subsurface water off the west coast of Vancouver Island in summer also contributes to the lower summer temperatures.

Mean daily maximum air temperatures in July are cool to mild throughout the Island (Figure 3,4). The maximum temperature is presented because human outdoor activities usually take place during the day and are affected more by the daily maximum temperature than by the daily mean or minimum temperatures. Inland stations have the warmest summer temperatures. East coast stations have temperatures that are distinctly higher than those on the west coast because they are somewhat sheltered from the influence of the Pacific and are adjacent to warmer waters. The sea surface temperature in the open Pacific is about 14.2°C in July and 15°C in August.[17] Water temperatures measured at the

TABLE 1,4 Mean Daily Total Solar Radiation in MJ m^{-2} day^{-1}

	Jan.	Feb.	Mar.	Apr.	May	June	July	Aug.	Sept.	Oct.	Nov.	Dec.
Alberni, Lupsi Cupsi	2.16	4.58	8.16	12.90	19.08	19.18	22.26	17.83	15.80	5.99	2.86	1.72
Campbell River	2.60	5.68	9.05	13.85	20.29	19.59	23.33	18.20	12.25	6.57	3.32	1.88
Cowichan Lake Forestry	2.36	4.96	8.03	12.15	16.59	16.77	19.92	16.51	12.08	6.61	3.26	1.93
Nanaimo, Departure Bay	2.92	6.29	10.66	15.91	21.50	22.12	24.05	19.91	14.26	7.76	3.75	2.36

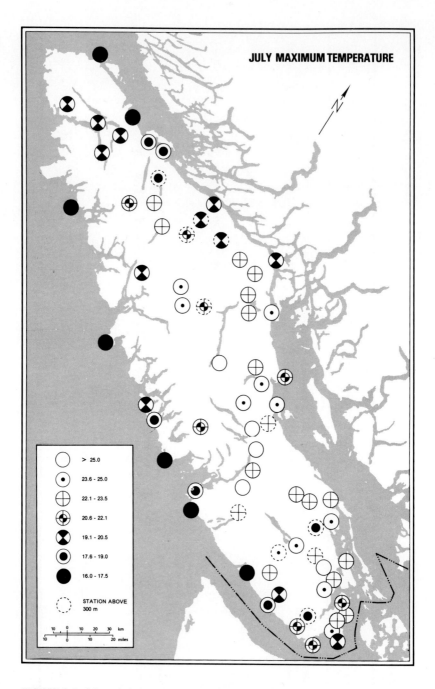

FIGURE 3,4 Mean daily maximum temperature in July.

78

Kains Island and Amphritite Point lighthouses on the west coast average 12.6°C in July and 13.2°C in August.[18] At the same time, water temperatures along the east coast of the Island vary between 14°C and 18°C.[19] Summer advection fog produced over the cold, upwelling zone helps to reduce further the summer maximum air temperature on the west coast. The mean daily maximum summer air temperatures are well below those of southern Canada, with the exception of the Atlantic Provinces. The low temperature, coupled with relatively low humidity, gives Vancouver Island a summer climate where heat stress is not a problem. Extremes of maximum temperature also are moderate. The highest recorded temperature at Gonzales Heights in Victoria, which has over seventy years of record, is 35.0°C. Other examples of extreme maximum temperatures up to 1970 are Nanaimo, 40.6°C; Comox Airport, 34.4°C; Port Hardy Airport, 31.7°C; Port Alice, 34.4°C; Estevan Point, 28.9°C; and Port Alberni, 41.1°C.[20]

Winter temperatures are more uniform over Vancouver Island than are summer temperatures. Low altitude inland stations have January mean daily temperatures near the freezing point. West coast stations then are beneficiaries of heat stored in the ocean water. Open ocean temperatures are in the 7.2°C to 8.6°C range west of Vancouver Island in January and February.[21] The west coast lighthouses report water temperatures of about 7.6°C,[22] whereas those off the east coast are in the 5°C to 7°C range.[23] January mean daily air temperatures are about 3°C to 5°C on the west coast and 2°C to 4°C on the east coast. Thus, Vancouver Island has a very mild winter by Canadian standards.

Extreme minimum temperatures also are relatively mild and occur when an outbreak of cold Arctic air from the interior covers the Island. Examples of record minimum temperatures at a number of stations up to 1970 are Victoria, -15.6°C; Nanaimo, -17.2°C; Comox Airport, -21.1°C; Port Hardy Airport, -14.4°C; Port Alice, -12.8°C; Estevan Point, -13.9°C; and Port Alberni, -21.7°C. Hence, the lowest temperatures on record at Victoria, Port Hardy and along the west coast are higher than the mean daily January temperatures in Saskatchewan and Manitoba.

The freeze free period on Vancouver Island is relatively long and somewhat compensates for the lack of summer heat. Coastal stations have a freeze free period of up to 230 days, though 150 days is more typical of the inland stations. Local relief, of course, creates a great deal of variability. Gonzales Heights in Victoria is a prime example of a site factor producing a long freeze free period. This station, situated on top of a small hill, is immediately adjacent to the Strait of Juan de Fuca. The freeze free period at Gonzales Heights is 283 days (February 28 — December 9).[24] The Victoria, Tillicum station, situated somewhat inland and not possessing the benefits of free air drainage, has a freeze free period of only 164 days (May 8 — October 20). Other examples of freeze free periods are: Duncan, 167; Nanaimo, Departure Bay, 216; Comox Airport, 180; Port Hardy Airport, 175; Port Alice, 229; Estevan Point, 226 and Port Alberni, 170. Inland areas and the northeast coast of the Island have a freeze free period about equal to that of the southernmost part of Ontario. The west and southeast coasts have the longest freeze free periods in Canada.

HUMIDITY

The amount of water vapour in the air is the atmospheric response to the evaporation process. Important controls of atmospheric humidity are the effective distance from a source of evaporative moisture, air temperature and elevation. The oceans usually are more important sources of water vapour than are land areas and warm ocean surfaces evaporate more water than do cold ones. Knowledge of the sources of the air masses that affect a region is necessary in order to explain the humidity regime.

Vancouver Island is well exposed to and constantly under the influence of a cool ocean surface. Air temperatures are moderate throughout the year. The humidity, therefore, also is moderate and lacks the seasonal extremes of other parts of Canada. All Atmospheric Environment Service stations which have humidity data published in the climatic normals are situated near the coast. The west coast, with its higher air temperatures, protection from cold, dry air from the interior, and nearness to the relatively warm water surface, has higher winter humidity than does the east coast (Table 2,4). Humidity over the Island is fairly uniform in spring and summer, with the west coast maximum becoming noticeable again in the fall.

Winter humidity on Vancouver Island is much higher than that in the rest of Canada, which is largely under the influence of dry, cold continental air. Summer humidity is lower than that in southern Ontario and Quebec, which have higher air temperatures and receive moisture from the warmer Atlantic Ocean and even the Gulf of Mexico. Vancouver Island humidity is slightly lower than that of the Maritimes. On the Prairies, Alberta has a lower humidity than the Island, whereas Manitoba's is somewhat higher. Eastern Saskatchewan provides the best Prairie analogy for Vancouver Island's summer humidity.

80

TABLE 2,4 Mean Vapour Pressure at Selected Vancouver Island Stations During Mid-Season Months in Millibars

Station	January	April	July	October
Alert Bay	6.61	8.38	13.21	10.57
Bull Harbour	7.16	9.05	13.70	10.98
Comox	6.61	8.38	13.70	10.16
Estevan Point	7.74	8.72	13.70	10.98
Nanaimo (A)	6.38	8.07	13.70	10.16
Port Hardy	6.90	8.38	13.21	10.16
Spring Island	8.07	8.72	13.70	11.39
Tofino	7.75	8.72	13.70	11.39
Gonzales Heights	7.16	8.72	12.73	10.98
Victoria International Airport	6.90	8.38	13.21	10.57

PRECIPITATION

Most of Vancouver Island's precipitation falls during the winter and December is the month of maximum precipitation at most stations (Figure 4,4). That month successfully combines the two factors necessary for abundant precipitation: dynamic lifting mechanisms and water vapour in the air. Almost all of the precipitation along the British Columbia coast originates from storm systems. Walker found that ninety-three percent of the January precipitation at Port Hardy and ninety-nine at Vancouver occurred with fronts present.[25] Comparable values in July were ninety-five and ninety-two percent, respectively, for Port Hardy and Vancouver. Cyclonic storms or frontal systems are common throughout the winter.

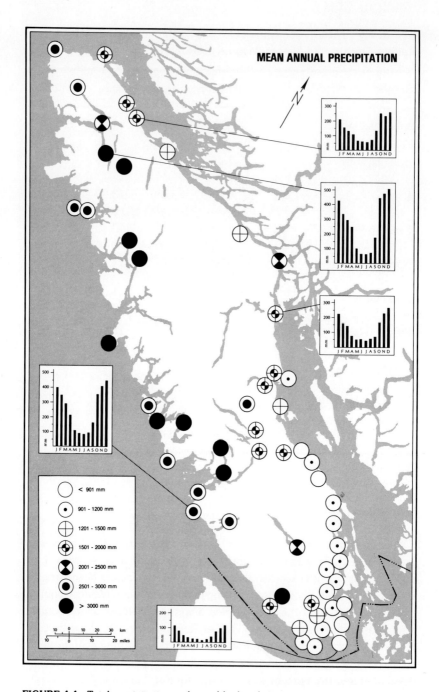

FIGURE 4.4 Total precipitation and monthly distribution.

82

Although Klein[26] found more days with cyclones present in the Vancouver Island area in January, the precipitable water vapour is higher in December.[27] In fact, mean monthly precipitable water does not reach December levels again until April.

Winter and mean annual precipitation generally increase from south to north and from east to west over Vancouver Island (Figure 4,4). Orographic effects are of prime importance in controlling the precipitation distribution. Walker reported that most of the precipitation throughout the year occurs with 700 millibar flow from the southwest quadrant.[28] The southwesterlies are relatively moist and the mountains of Vancouver Island, oriented at right angles, augment precipitation with air flow from this direction. The west coast, therefore, is the area of maximum precipitation. The mountains not only provide extra lift, but also help to retard cyclonic storms and create areas of horizontal convergence in valleys or passes. Perhaps the most famous precipitation station on Vancouver Island is Henderson Lake which operated for fourteen years between 1923 and 1936. Henderson Lake holds the North American record for the highest mean annual precipitation, 6,658 millimetres. The station was situated at the head of the lake where horizontal convergence and orographic uplift could combine to greatly augment precipitation.[29]

The east side of the Island usually is in a rain shadow. The southern part, especially the Victoria area, is further protected by the mountains of the Olympic Peninsula which lie to the west and south. A transect of stations along the southwest coast of the Island shows an increase in precipitation from south to north, as each station, successively, receives less protection from the Olympic Mountains. Becher Bay records 1,005 millimetres of annual precipitation, whereas the total is 1,305 at Milnes Landing, 1,989 at River Jordan, and 2,988 at Pachena Point. The southern part of the Island also receives fewer cyclonic storms throughout the year than the northern part and is especially well protected in the summer months when it comes under the influence of the subtropical high pressure system.

The reduced number of cyclonic storms, the influence of the subtropical high pressure cell and the stabilizing effect of the ocean waters combine to produce a marked summer minimum in precipitation.[30] Unlike the Prairies and in much of eastern Canada, water vapour is not lacking on the Pacific Coast at any time of the year. The precipitation regime is controlled by the availability of dynamic mechanisms to produce lifting and the conversion of the water vapour into measurable precipitation. The northward extension of the subtropical high pressure cell along the British Columbia coast, with its associated subsidence inversion, is the most important factor in restricting the vertical movement needed to produce precipitation. The Mediterranean type of climate, with its dry summer condition, finds its most poleward extension (land areas) along the east coast of Vancouver Island.[31] Depending on the particular definition of annual precipitation needed to qualify as a true Mediterranean climate, this zone may extend anywhere from the Saanich Peninsula north to Comox. The areal distribution pattern of summer precipitation over Vancouver Island is similar to that of annual precipitation (Figure 5,4). Data for the May-September period from a number of stations operated by the Resource Analysis Branch of the provincial government supplement the regular network and help to give a more complete picture.)

Snowfall generally is light in the lowland areas of Vancouver Island and does not last long in the south and west. Although abundant moisture is available and heavy falls of snow can occur in the mountains, the temperatures are too warm for much snow in areas near sea level. The storms which bring the precipitation inevitably are accompanied by warmer air, so that snow usually turns to rain after a short time. Almost all of the snow at lowland stations falls between November and March, with the maximum usually occurring in January. Snowfall increases inland from the coast and is greater in the central and northern parts of the Island than in the south. Some examples of mean annual snowfall measured at Atmospheric Environment Service stations are: Victoria International Airport, 45.5 centimetres; Duncan, 74.9; Nanaimo, 69.9; Courtenay, 119.4; Port Hardy Airport, 70.6; Estevan Point, 34.3; Port Alberni, 81.0; and Cowichan Lake Forestry, 179.8.[32]

The mean April 1 snow depths measured at higher elevation snow courses in the centre of the Island generally are between 350 and 450 centimetres, representing water equivalents of between 1,600 and 1,800 millimetres.[33] Forbidden Plateau, for example, which lies inland from Campbell River at an elevation of 1,130 metres, has a mean April 1 snow depth of 430 centimetres, with a water equivalent of 1,802 millimetres.

In many practical applications the intensity of precipitation is of more concern that the total amount over an extended period. Most Vancouver Island precipitation originates from cyclonic storms, many of which are in the occluded stage. Marked cold fronts and heavy, short duration, convective precipitation are rare. The mean number of days per year with thunder at Atmospheric Environment Service reporting stations varies from 0.7 at Alert Bay, just off the northeast coast of the Island, to 4.0 at Victoria, Gonzales Heights.[34] Most of the Prairies, Ontario and southern Quebec record 15 to 25 days and Nova Scotia and New Brunswick 10 to 15 days of thunder per year.

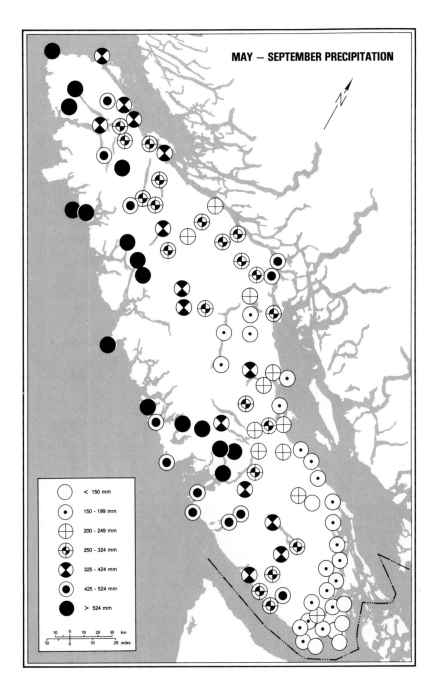

FIGURE 5,4 Growing season precipitation.

Rainfall intensity increases from east to west over Vancouver Island. Fifteen minute rainfall intensities on the west coast are equivalent to those in the rest of British Columbia, southern Alberta and western Saskatchewan, but are only about one-half of those in southern Ontario and Quebec. The east coast of the Island has the lowest fifteen minute rainfall intensity of any region in southern Canada (generally below 7.5 millimetres).[35] Intense cyclonic storms can bring very heavy one day rainfall totals to the west coast, however. The highest recorded one day totals there are exceeded in Canada only by those of other areas of the British Columbia coast. Most west coast stations have recorded over 140 millimetres of precipitation in one day. Estevan Point has received 219 millimetres, while Bear Creek, in the uplands west of Victoria, has recorded 363 and Henderson Lake 422. Values for east coast stations are much lower, ranging between about 80 and 100 millimetres. All stations received their highest one day rainfall totals sometime during the fall or winter, showing the importance of cyclonic storms as the producer of Vancouver Island's precipitation. December and January are the months in which most stations received their record one day totals, although the record at some stations occurred in September, October, November or February.

Although Vancouver Island receives ample annual precipitation, the summer dry period comes at the time when evaporative demand is at a maximum. Most of the Island has a water deficit during the summer, with the southeast being the most severely affected. As a result, the seasonal distribution of precipitation is not the most favourable for agriculture.

CONCLUSION

If one had to summarize the climate of Vancouver Island in one word it would be "humdrum." The Island possesses a mild, unexciting, unspectacular, maritime climate. The populated lowlands do not experience extremes of heat or cold. The seasons are not marked by either dry air in winter or high humidity in summer. Severe weather events, such as tornadoes or tropical cyclones, are almost unheard of. Vancouver Island is noted for its high precipitation, but long duration is a more important feature of the regime than is intensity. Destructive, memorable, high intensity rainstorms are rare. The southeast, moreover, has only a moderate annual precipitation and the bulk of the Island has a relatively dry summer. An uninspiring, unspectacular, humdrum climate, however, does offer advantages and Vancouver Island possesses a comfortable and generally benevolent climate which is quite favourable for human habitation.

REFERENCES

1. Data supplied by the Resource Analysis Branch of the British Columbia Ministry of the Environment greatly aided in the preparation of this chapter. Rodney Chilton and Mauro Coligado of the Resource Analysis Branch deserve special thanks for their assistance.

2. LAHEY, J.F., BRYSON, R.A., CORZINE, H.A. and HUTCHINS, C.W. *Atlas of 300 mb Wind Characteristics for the Northern Hemisphere.* Madison: University of Wisconsin Press, 1960; and LAHEY, J.F., BRYSON, R.A., WAHL, E.W., HORN, L.H., and HENDERSON, V.D. *Atlas of 500 mb Wind Characteristics for the Northern Hemisphere.* Madison: University of Wisconsin Press, 1958.

3. *Ibid.*

4. MAUNDER, W.J. "Synoptic Weather Patterns in the Pacific Northwest," *Northwest Science*, 42, No. 2 (1968), pp. 80-88.

5. REED, R.J. "Principal Frontal Zones of the Northern Hemisphere in Winter and Summer," *Bulletin of the American Meteorological Society*, 41, No. 11 (1960), pp. 591-598.

6. REITAN, C.H. "Frequencies of Cyclones and Cyclogenesis for North America, 1951-70," *Monthly Weather Review*, 102, No. 12 (1974), pp. 861-868.

7.   KLEIN, W.H. *Principal Tracks and Mean Frequencies of Cyclones and Anticyclones in the Northern Hemisphere*. Washington: Government Printing Office, Weather Bureau Research Paper No. 40, 1957.

8.   NAMIAS, J. "Seasonal Interactions between the North Pacific Ocean and the Atmosphere during the 1960's," *Monthly Weather Review*, 97, No. 3 (1969), pp. 173-192; NAMIAS, J. "Climatic Anomaly over the United States during the 1960's," *Science*, 170, No. 3959 (1970), pp. 741-743; and NAMIAS, J. and BORN, R. *Empirical Techniques Applied to Large-Scale and Long-Period Air-Sea Interactions*. La Jolla, California: Scripps Institution of Oceanography, 1972.

9.   NEIBURGER, M., JOHNSON, D.S. and CHIEN, C-W. *Studies of the Structure of the Atmosphere over the Eastern Pacific Ocean in Summer. I. The Inversion over the Eastern North Pacific Ocean*. Berkeley: University of California Press, 1961, pp. 43 and 46.

10.   *Ibid.*, p. 84.

11.   Canada, *Canadian Normals, Volume 3, Wind, 1955-1972*. Downsview, Ontario: Environment Canada, Atmospheric Environment, 1975.

12.   Data for these two stations were supplied by Dr. John E. Hay, Department of Geography, University of British Columbia, Vancouver, October, 1977.

13.   Personal Communication, Mauro Coligado, Resource Analysis Branch, Ministry of the Environment, Victoria, November, 1977. The regression constant and coefficient used in the equation were supplied by M. Coligado.

14. SELLERS, W. *Physical Climatology*. Chicago: University of Chicago Press, 1965, pp. 54-58.

15. Canada, *Climatic Normals, Volume 3, Sunshine, Cloud, Pressure and Thunderstorms*. Toronto: Department of Transport, Meteorological Branch, 1968.

16. HARE, F.K. and HAY, J.E. "The Climate of Canada and Alaska," in BRYSON, R.A. and HARE, F.K. (eds.) *Climates of North America*. New York: American Elsevier, pp. 104 and 105.

17. United Kingdom, *Monthly Meteorological Charts of the Eastern Pacific Ocean*. London: Meteorological Office, 1968; and United States, *Climatological and Oceanographic Atlas for Mariners, Volume II, North Pacific Ocean*. Washington: Office of Climatology, 1961.

18. HOLLISTER, H.J. *Observations of Seawater Temperature and Salinity at British Columbia Coastal Stations in 1964 and 1965*. Nanaimo: Fisheries Research Board of Canada, Pacific Oceanic Group, Manuscript Report Series No. 226, 1966, pp. 38 and 42. Data presented include thirty year averages.

19. WALDICHUK, M. "Physical Oceanography of the Strait of Georgia, British Columbia," *Fisheries Research Board of Canada, Journal*, 14, No. 3 (1957), pp. 321-486.

20. British Columbia, *Climate of British Columbia, Tables of Temperature and Precipitation, Climatic Normals, 1941-1970, Extremes of Record*. Victoria: Department of Agriculture.

21. United Kingdom, *op. cit.*; and United States, *op. cit.*

22. HOLLISTER, H.J., *op. cit.*, pp. 36 and 40.

23. WALDICHUK, M., *op. cit.*

24. HEMMERICK, G.M. and KENDALL, G.R. *Frost Data 1941-1970.* Downsview: Atmospheric Environment Service, 1972. All freeze free period data are from this source.

25. WALKER, E.R. *A Synoptic Climatology of Parts of the Western Cordillera.* Montreal: McGill University, Arctic Meteorology Research Group, Publications in Meteorology No. 35, 1961.

26. KLEIN, W.H., *op. cit.*

27. TULLER, S.E. "Mean Monthly and Annual Precipitable Water Vapour in Canada," *Weather*, 27, No. 7 (1972), pp. 278-289; and HAY, J.E. "Precipitable Water over Canada: II. Distribution," *Atmosphere*, 9, No. 4 (1971), pp. 101-111.

28. WALKER, E.R., *op. cit.*

29. DENISON, F.N. "The Remarkably Heavy Precipitation at Henderson Lake, Vancouver Island, B.C.," *Monthly Weather Review*, 60, No. 12 (1932), p. 252.

30. KERR, D.P. "The Summer-dry Climate of the Georgia Basin, British Columbia," *Royal Canadian Institute, Transactions*, 29, No. 1 (1951), pp. 23-31.

31.   TREWARTHA, G.T. *The Earth's Problem Climates*. Madison: University of Wisconsin Press, 1961, pp. 268 and 269.

32.   British Columbia, *op. cit.*

33.   British Columbia, *A Summary of Snow Survey Measurements 1935-1975*. Victoria: Department of Lands, Forests and Water Resources, Water Investigations Branch, 1975.

34.   Canada, *Climatic Normals, Volume 3, Sunshine, Cloud, Pressure and Thunderstorms, op. cit.*

35.   BOYD, D.W. *Climatic Information for Building Design in Canada*. Ottawa: National Research Council, 1970.

PLATE 9   Riverine vegetation.   *C. Morley Photo* ▶

5 VEGETATION

Michael C.R. Edgell

Vast, unbroken forests, stretching almost to the highest peaks, greeted the early European explorers and colonists who probed the coastlines of Vancouver Island. Only in scattered alpine areas, waterlogged swamps and bogs, or in open woodlands of the southeastern part of the Island, was that forest cover interrupted. By the 1850's, the immense forests had begun to yield to the impact of settlement and agriculture. Later, they were to fall more readily before the swing of the logger's ax. Today, most of the southeastern part bears only residual evidence of its former forested nature, and the forests that cover the rest of the Island have been transformed by logging activities.

But Vancouver Island remains overwhelmingly a forested land, part of the great coniferous, hemlock-cedar-spruce biome that extends for 3,680 kilometres (2,300 miles) along the Pacific coast from central California to southern Alaska.[1] The tall trees of this biome typically form dense canopies in mature forests, which allow little development of shrub and herb layers. Between the extreme north and south of those 3,680 kilometres, the dominant trees may be western hemlock (*Tsuga heterophylla*), western red cedar (*Thuja plicata*), Sitka spruce (*Picea sitchensis*), coast redwood (*Sequoia sempervirens*), Douglas fir (*Pseudotsuga menziesii*) or grand fir (*Abies grandis*). On Vancouver Island, the major conifers are confined to western hemlock, western red cedar, Douglas fir and silver fir (*Abies amabilis*), with grand fir and Sitka spruce of lesser importance.

Lying transverse to the main movements of air masses from the Pacific Ocean, the mountainous terrain of Vancouver Island produces great environmental diversity. Zones of forest types, arranged approximately parallel to the Island's axis, and ranging from dense rainforests on the west coast to drier forests on the east, reflect the major environmental gradients associated with elevation and amounts of effective precipitation. Finer divisions are imposed by the details of topographic, parent material and drainage conditions that effect soil moisture and nutrient differences. This complex of forest types can be classified into four biogeoclimatic zones, and five sub-zones[2] (Figure 1,5).

93

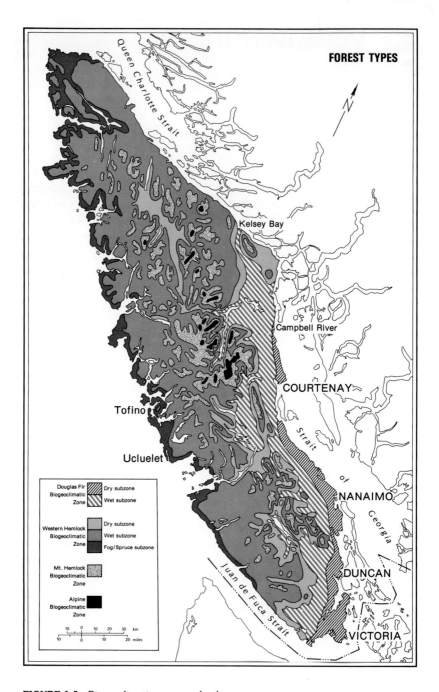

FIGURE 1.5 Biogeoclimatic zones and sub-zones.

94

Within each biogeoclimatic zone, macro-climatic influences on soil and vegetation are similar. Over time in any one zone, similar climatic climax ecosystems will develop on normal or mesic sites.[3] These zones are a very broad level of ecosystem classification, and may be subdivided into sub-zones reflecting more specific environmental conditions. In turn, each sub-zone contains a number of forest communities which develop in response to local soil and relief, and which occur repeatedly in clearly defined landscape patterns.

Throughout the following brief summary of Vancouver Island's vegetation, it should be borne in mind that biogeoclimatic zones are based on the concept of potential climatic climax vegetation. Therefore, the ecosystems used to classify the zones are not necessarily the most widespread, due to the often overriding influence of local environmental conditions and, particularly, man's modification of the vegetation cover.

DOUGLAS FIR BIOGEOCLIMATIC ZONE

Douglas fir was once the dominant forest species on much of the southern and eastern parts of the Island as far north as Sayward. It also extended westward along many of the larger valleys, notably to Buttle Lake and the head of Alberni Inlet. Many of these forests seem to have originated after extensive fires during the last 1,200 years, the last of which occurred approximately 400 years ago.[4] This zone is the driest area on the Island, but two sub-zones are recognized, due to the variation in environment and forest ecosystems.

Garry Oak-Douglas Fir Dry Sub-zone

The rain shadow of the Vancouver Island and Olympic mountains creates a warm, dry zone along the eastern coastal strip, with annual precipitation between 658 and 1,143 millimetres (26 and 45 inches). There, annual soil water deficits, in soils that are generally concretionary Dystric Brunisols, may be more than 200 millimetres (eight inches) and can appear in May. Forest potential is good only on the moister sites. Originally the vegetation ranged from open woodlands of Douglas fir, Garry oak (*Quercus garryana*), madrone (*Arbutus menziesii*) and lodgepole pine (*Pinus contorta*) on xeric sites to forests of grand fir and western red cedar on seepage zones. Mesic sites were occupied by Douglas fir stands, with an understory of salal (*Gaultheria shallon*) and

95

Oregon grape (*Mahonia nervosa*). Most of this vegetation has disappeared because of the high settlement and agricultural value of the region. But residual woodland and forest, especially the madrone-Garry oak woodlands, with their associated spring-flowering bulbs, have high aesthetic and conservation values.[5]

Madrone-Douglas Fir Wet Sub-zone

Garry oak, which gives so much of the character to the drier Douglas fir sub-zone, is absent from the forests of this unit, although madrone is frequent, particularly in young coniferous stands and on well drained sites. Although western hemlock occurs, it is confined to poorly drained, acidic soils, and rarely reaches importance, due to the frequency of severe drought. Soil water deficits, however, are not as severe as in the dry sub-zone, reaching an annual level of 150 millimetres (six inches), and appearing by June. Due to the higher precipitation, 1,143 to 1,905 millimetres (forty-five to seventy-five inches) podsolization is stronger, producing degraded Dystric Brunisols or weak humoferric podzols. These support a closed forest of Douglas fir, with an understory of salal on mesic sites. Grand fir is frequent as an edaphic climax species, and western red cedar is common. The productivity of Douglas fir is good, and the original stands were the main source of timber for early logging on the Island. Most areas now are occupied by mosaics of regrowth communities which, on xeric sites, may be dominated for up to 100 years by lodgepole pine.

WESTERN HEMLOCK BIOGEOCLIMATIC ZONE

A shade tolerant tree, adapted to heavy precipitation and mineral-poor soils, western hemlock is the major climax dominant over most of the forest land of Vancouver Island. These forests exhibit great variation over their range, and three sub-zones can be recognized.

Western Hemlock-Douglas Fir Dry Sub-zone

Differentiated from the adjacent Douglas fir zone mainly by lower soil moisture deficits, this sub-zone overlaps it considerably in temperature and precipitation regimes. Many species of the Douglas fir zone, such as madrone and grand fir, occur in the drier areas. Although western hemlock is abundant throughout these forests, Douglas fir can outgrow it, and, in fact, it is in this hemlock zone where Douglas fir shows the maximum growth of any tree on any site in Canada. The resulting mixed stands are some of the most imposing forests on the Island. But Douglas fir is shade intolerant under these conditions, and can only regenerate in openings. In the absence of these, it is replaced by western hemlock or western red cedar after 400 years. The high timber volumes in the forests of this sub-zone, for instance in the Nimpkish valley, were the main source of timber when logging moved inland from the eastern coastal plain in the 1930's and 1940's.

Western Hemlock-Silver Fir Wet Sub-zone

This is the most extensive sub-zone on the Island, and is dominated by forests of western hemlock, silver fir and western red cedar on well developed ferric or humic podzols, with thick mor humus. Summers of the western and northern parts of the Island are cool and in this season up to ten percent of the area's annual precipitation may be received. Soil moisture deficits, therefore, usually are less than fifty millimetres (two inches) and are not experienced until July or August. Western hemlock and western red cedar show their maximum growth in these forests, but the climax stands are, from a silvicultural viewpoint, overmature and decadent. Above 550 metres (1800 feet), precipitation falls mostly as snow, and the shorter vegetative season curtails productivity. Although these forests were not used appreciably as a timber source until the 1950's, they now form the main supply of timber for the Island's forest industry.

Western Hemlock-Sitka Spruce Fog Sub-zone

From Port Renfrew north along a narrow coastal strip frequent summer fogs are normal. High relative humidities and low summer temperatures are characteristic, and soil water deficits low or non-existent. Sitka spruce is an important constituent of the forests and it can withstand salt concentrations in wind blown spray that other trees, especially western hemlock, cannot tolerate. A narrow band of pure spruce, much deformed by the wind's mechanical action is, therefore, a characteristic feature of the immediate coastal fringe. Away from the coast, spruce occurs mainly in seral communities, or along alluvial flats, and is less common in the climax western hemlock-silver fir-western red cedar stands.

97

MOUNTAIN HEMLOCK BIOGEOCLIMATIC ZONE

Western hemlock is replaced by mountain hemlock (*Tsuga merten-siana*) as the dominant forest tree at elevations ranging from 600 to 1000 metres (1,960 to 3,280 feet), depending on particular site exposure. Above these altitudes, and concentrated along the main mountain backbone of the Island northwest of Great Central Lake, are forests in which silver fir and mountain hemlock are climax dominants over weakly gleyed humic podzols. Yellow cypress (*Chamaecyparis nootkatensis*) also occurs as a dominant in some stands. The productivity of these stands is low, due to adverse climatic conditions and the short growing season, but they are logged. At elevations of 1,200 to 1,500 metres (3,925 to 4,920 feet), the closed forests are replaced by open parklands of mountain hemlock and ericaceous shrubs.

ALPINE BIOGEOCLIMATIC ZONE

The only non-forested zone is confined to elevations generally in excess of 1,600 metres (5,250 feet) on the northern part of the Island in the Strathcona Park and Sutton Range areas. The tree line may vary as much as 200 to 300 metres (656 to 984 feet), depending upon aspect. Considerable variation exists in these alpine ecosystems, and the vegetation may consist of sedge, grass or herb turfs, ericaceous shrub communities, or sparsely vegetated boulder and scree areas. The recreational value of these areas is high, but inaccessibility limits the amount of use they receive.

CONCLUSION

The impact of man upon the vegetation of Vancouver Island, whether imposed through urbanization, agriculture or logging, has been heavy. In places it is difficult to find the original climax communities which characterize the various biogeoclimatic sub-zones. Particularly is this true in the dry Garry oak-Douglas fir sub-zone. Even as one moves away from the eastern coastal plain into the wet Douglas fir and dry western hemlock sub-zones, the present forests are not pristine, but have sprung from logged-over areas. Only in the western and northern parts of the Island, and in the higher mountain hemlock areas, do there remain extensive natural forest stands. But at the present rate of logging, most of these will be gone within sixty years. The only natural vegetation on the Island by then will be confined to alpine areas, the more inaccessible parts of the mountain hemlock zone, and the major provincial parks, notably Strathcona. In the two hundred years of European settlement since the 1840's, most of Vancouver Island will have been transformed from a wilderness to a varied complex of humanized landscapes.

REFERENCES

1. SHELFORD, V.E. *The Ecology of North America*. Urbana: University of Illinois Press, 1963, Chap. 8.

2. Biogeoclimatic zones are now widely used by ecologists and foresters as the most satisfactory ecological and management classification of British Columbia's vegetation. For the initial application of the concept, see KRAJINA, V.J. "The Biogeoclimatic Zones and Classification of British Columbia," *Ecology of Western North America*, 1 (1965), pp. 1-17; and "Ecology of Forest Trees in British Columbia," *Ecology of Western North America*, 2 (1969), pp. 1-147. This chapter follows more recent revisions of Krajina's work by PACKEE, E.C. *The Biogeoclimatic Sub-zones of Vancouver Island and the Adjacent Mainland and Islands* [revised]. Vancouver: MacMillan Bloedel, Research Note No. 1, 1974; and KLINKA, K. *Guide for the Tree Species Selection and Prescribed Burning in the Vancouver Forest District*. Victoria: British Columbia Forest Service, Research Division, 1977.

3. Mesic sites occupy an intermediate position in a range from excessively drained xeric to very poorly drained subhygric sites. Soils and vegetation on mesic sites are considered to be the products of the region's macroclimate, rather than of local edaphic or topographic conditions. Thus, these mesic ecosystems are used to typify the vegetation within each biogeoclimatic sub-zone.

4. SCHMIDT, R.L. *The Silvics and Plant Geography of the Genus Abies*. Victoria: British Columbia Forest Service, Technical Publication T. 46, 1957, p. 7.

5. EDGELL, M.C.R. "Humanizing the Urban Forest" in FOSTER, H.D. (ed.), *Victoria Physical Environment and Development*. Victoria: University of Victoria, Department of Geography, Western Geographical Series, Vol. 12, 1976, pp. 45-92.

PLATE 10   Sorting logs.   *Jim Ryan Photo* ▶

PRIMARY RESOURCE INDUSTRIES

INTRODUCTION

The transition is easy from the topic of physical environment to the intimately connected primary industries. The basic contrast between developed coastal plain and wilderness interior is well exemplified by the sharpness of agricultural area boundaries. Several attempts to establish agricultural settlements in remote, frontier areas ended in failure. The forest industry is divided into two generalized zones of wilderness logging, on the one hand, and wood processing industries, on the other. Within the mining industry the long dominant coal exploitation of the coastal sedimentaries is in contrast with the scattered occurrence of metallics in the igneous rocks to the west and north. Vancouver Island is noted, both for its abundant commercial fishery, particularly off the west coast, and its legendary sport fishery, especially along the southeast coast.

In recognition of the overwhelming importance of the forest industry to Vancouver Island, Chapter 6 has been expanded to adequately cover the primary activity of forestry, as well as the manufacturing phases. An historical account establishes the foundations of the industry, indicating the complex evolution of the forest management system that involved a plethora of grants, tenures, leases and licences. This is followed by an outline of the present organization of the industry and its role in the Island's economy. Certain aspects of the forest industry's future are investigated, especially forest management, log supply and industrial structure. As a background to the study of mining in Chapter 7, a brief survey of the geologic structure is presented. The long history of coal mining is traced from its beginning in the early days of European settlement to its demise in recent times and its imminent rebirth. Attention is given, also, to the mining of placer gold, lode deposits of metallic ores, including copper, zinc and lead, and structural materials. The importance of agriculture as a landscape feature and way of life is far greater than its dollar value, as indicated in Chapter 8. Among major topics considered are the economic and political setting, the pattern of farming, and recent trends in agriculture. Chapter 9 is concerned with the development and present characteristics of the fisheries. The evolution of management and processing arrangements in the commercial fishery is outlined and the significance of salmon migration patterns is indicated. Other topics include the impact of the sport fishery and the future prospects of the federal government's ongoing salmon enhancement program.

PLATE 11   Early logging using drag chute and donkey engines.   *B.C. Archives Photo* ▶

PLATE 12   Modern logging operation.   *B.C. Government Photo* ▶

6 FOREST INDUSTRY

Michael C.R. Edgell

The landscapes and economy of Vancouver Island are dominated by forests and the forest industry. Only in the vast Cariboo-Fort George economic region is the relative contribution of forestry to the regional manufacturing structure greater than it is on Vancouver Island and the adjacent mid-coast region (Figure 1,6). But even in that rapidly growing, forest-based economy, the actual value added by wood manufacturing and processing industries in 1974 was only 325,000,000 dollars, compared with 421,000,000 in the Vancouver Island-Coast economic region.[1] Production from highly concentrated wood industries in the lower mainland approaches that from the more widely scattered establishments on Vancouver Island, but its impact on the regional economy is diluted by a wide range of other industrial activities. It is the combination of production volume and the hegemonic position of that production relative to all other economic activities that characterizes the preeminent role of forests and forest-based activities on Vancouver Island.

That hegemony is the most extreme example of the paramount and pervasive role that forest-based activities have played in the Province's social and economic development. Until the early 1950's, forestry in British Columbia was dominantly forestry on Vancouver Island and the adjacent lower mainland coast. During the first forty years of this century, coastal forests accounted for at least eighty-five percent of the provincial timber cut, and the bulk of this came from the accessible valleys and slopes of eastern Vancouver Island. Although the last three decades have witnessed tremendous surges in the forest industry of British Columbia's central, and more recently, northern interior, historically the foundations of the economic giant that the forest industry has become were laid in the Georgia Strait region.

But in many ways, those early foundations, and the more recently evolved industrial structure, now seem inadequate to the task of supporting the industry's changing fortunes. The unbridled timber speculations of the turn of the century, the boom days and unregulated harvesting of

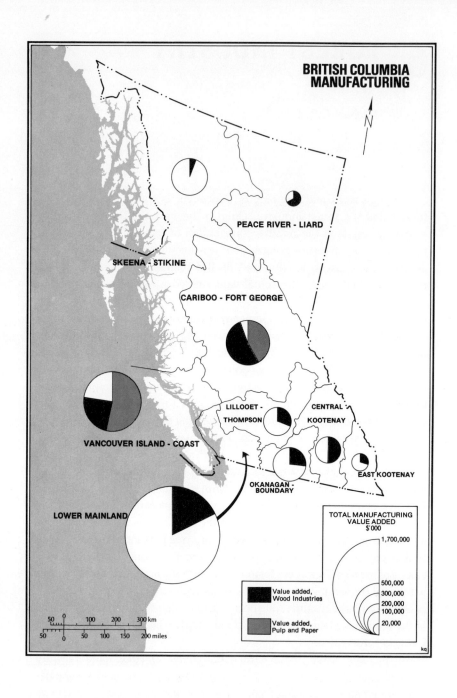

FIGURE 1,6 Manufacturing industry, by value added, economic regions, 1974.

the 1900-1930 period, and the superb, old growth Douglas fir stands on the Island that supported them are long past. More recently departed are the ever optimistic and expansionist 1950's and 1960's which saw the consolidation of the present industrial structure in the Georgia Strait region, and the implementation of sustained-yield management policies and regulated harvesting designed to assure future wood supplies and regional economic stability. The confidence of those years has been replaced in the 1970's by a mood of guarded pessimism, and the industry has grown from a boisterous teenager to a worried and harassed adult.

The establishment of a fourth Royal Commission on Forest Resources in 1975,[2] at a time when forest management and industry faced serious challenges, was, perhaps, more symptomatic of a deeper concern with the future of forestry than was the case when the 1945 and 1957 royal commissions were established.[3] Yet, even in this current period of great change, problems and potentials, the past is always present.

FOUNDATIONS

The linchpin of early forest utilization on Vancouver Island was forged in the colonial and provincial legislation on land tenure and resource rights enacted between 1865 and 1907. In particular, the emergence of two classes of land, that alienated from the Crown and that to which the Crown retained title, was to play a central role in the growing forest scene. Together with the nature and location of the timber resources themselves, early tenure and land grant policies provided the foundations of the forest industry (Figure 2,6). They shaped the subsequent distribution of timber extraction and processing by concentrating them in and around the Georgia Strait region; they determined access to and changing availability of logs; and they profoundly affected later forest management attitudes in the 1940's and 1950's, so that today their legacy remains stamped indelibly upon the Island's forest industry.

After 1858, the alienation of Crown lands, by sale and homesteading, proceeded as the normal means of promoting settlement and economic development. But the colonial, and after 1871, provincial governments also used their power to grant, in fee simple, land and resources on a large scale as an inducement to particular activities, notably railroad construction. In 1883 the province deeded approximately 7,689 square kilometres (2,970) square miles) on the east side of Vancouver Island to the Dominion for the construction of an Island railroad. The Dominion

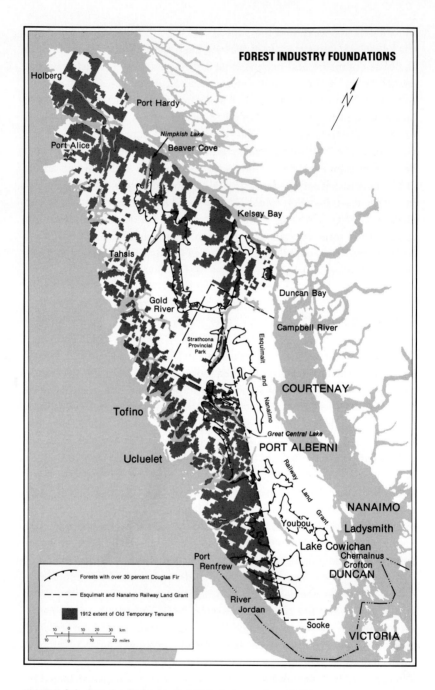

FIGURE 2,6 Douglas fir forests and historic tenure boundaries.

108

then negotiated a contract with coal baron Robert Dunsmuir to build the 120 kilometre (75 mile) railroad from Esquimalt to Nanaimo, and after its completion the land was conveyed to the Esquimalt and Nanaimo Railway Company in 1887.

This outright grant of land removed almost one-quarter of the Island's area, along with much of the Province's best timber, from Crown control and essentially placed it on a speculator's market (Figure 2,6). The land's value was seen primarily in its mineral rights and secondarily in its settlement potential; the superb timber resources more often than not were regarded as an obstacle to settlement and agriculture. But within the next twenty years the real value of the timber was recognized. Resulting sales to land and timber speculators provided one of the two resource bases for the Island's logging industry until 1940.[4] Even in 1974, timber harvested from Crown grant lands, dominantly those of the Esquimalt and Nanaimo, accounted for twenty-four percent of the total harvest in the Vancouver Forest District.[5] Thus, while today the Province's forest industry is dominated by the regulated harvesting of timber under licence from Crown-owned land, its early growth occurred largely because of unregulated harvesting of timber from granted fee simple land.

Along with crown grant timber, the other source of logs was timber harvested under cutting rights on certain classes of land maintained in Crown ownership. In 1865, the Crown Colony of Vancouver Island issued a Land Ordinance that established a policy of retaining Crown title to land and resources while granting the timber harvesting rights to private interests. The philosophy behind this Ordinance, strengthened by an 1887 amendment to the Land Act preventing outright grants of land "chiefly valuable for timber," gradually emerged as the cornerstone of provincial land tenure policy, especially after 1900. Its ultimate legacy is the ninety-five percent of British Columbia's land area to which the Crown today holds title, and the control which the provincial Forest Service exerts over management and utilization of the Crown's forest resources.

The more immediate effect of the Ordinance, however, was the allocation of timber harvesting rights on Crown land through various timber and pulp leases and licences, now collectively known as the "old temporary tenures."[6] Although "temporary," many were renewable indefinitely until the commercial timber on them was extracted. Like the Esquimalt and Nanaimo grant, temporary tenures contained the better and more accessible timber on the Island. They encompassed the remaining Douglas fir stands not already alienated by the railway grant, as well

109

as high quality coastal and river valley stands of cedar, hemlock, silver fir and spruce (Figure 2,6). Varying considerably in size, initial length of term, charges levied and conditions imposed, they were the only means by which timber could be extracted from Crown land. Many temporary tenures were held for speculative purposes, but others contributed significantly to log supplies, especially those in the south central, and northeast coastal regions of the Island. Unlike Crown grants, these tenures represented the first attempt by the government to retain resource rights while directly stimulating the forest industry. Holders of many tenures were required to operate mills as a condition of tenure, and financial incentives, backed by legislation in 1901 and 1906, were given to promote manufacturing. This dual use of the forest resource as a revenue source in the form of royalties and annual payments, and as an instrument to promote economic development was to emerge later as the rationale underlying sustained-yield policies in the 1950's and 1960's.

Sawmill development in the nineteenth century was confined to the southeastern part of Vancouver Island. The mills themselves were small and often short-lived, as at Shawnigan, Mill Bay and Nanaimo. Lumber was exported to the California gold fields from mills at Victoria and Sooke, and to Peru and Australia from Alberni. Feverish speculation from 1890 to 1910, in both Esquimalt and Nanaimo grant land and temporary tenures, coupled with the appurtenant mill clauses of many of those tenures, more firmly established the nuclei of the embryonic forest industry on the southeast coast of the Island. Mills drawing upon local log hinterlands were operating by 1900 at Victoria, Nanaimo, and most notably, Chemainus, where the Victoria Lumber and Manufacturing Company had built a large mill utilizing logs from areas granted to it by the railway company. At the same time, Vancouver mills were drawing logs from the northeastern part of the Island. The total harvest from these operations in 1900 was small, about 500,000 cunits, compared with the present Island total of almost 6,000,000 cunits, but the impetus for a massive onslaught upon the Island's forests was now underway.[7]

INDUSTRIAL EXPANSION AND FOREST LIQUIDATION

During the first thirty years of this century the industry expanded greatly on eastern Vancouver Island. The result was the depletion of the magnificent stands of large timber, gone forever as a part of the Island's eastern landscapes. The influence of the Esquimalt and Nanaimo grant and the old temporary tenures during this period was paramount, as they accounted for the bulk of the harvest. Offering the best stands of the one tree demanded by mills above all others — prime Douglas fir, they also provided either the security of tenure or the speculatory incentives to attract capital investment. They lay close to the growing markets and export facilities of the Georgia Strait region. Also, the gentle valley slopes of the eastern Island posed no access problems and were close to tidewater transportation. The advent of the steam donkey and high lead techniques accelerated the rate at which individual stands could be cut, and the development of logging railroads rapidly pushed logging back into all of the major valleys as far north as Duncan Bay.[8] Sawmills initially established close to their log sources were able to remain closely associated with their supply areas because of the accessibility of their expanding hinterlands.

In retrospect, this period has been variously condemned as one of "capitalist" exploitation, forest mining and liquidation, and clear-cut logging at its worst in which the coastal forests were used, not as a continuous crop, but as a quick cash return to help the opening of the rest of the Province.[9] These judgements may well be true in the light of present conditions, and perhaps both industry and the provincial Forest Service can look back and wish that different viewpoints of the forest resource had prevailed. Be that as it may, the human geography of Vancouver Island, always so intimately associated with forest activities, was largely moulded in this period. In spite of later changes in the number, character and importance of mills, the forest industry today still reflects the general pattern that had emerged by 1925 (Figure 3,6).

Sawmill activity was concentrated almost exclusively in the Douglas fir stands of the Georgia Strait region, with major clusters of mills oriented to markets or railroad and port facilities at Port Alberni-Great Central Lake, Cowichan, Chemainus and Victoria. Logging operations in the Comox-Courtenay-Bloedel area rafted logs to the lower mainland, especially Fraser Mills above New Westminster. Outside the Georgia Strait and Alberni Inlet regions, logging was mostly confined to those few areas where there were stands of Douglas fir, such as Port Renfrew, and in the Nimpkish valley which fed a sawmill and intermittent pulp mill at Beaver Cove. The only use of species other than Douglas fir at this stage was at Quatsino Sound where a pulp lease granted in 1901 eventually resulted in the establishment of the Port Alice pulp mill in 1918.

For the myriad small and medium-sized logging concerns and speculators this was a "boom and bust" era. The market fluctuated widely and

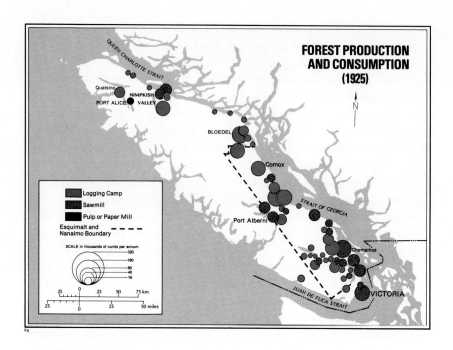

FOREST PRODUCTION
AND CONSUMPTION
(1925)

Logging Camp
Sawmill
Pulp or Paper Mill
Esquimalt and
Nanaimo Boundary

SCALE in thousands of cunits per annum

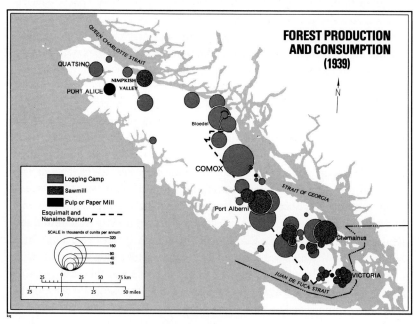

FOREST PRODUCTION
AND CONSUMPTION
(1939)

Logging Camp
Sawmill
Pulp or Paper Mill
Esquimalt and
Nanaimo Boundary

SCALE in thousands of cunits per annum

FIGURE 3,6   Prewar changes in the forest industry structure.

112

was always dominated by Douglas fir: too much cedar or grand fir in a stand could make all the difference between success and failure for a logger.[10] Yet, a surplus of sawmill capacity evolved, due both to the general speculatory atmosphere and the government's insistence on conversion plants as an adjunct to harvesting rights. This problem was to grow to a much larger scale in the late 1960's, and plagues the coastal industry today. Expansion did suffer a temporary setback in the Depression years when marginal operators were forced out, the number of mills was reduced, and the position of the larger and more flexible operations was consolidated, as they acquired mills and timber holdings at absurdly deflated prices. The move toward the present integrated corporate dominance of the industry had begun. By 1936, recovery was complete and forest liquidation continued at an unprecedented rate. The industry in 1940 was a more consolidated and integrated version of what it had been fifteen years earlier, dominating the Island's infrastructure (Figure 3,6).

Somewhat paradoxically, the start of the liquidation era also produced the first comprehensive review of British Columbia's forest resources and their management. The first Royal Commission of Inquiry into Forest Resources submitted its report in 1910.[11] By that date speculation in temporary tenures and Crown grants had alienated approximately seventy-five percent of the Province's then crudely estimated commercial timber. The Commission concluded that such a degree of alienation was adequate to support the industry for the next few decades, and recommended the establishment of forest reserves as a means to prevent further alienation. To maintain balanced harvesting and market competition, however, some Crown timber would be made available through competitive bids for Timber Sale Licences, which were to replace the various temporary tenures as the means for allocating Crown timber rights. These recommendations were put into effect by the 1912 Forest Act which also established the provincial Forest Service.

Timber Sale Licences became the sole means of providing new timber rights to the expanding provincial industry. Nevertheless, harvesting on Vancouver Island during the 1920's, 1930's and 1940's still remained concentrated in the existing old temporary tenures, the Esquimalt and Nanaimo grant and other smaller Crown grants. The Douglas fir stands in these areas were massively overcut, but the extensive, mature and over-mature forests of cedar, hemlock and silver fir on the western and northern parts of the Island remained almost untouched. The scale of logging and its often destructive effects on soil stability and watersheds, the poor regrowth of the forest in many areas, and the increasing scarcity

113

of accessible Douglas fir gradually emerged as serious concerns. In 1939, the Chief Forester, E.C. Manning, drew attention to these problems, suggesting also that at the prevailing rate of harvesting the Douglas fir lumber industry would be "going downhill" within fifteen years.[12] A more extensive review of the Province's forest resources also expressed concern for the future of local, forest-based economies.[13] And to these concerns industry added its own voice, arguing that short-term Timber Sale Licences were insufficient supplements to Crown grant and temporary tenure timber if long-term industrial stability and planning were to be assured. Such uncertainty about the provincial economic base and regional stability precipitated, in 1943, the second Royal Commission of Inquiry into Forest Resources, which heralded the end of this period of unregulated liquidation.[14]

SUSTAINED YIELD AND INDUSTRIAL CONSOLIDATION

Two major questions faced the Royal Commission. How could as much forest land as possible be brought under sustained-yield management? And how could industry be assured of the permanent timber supply deemed necessary to encourage capital investment in processing plants? The solutions to these questions formulated in the Commission's 1945 report, their subsequent implementation in 1947 and their modification in 1957 were, irrevocably, to commit future provincial forest policy to a primary role of accommodating and promoting forest industrial development.

Those solutions were embodied in the concept of perpetual, sustained-yield management of forest land within discrete areas or "working circles." The general problem was to regulate the harvest of old growth timber so that when it was finally removed the first regrowth rotation crops would be available for harvest. The balance between cutting and forest increment would thus provide "a perpetual yield of wood...from regional areas in yearly or periodic quantities of equal or increasing value."[15] Working circles were both "public" and "private" and later became known as Public Sustained-Yield Units (PSYUs) and Tree Farm Licences (TFLs), respectively.

Public Sustained Yield Units are confined to unalienated Crown land, and in the north-central part of British Columbia many are over 1,000,000 hectares (2,470,000 acres) in extent. Managed by the Forest Service, timber from them is sold to loggers and mills through Timber Sale Harvesting Licences and Quotas.

114

Tree Farm Licences, on the other hand, are cooperative management ventures between industry and the Forest Service, occupying both private and Crown land. Although generally smaller than PSYUs, they occupy more of the southern coast of the Province, including Vancouver Island. Intended to benefit large companies with existing processing plants and timber holdings, TFLs were viewed, also, as stabilizers of regional, forest-based economies. In return for subjecting portions of their existing private holdings and temporary tenures to sustained-yield management under Forest Service guidance, companies have been granted exclusive harvesting rights over large tracts of Crown timber. The various parcels included in one licence are managed as a single sustained-yield unit, whether or not they are contiguous, and the actual harvest is regulated according to a calculated annual allowable cut. TFLs are intended to satisfy the major log requirements of the licensee's processing plants, and most of the coast TFLs are appurtenant to integrated mill complexes. All TFLs are now on twenty-one year renewable terms.[16] Conditions of management are laid out in five year working plans prepared by the company and approved by the Forest Service that cover timber inventory and allowable cut, harvesting regulations, reforestation, road building, fire control and environmental protection.

Between 1948 and 1962 eleven TFLs were granted on Vancouver Island, ranging in size from 14,500 to 260,000 hectares (35,870 to 642,450 acres). Five of them included portions of the old Esquimalt and Nanaimo grant (Figure 4,6).[17] PSYUs in the relatively low quality and less accessible stands of the northern and western coasts, along with remaining private holdings in the railway grant, make up the residue of commercial forest.

Old temporary tenures that were incorporated into the new licences account for about sixty percent of TFL area on the Island. The location of these old tenures, and of early Crown grants, had a significant influence on the eventual allocation of TFLs, for some companies were strategically positioned to control access to, and to bid for, additional Crown timber. The present distribution and allocation of TFLs, therefore, does not necessarily reflect an optimum spatial orientation of log supply areas to processing plants and regional economies. In many cases it reflects, rather, the nature of a company's prior holdings and bargaining power with the provincial government.

For example, the companies that eventually merged in 1959 to form MacMillan Bloedel had, over the previous years, purchased sizeable portions of the railway grant from Canadian Pacific, and also controlled extensive private holdings and temporary tenures throughout the Island,

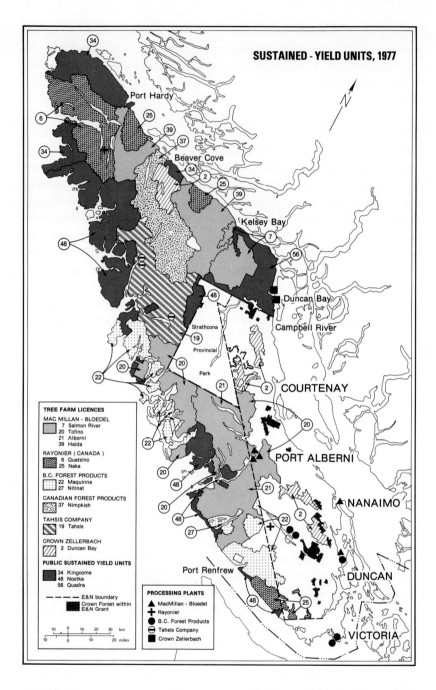

FIGURE 4.6 Tree Farm Licences by company, and Public Sustained Yield Units, 1977.

116

particularly in the Alberni-Great Central and Sproat Lake areas. Portions of these private holdings were combined with Crown land into two of the Company's TFLs, Alberni and Tofino, which are composed of a number of separated blocks, but together occupy most of the central part of the Island (Figure 4,6). They are closely integrated as a regional supply-processing unit centred on MacMillan Bloedel's pulp, paper, plywood and lumber complex at Port Alberni. In contrast, the company's Salmon River and Haida TFLs on the northeastern part of Vancouver Island are far removed from the processing plants that they supply on the lower mainland.

Of the other TFLs only Quatsino (Rayonier Canada), Tahsis (Tahsis Company), Nimpkish (Canadian Forest Products) and Nitinat (British Columbia Forest Products) are composed of single contiguous blocks. The first two function as regional supply areas for the Port Alice pulp mill, on the one hand, and the Tahsis Company's Gold River pulp mill and Tahsis sawmills, on the other. The Nitinat TFL, although on the west coast, supplies processing plants at Cowichan and Crofton on the east side of the Island. But the Nimpkish TFL, like the adjacent Mac-Millan Bloedel TFLs, continues a long established tradition of rafting logs from the northeastern area to processing plants on the mainland, 350 kilometres (215 miles) distant. The three remaining TFLs (Duncan Bay, Naka and Maquinna) each contain widely separated units, reflecting the companies' scattered holdings prior to TFL establishment. All three supply processing plants on the Island, as well as on the lower mainland.

TFLs and, in one case, PSYUs, were largely responsible, along with a rise in market demand for newsprint, for the imposition of a large scale pulp and paper industry upon the Island's preexisting sawmill complex. Four large pulp and paper mills, dwarfing the old Port Alice mill, were built between 1946 and 1958 at Crofton, Duncan Bay, Harmac (Nanaimo) and Port Alberni. The 1967 opening of the Tahsis Company's Gold River pulp mill in its west coast TFL marked the only major industrial expansion outside of the Georgia Strait-Port Alberni region. Logging activity, however, did not remain concentrated in the Georgia Strait region. Sustained-yield entailed a curtailment of harvesting in the Douglas fir stands of the eastern Island, and a dispersal to the TFLs and PSYUs of the central, western and northern parts. The established short distance links between Island mills and log supply areas were replaced by longer distance movements of logs from these previously peripheral areas.

Because of the benefits of mill integration, pulp mills, with the exception of the Gold River mill, were established at or close to existing saw-

mill sites. Wood chips and sawdust, by-products of sawmilling operations, could be used to supplement raw material needs, and tidewater
location was essential for log inputs and produce export. Integrated mill
complexes developed, on a large scale at Port Alberni and on smaller
scales at Duncan Bay and Harmac. More diffuse integration developed,
via complex log and wood chip flows, between the various mills in the
Nanaimo-Chemainus-Crofton-Victoria region, which is characterized by
scattered and relatively distant locations of various resource supplies.
Technological innovations, such as gang mills which can use small diameter logs; chippers and barkers that were built at most larger sawmills
expressly for the purpose of producing pulping material; and kiln drying
of hemlock for lumber to compete with the traditional Douglas fir increased the industry's ability to use the varied flow of log species and
grades now available from sustained-yield units on Vancouver Island.

Regional economies were significantly affected by the establishment of
TFLs and PSYUs. Port Alberni, previously dependent upon ailing lumber
and cedar shingle mills, was revitalized as a forest industrial centre by
the complex integration of its numerous mills with an expanded and
varied log hinterland. A smaller self-contained unit developed in the
Tahsis TFL, where a sawmill gave rise to the company town of Tahsis in
the early 1960's, and a pulp mill produced the "instant town" of Gold
River in the late 1960's. On the northern part of the Island, increased
investment by Rayonier Canada and Canadian Forest Products in road
networks and communities, such as Port Hardy, Port Alice, Beaver Cove,
Port McNeill and Woss, was bolstered largely by the security that TFLs
provided. However, it may be noted that, with the exception of the Port
Alice mill, there is no significant processing capacity to stabilize the
north Island economy. In the established Georgia Strait region, Nanaimo
took on a new lease of life as an industrial service and sawmill centre, and
expanded its port facilities. The Cowichan-Ladysmith mills were now
able to draw upon logs from a much wider area to supplement the fast
dwindling resources of the adjacent Esquimalt and Nanaimo grant.
Victoria sawmills and plywood plants, far removed from significant timber supplies, were able to draw logs from west coast sources once the
technical problems of exposed water transport had been overcome.

In addition to enabling industrial expansion, TFLs and PSYUs were
successful management instruments for bringing much alienated land, as
well as Crown land, under sustained-yield management. This was particularly important on the Island because of the large areas of Crown grant
and temporary tenures. As a result, the already preeminent position of a

relatively small number of large companies was enhanced. Six companies control all of the TFLs, and of these, MacMillan Bloedel accounts for about forty-five percent of productive land and harvest (Table 1,6). Between them, four of the six also hold approximately sixty percent of cutting rights in PSYUs, further enhancing their control of the regulated harvest on the Island.

THE INDUSTRY AND THE ISLAND ECONOMY, 1977

The two essential components of the industrial structure on Vancouver Island are log supply and log processing (Figures 5,6 and 6,6). Many Island log supply areas and processing plants are connected, via log and by-product flows, with their mainland counterparts and are, therefore, included within an integral coastal forest industry and management system. Some of the sustained-yield units encompass both Island and mainland areas, and Forest Service administration at regional and district levels also incorporates the Island with the adjacent coast.

One central fact has remained constant throughout the many developments in the forest industry. The growth of the industry has always been based upon the liquidation of a standing crop of natural, old growth timber. Therefore, the 1977 harvest was cut from a resource which, on the Island as a whole, is limited to only about thirty years' supply, mainly in TFLs and PSYUs. The extensive regrowth stands that have filled in logged areas, especially in the railway grant, have not been used as a significant timber supply, or been managed as the critical future resource that they represent.

Almost seventy-six percent of the 5,800,000 cunits harvested on the Island in 1977 came from sustained-yield units, with TFLs outranking PSYUs by six to one (Table 2,6). Although the harvest from these units must, over time, fall within limits set by the allowable cut, there are considerable variations from year to year, depending on market and labour conditions. In 1976, for example, cuts in TFLs 19 (Tahsis) and 21 (Alberni) were twenty percent above the approved annual allowable amount, but in 1975 were below it. Similar trends were shown by other TFLs. For the Island as a whole, the 1975 harvest fell twenty-one percent below the previous year, and was thirty-one percent below the 1972-1976 average. Due to a return of buoyant market conditions and stable labour relations, the 1976 harvest jumped to twenty-nine percent above the 1972-1976 average.

119

TABLE 1,6 Summary of Tree Farm Licences, Vancouver Island

Licence Number, Name and Licencee	Productive Area		Annual Allowable Cut 1975-76 Average		Actual Harvest 1972-76 Average	
	Hectares	Percent	Cunits	Percent	Cunits	Percent
7, Salmon River, MacMillan Bloedel	70,944	4.7	190,000	5.0	145,462	4.9
20, Tofino, MacMillan Bloedel	144,166	9.6	421,560	11.0	285,264	9.6
21, Alberni, MacMillan Bloedel	216,154	14.4	726,710	19.0	570,384	19.2
39, Haida,* MacMillan Bloedel	255,510	16.9 } 45.6	349,612	9.1 } 44.1	318,991	10.8 } 44.5
6, Quatsino, Rayonier Canada	143,941	9.6	443,215	11.2	339,525	11.4
25, Naka,* Rayonier Canada	91,291	6.1 } 15.7	214,000	5.6 } 16.8	158,296	5.4 } 16.8
22, Maquinna, British Columbia Forest Products	151,534	10.1	363,044	9.5	304,551	10.3
27, Nitinat, British Columbia Forest Products	12,988	0.9 } 11.0	40,639	1.0 } 10.5	38,365	1.3 } 11.6
2, Duncan Bay, Crown Zellerbach	168,916	11.2	390,560	10.3	147,460	5.0
37, Nimpkish, Canadian Forest Products	135,532	9.0	395,500	10.4	371,895	12.5
19, Tahsis, Tahsis Company	113,155	7.5	302,000	7.9	285,738	9.6
	1,504,131	100.0	3,836,840	100.0	2,965,951	100.0

*Parts of these TFLs within the Vancouver Forest District are on the mainland.

SOURCE: British Columbia Forest Service, annual reports and unpublished data.

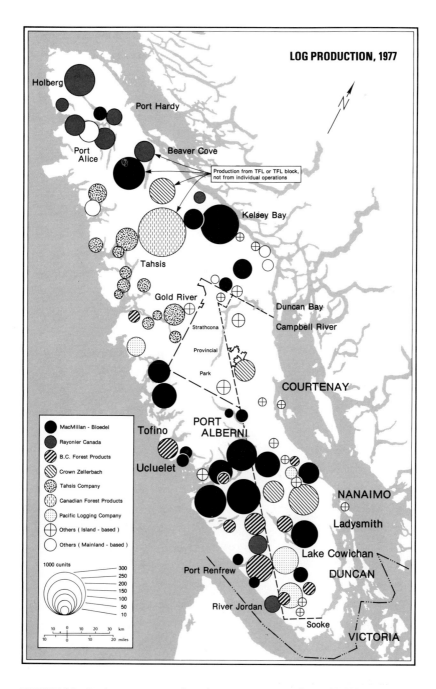

FIGURE 5,6 Production in cunits from logging operations of over 10,000 cunits.

121

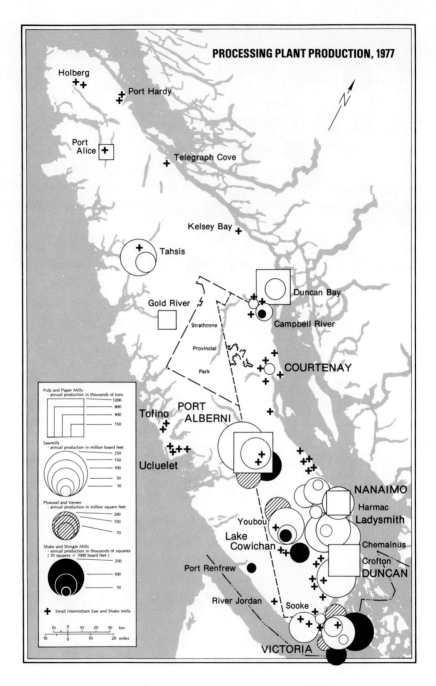

FIGURE 6.6 Production capacity of wood processing plants, 1977.

122

Besides their strong control of the regulated harvest, the "big six" also control sixty percent of the unregulated cut from private lands (Table 2,6). Two of them, MacMillan Bloedel and Crown Zellerbach, own large tracts within the former Esquimalt and Nanaimo grant which are not included in their TFLs, and British Columbia Forest Products has smaller holdings. Pacific Logging, a Canadian Pacific subsidiary, owns 121,500 hectares (300,100 acres), mainly south of Cowichan Lake. Collectively, these four companies own sixty-five percent of the original land grant and control eighty percent of the harvest from these lands. Other major forest companies also have holdings in the railway grant, although some of these properties are not currently logged. They include Scott Paper which controls holdings north of Parksville almost equal in extent to those of British Columbia Forest Products; Weldwood, another of the ten largest timber holding and manufacturing companies in the Province; and Rayonier Canada.

A number of small companies accounted for a total of eight percent of the harvest, in Timber Sale Harvest Licences on PSYUs, old temporary tenures and private holdings (Table, 2,6). Mainland-based interests include the lumber manufacturers, Bay Forest Products and Whonnock. Island-based companies, including one that annually cuts approximately 40,000 cunits in Strathcona Provincial Park, own or supply mills ranging from small, intermittent operations to mills with a respectable annual capacity of 50,000,000 board feet.[18]

Within the Georgia Strait region a combination of inertia, benefits of horizontal integration and the advantage of tidewater location have maintained established sawmill centres in the face of increasing distance from log supplies (Figures 5,6 and 6,6). Many of these mills that were established for the processing of Douglas fir now specialize in hemlock lumber. Five nodes of activity, at Victoria, Crofton-Chemainus, Cowichan Lake, Nanaimo and Campbell River-Courtenay, have consolidated their position, although Cowichan Lake increasingly suffers from inadequate timber supplies and its non-coastal location (Figure 6,6). Within each of these nodes the number of mills has decreased in the past thirty years, while total production has increased, and all but Victoria and Cowichan Lake have been augmented by pulp and paper mills. Port Alberni, the largest single forest industry complex on the Island, maintains its position at the transition of the Georgia Strait and west coast regions. Beyond the periphery of the Georgia Strait region, there are isolated nodes of activity at Gold River, Tahsis and Port Alice.

123

TABLE 2,6 Vancouver Island Timber Harvest,
By Company and Tenure, 1977 Estimates in Percentage

Company	TFL	PSYU	Private*	Other**	Total
MacMillan Bloedel	29.3	0.7	6.7	-	36.7
Rayonier	10.8	0.3	1.0	-	12.1
Tahsis Company	5.8	4.3	-	-	10.1
British Columbia Forest Products	6.5	0.8	2.5	-	9.8
Crown Zellerbach	5.2	-	3.0	-	8.2
Canadian Forest Products	7.9	-	-	-	7.9
Pacific Logging	-	0.9	5.6	-	6.5
Bay Forest Products†	-	0.7	1.9	-	2.6
Whonnock†	-	0.6	-	-	0.6
Weldwood†	-	0.4	-	-	0.4
Other	-	1.4	2.6	1.1	5.1
Total	65.5	10.1	23.3	1.1	100.0

*Unregulated harvest from private land in the Esquimalt and Nanaimo grant and old temporary tenures not included in TFLs.

**Mainly Vancouver Island Plantation and timber rights in Strathcona Provincial Park.

†Companies owning or supplying processing plants on the mainland.

SOURCE: British Columbia Forest Service, unpublished data.

The degrees of inter-mill integration at each of these nodes, and relationships with regional log supplies, differ markedly. Port Alberni has attained regional self-sufficiency and integration of supplies and processing. On a smaller scale, Port Alice and Tahsis-Gold River also exhibit regional self-sufficiency. All other nodes exhibit lesser degrees of internal integration. Although Crown Zellerbach's pulp and paper mill at Duncan Bay is integrated with a gang mill, log supply areas for both mills stretch from the Nitinat valley on the west to points on the northeast coast of the Island. The MacMillan Bloedel mills at Harmac, along with the Company's Chemainus sawmill, draw logs from a wide area. The remaining sawmills in the Chemainus-Nanaimo area form a loosely integrated complex and are operated by companies which, in their PSYU or private holdings, do not control the volumes of timber that support the "big six." The British Columbia Forest Product's mills in Victoria draw logs from west coast flows directed toward Vancouver, but are integrated with the Crofton pulp mill to which they supply chips, and the Youbou mill from which is received veneer for plywood manufacture. Part of the wood supplies for the Youbou mills, however, may be threatened by park alienation. On the other side of Lake Cowichan at Honeymoon Bay, the large Western Forest Industries (Rayonier Canada) saw and shingle mill is facing depletion of mature stands in its Gordon River holdings.

Control of forest manufacturing on the Island is even more concentrated than control of timber holdings (Table 3,6). Of the "big six," only Canadian Forest Products does not operate processing plants on the Island, and the remaining five control all pulp and paper, seventy percent of lumber and eighty-seven percent of plywood. Doman Industries is a rapidly expanding, Island-based company that augmented its existing mills with a large, new sawmill at Cowichan Bay in 1976, and recently has announced the pending construction of a similar-sized mill at Nanaimo. It is also searching for a site for a thermo-mechanical pulp mill. Most of Doman's timber supplies come from off-Island PSYUs, although the company's past development has been due to its competitive bidding for logs on the open market, largely originating from the railway grant. Mayo Lumber also gets most of its timber supplies from the mainland. Pacific Logging, mainly a timber harvester until the mid 1960's, has moved increasingly into lumber manufacture by obtaining joint interests in existing mills. The CIPA mill at Nanaimo, eighty percent Japanese owned, receives hemlock logs from Pacific Logging which it processes into lumber specifically for the Japanese market. Smaller mills, also often shipping directly to overseas markets, may employ up to 100 workers and are very important to local economies.

125

TABLE 3,6 Manufacturers and Major Forest Products
By Capacity, Vancouver Island, 1977, in Percentage

Company	Lumber*	Pulp	Paper	Plywood and Veneer
MacMillan Bloedel	41.9	42.0	47.0	32.0
British Columbia Forest Products	9.3	20.3	23.5	55.2
Crown Zellerbach	2.3	22.3	29.5	-
Tahsis Company	10.0	9.6	-	-
Rayonier Canada	6.5	5.8	-	-
Doman Industries	9.4	-	-	-
Pacific Logging	5.1	-	-	-
Mayo Lumber	2.6	-	-	-
CIPA	2.6	-	-	-
Others	10.3**	-	-	12.8
Total	100.0	100.0	100.0	100.0

*Excludes shingle mills and sawmills with less than 25,000 board feet per eight hour shift capacity.

**Nine mills share this capacity on a roughly equal basis.

SOURCE: British Columbia Forest Service and industry data.

On a larger scale, it is difficult to overstate the importance of the forest industry complex to the Island's economy.[19] Logging and wood processing activities directly employ twenty-two percent of the Island's total work force. Wood processing accounts for seventy-six percent of the total manufacturing work force, and logging provides over three times the amount of employment as do fishing, agriculture and mining combined. Many communities, especially on the west and north coasts, such as Gold River, Tahsis, Zeballos and Port Hardy, owe their very existence to logging or mill activities. In 1973 there were approximately 500 contract logging, trucking, road building and log booming firms operating on the Island, concentrated, particularly, in Duncan, Port Alberni and Campbell River.[20] These ranged in size from small operators owning a single truck and power saw to large "stump-to-dump" operators, usually contracted to a major timber licencee and employing perhaps 150 men. Whole regional economies are founded on the forest resource: in the Alberni-Clayoquot census division, logging and wood processing provide sixty-one percent of all employment, and in the Cowichan valley division, forty percent.[21] Even if pulp mill and sawmill employment at Tahsis, Gold River, Port Alice, Campbell River and Duncan Bay is excluded, logging alone accounts for forty percent of the total work force on the Island north of a line from Gold River to Courtenay.[22] Only in Victoria, where the forest industry accounts for thirty-six percent of manufacturing activity, does the portion of the total work force directly employed by forest-related activities fall to the much lower level of seven percent.[23]

Within individual communities, forestry often provides the bulk of "basic" (export of products outside the community) industry and employment and, therefore, influences the amount of "non-basic" employment provided by activities producing goods and services for the local market. This "employment multiplier" averages about two in medium-sized forest-based communities: in other words there is one non-basic job for every basic job.[24] Employment multipliers have been calculated at 2.7 for Nanaimo where forestry represents half of basic employment and 1.9 in Port Alberni where it represents ninety percent.[25]

Above the community level, the industry has a tremendous indirect impact on regional and provincial economies through its use of goods and services necessary to support its operations. At all stages, from logging through to movement of wood chips and manufactured products, the industry is a heavy user of road, rail and water transport. Capital and repair construction in the forest industry accounts for fourteen percent of the provincial construction industry.[26] The manufacture, purchase and servicing of machinery and equipment, especially in Alberni, Nanaimo and Victoria, are other sources of employment and income. It has been estimated, on a provincial basis, that employment from these indirect

127

effects of the industry is at least equal to half of its direct employment.[27] Additionally, employment in services generated or induced by direct and indirect industrial activity at least equals that in both of these combined. If this reasoning is applied to the approximately 20,000 workers directly employed in logging and wood processing on the Island a total work force of 60,000, or sixty-five percent of all employment, may stem from the forest industry. This compares with a provincial average of twenty-five percent.[28]

THE FUTURE

Much of the past and present of Vancouver Island has been and is wedded to the fortunes of the forest industry. A future Island economy in which that industry does not play a significant role is unthinkable. But the degree of future economic dependence on the industry, the manner in which the forest resources are utilized, and the relationship between forestry and other economic and social needs, are not necessarily predetermined by historical precedent. Currently there are developments, both "internal" and "external" to the industry and the Island, that portend significant future changes in forest management and industrial operations. Many see these developments as more significant than those vicissitudes that have surfaced periodically in the past to be dealt with by successive commissions and amendments to the 1912 Forest Act. Public debate on the role of forest resources in the Province's development has intensified in the 1970's, and there is criticism that in the new Forest Act passed by the Legislature in 1978 there is not sufficient attention paid to the findings of the 1975 Pearse Commission. Forest management and industry face a transitional period, and in coming years significant changes in both established and emerging attitudes toward the forest resource must be accommodated.

While it is beyond the scope of this chapter to review all of these changes, particularly those that are external in origin, an attempt is made to deal with a few topics of an internal nature.[29] These have been chosen to illustrate some aspects of the two components outlined in the previous section, those related to log supply and forest management and those related to the structure of the Island's forest industry complex. The major external factor may be mentioned in passing, however; British Columbia's share of a fluctuating international wood products market is decreasing in the face of competition from other wood producing regions. Present developments in wood production, harvesting and processing in the southeastern United States and Scandinavia, and future developments in Russia, Brazil and Southeast Asia, promise to change significantly wood product trade patterns. Many of these areas have advantages over British Columbia in terms of forest growth rates, costs and market proximity. And some of the larger forest companies operating in the Province have significant investments in many of these competing areas.

Forest Management and Log Supply

Much controversy surrounds the calculation and allocation of allowable cut, the mechanism by which the harvest in sustained-yield units is regulated.[30] There is concern over the narrowing gap between cutting rates and the sustainable supply of harvestable timber. This has happened in spite of continued upward revisions in allowable cuts for TFLs and PSYUs since their establishment, due to improved timber inventory data and the employment of closer utilization standards. In some TFLs, these revisions were in the order of 200 percent over the originally established cuts. PSYUs on the Island are harvested at only about seventy percent of theoretical allowable cut, but this harvest may be close to the maximum possible. When timber inventory data are transformed into actual harvest rates, insufficient account is taken of rough terrain, decadent timber with high unavoidable losses in harvesting, and economic and environmental constraints on closer utilization.

In general, the consensus of opinion seems to be that allowable cuts in old growth TFL and PSYU timber on Vancouver Island are at the maximum possible under sustained-yield. Obtaining greater utilization of many stands during harvesting, even when the allowable cut would indicate that this is possible, is thwarted by the nature of the stands themselves. As the logging frontier on the Island has shifted to the west and north, the move from accessible, high quality stands into less accessible, low quality stands has imposed strains on extractive, transportation and processing techniques, and raised the cost of obtaining a less valuable raw product. The supply situation on the Island, therefore, is one of mature, often decadent, stands committed to the maximum possible cut. In relation to existing processing plant capacity, however, these supplies are overcommitted. One study has demonstrated that if coastal pulp and paper mills were to operate at full rated capacity, coastal wood supplies would fall short of satisfying their needs by over 420,000 cunits.[31] Similarly, if coastal sawmills were to operate at rated capacity their needs would exceed coastal wood supplies.[32]

Current allowable cuts are high because of the large volume of timber in old stands, although much of that timber is not economically usable. As these high volume stands are removed and progressively replaced by lower volume, regrowth stands, calculated allowable cuts will fall short of present levels. This will result in an inescapable reduction in harvest rates.[33] Among other effects, this would exaggerate the present excess processing capacity of Island mills relative to local timber supplies, and dictate that no additional processing capacity be constructed. But, even if present allowable cuts were to be reduced to lessen the eventual impact of the reduction in harvest, that excess processing capacity would be further exaggerated. In those areas of the Province where the reduction will not occur for seventy years or more, silvicultural advances may offset its impact. But on Vancouver Island, it is more imminent due to the limited remaining inventory of mature timber; some TFL divisions contain up to sixty years' remaining old growth supply, but many have as little as ten or twenty years' supply. Yet, these old growth stands occupy some of the most productive sites, and after logging and reforestation, the regrowth stands on them will provide much of the future forest resource. Young planted stands are progressively filling in sustained-yield units as they are logged, but in much of the Esquimalt and Nanaimo grant, this resource is already available in the form of advanced regrowth stands up to ninety years old. Intensive management of this future harvestable standing crop is essential.

The economic advantages of utilizing these stands even now are considerable, and many are past the rotation age planned for managed crops. Established on the earliest logged areas which, generally, were the most accessible and fertile sites, they contain high timber volumes, yielding potentially higher returns than many old growth stands. Most of them are close to tidewater and the processing plants of the eastern Island. Some of the most productive areas, however, are being significantly eroded by urban development. In many younger stands silvicultural techniques, such as fertilization, spacing and thinning, could greatly increase timber quality and future yields. Forest Service experiments in the Sayward Forest, north of Campbell River, indicate a 100 percent greater annual increment in thinned and fertilized immature Douglas fir than in similar-aged, unmanaged stands.[34] But the conservatism and inertia imposed on management policies by the past availability of old growth timber is reflected in the Forest Service's policy of requiring all mature timber to be cut before younger stands. On Crown land the industry is thus forced to harvest the less accessible and often lower quality stands in areas that are more expensive to log. One rationale for this is to replace these stands, which show no positive annual increment, with productive regrowth. Yet, because of the budgetary priorities given to reforestation, there are no provisions in TFL agreements for the Forest Service to support either non-commerical regrowth stand improvements or commercial thinning.[35] The old growth has been divided among the big companies, the timber is cut, seedlings are planted, but systematic silvicultural management of the growing crop is not undertaken.

Some tree-farm licencees have attempted limited non-commercial stand improvements, but the most intensive developments in second growth management on the Island appear to be those of Pacific Logging. On its private land it is free of the restrictions placed by the Forest Service on the activities of Crown land licencees. Pacific Logging has developed economical techniques for aerial fertilization that can increase productivity by twenty-five percent. With thinning, juvenile spacing and sanitation cutting, productivity increases by 100 percent. The company now has the largest area of fertilized second growth forest in Canada, 10,930 hectares (27,000 acres).[36] Like the large Crown land licencees, it operates a tree improvement orchard, and it also spends approximately $8.60 per hectare ($3.50 per acre) on silvicultural management, compared with an average expenditure by the Forest Service on Crown land, exclusive of TFLs, of only seventy-five cents per hectare.[37]

Pacific Logging, like other companies on private land, can operate with greater flexibility in balancing log supplies to the changing economic conditions that determine the output of processing plants. On Crown land tenures, regulation of the cut is based upon the objective of ensuring constant harvests over long periods. Generally, a licencee must harvest within fifty percent of the allowable annual cut each year and within ten percent in each five years. This imposes some limitations on the licencee's ability to respond to short-term economic fluctuations that determine the demand for wood products and, therefore, influence the economically optimum rate of log harvesting. In a long-term perspective, there is growing evidence that present harvest regulations on Crown land tenures, because they are based upon the physical volume of timber and an overriding concern with constant harvest rates and regional economic stability, are inadequate to meet the requisites of present and future predicted patterns of timber use.[38] With the changes in logging areas, transportation and utilization techniques over the past three decades, many sustained-yield units now patently do not act as regional timber supply areas. Indeed, on the Island, optimum timber supply regions, as now delimited by the location and structure of processing plants, often incorporate separately managed TFLs and PSYUs. Concentration of wood processing on the Island has resulted in the demise of many smaller logging and milling operations, while sustained-yield unit boundaries have remained constant. As the Pearse Report noted:

> ...developments in industrial structure render obsolete the timber supply regions appropriate for an earlier period; and...regulation of regional harvest rates does not secure the continuity of local economic activity.[39]

Industrial Structure

The general structure and distribution of wood processing on the Island has remained fairly constant over the past forty years, in spite of changes in timber supply regions and the problems associated with harvest regulations. Those mills and forest-based communities that disappeared in the face of industrial concentration and dwindling wood supplies were mostly situated within the Georgia Strait-Alberni region, precisely the area in which centralization has taken place. More fluctuation in regional economies has occurred on the northern part of the Island, but even there centres, such as Winter Harbour, Holberg and Port McNeill, have displayed remarkable stability. Are there likely to be any changes in this industrial structure over the next thirty years?

Many Vancouver Island mills, even those established only twenty-five years ago, are obsolete and becoming increasingly difficult to maintain economically in the face of costly renovations and pollution control measures. Twenty-seven percent of the Province's forest industry capital investment goes to meet pollution control guidelines, compared with a national average of twelve percent.[40] Recently, Rayonier has expended over 40,000,000 dollars on pollution control at the Port Alice mill, and all the major companies are undertaking smaller, but still multi-million dollar renovations. Increasing the efficiency of mills, particularly through the construction of hog fuel power boilers, is another major outlay, as at MacMillan Bloedel's Alberni and Harmac mills. There is general concern within the "big six" over their self-perceived inability to generate new investments, as labour and construction costs soar and returns on invested capital, at six percent, are the lowest of any major industry in Canada. Not only does the industry feel uneasy with the local and worldwide impacts of inflation and recession, it also has sharply criticized

132

many aspects of Forest Service policy, particularly those relating to harvest regulation and tenure security, costs of logging road construction and environmental constraints on industrial activities. One industrial spokesman was moved to comment on this plethora of problems in 1975:

> (the industry)...is confronted by bureaucracies intent on enforcing costly operating procedures totally divorced from practical economics.... (these trends) are perilously close to pricing the industry out of the market....capital is more mobile than labour and will quickly seek out the healthiest climate.[41]

Such prognostications concerning industrial closure or decline, and the impact this would have on regional and provincial economies, have appeared frequently in the past six years. Indeed, they were voiced even in the 1950's and 1960's, a very healthy period for the industry. A credibility gap seems to have been created by the industry. The public is skeptical as to whether or not these industrial problems exist, and there has been a tremendous growth in public awareness of other forest values, such as recreation, conservation and wildlife.

While the industry may have many real problems, there are enough new developments underway or proposed to indicate a considerable degree of industrial confidence in the future. This is, perhaps, surprising in view of the fact that the pulp mills on the Island have rarely operated at over eighty percent of capacity.[42] One of the fastest growing industrial concerns is Doman Industries, although it is small in comparison to the big companies. At present this company is looking for a site for a 300 ton per day thermo-mechanical pulp mill, initially to supply pulp to other mills, but eventually to be converted to paper and newsprint production.[43] Possible locations range from Cowichan Bay to Port Hardy.[44] Crown Zellerbach also is considering a thermo-mechanical mill which would be built at Duncan Bay. Thermo-mechanical mills have many advantages that make them more attractive investments, in many cases, than kraft mills. Their minimum economic size and establishment cost is twenty-five percent of that of a kraft mill. Because their efficiency of fibre conversion is twice that of a kraft mill, the wood requirements of a minimum-sized operation would be about thirteen percent of those for a large chemical mill, and their environmental impact as a result of mill effluent would be much less. The demand for lumber and plywood has been firmer than it has been for pulp and paper over the past ten years. This has led to the establishment of new mills by Doman Industries, CIPA and

Pacific Logging, and the current plans for a sawmill and plywood plant at Crown Zellerbach's Duncan Bay operations, as well as another sawmill to be built by Doman Industries at Nanaimo. As Island timber supplies are fully committed, the timber for most of these new developments will come from off-Island sources, particularly the north-central mainland coast PSYUs. The eastern side of the Island, with its tidewater access to these sources, is favourably placed to receive and process that timber.

Looking some twenty years ahead, there is another reason, besides the use of mainland timber, for predicting that the eastern Island will continue to be the major region of wood processing. By that time, many of the advanced regrowth stands in the old railway grant will be harvestable. These stands are considerable, and although the old grant lands now contribute less than twenty percent of the Island harvest, by then it will be far higher. This will hold, not only for the smaller industrial operators, but also for the large companies that control extensive Esquimalt and Nanaimo holdings, in addition to their western TFLs.

CONCLUSION

While the present geographical distribution of wood processing and the general boundaries of forest tenure and management units are not likely to change significantly in the foreseeable future, there will, undoubtedly, be changes in the way in which the forest resources are used and in the nature of wood processing. The province of Ontario, with only half the wood supply of British Columbia, and that of an inferior quality, manages to generate almost twice the return per cunit in value added as does British Columbia.[45] Of economic necessity, the historic dependence of the coastal wood industry upon incremental depletion of old forest growth and production of unfinished and semi-finished products will decline, and the industry will turn to more intensive forest management and greater output of high value manufactured products. This is particularly true for the pulp and paper segment of the industry, but significant changes also are likely in the Island's sawmill industry, which is now dominated by old, often obsolete mills designed to handle large diameter logs. At the present time, with the harvest still coming mainly from old growth timber, the choice between construction of small or large log handling capacity in new sawmills is fraught with economic difficulties. But as smaller logs (less than thirty-five centimetres or fourteen inches in diameter) become available from regrowth stands, investment in mills specifically designed to handle these logs will be necessary. Also to be expected is a greater production of high value-added products to supplement the lower value lumber that dominates the sawmill industry today.

New uses of the timber resources and even greater public concern about integrated forest use can be expected in future. Because of its biodegradability, natural cellulose may be more acceptable for many uses, and also cheaper, than existing synthetic polymers. Residual effluent from pulp processing can be transformed into biomass sediment containing forty-seven percent carbohydrate and thirty-eight percent protein. The possibilities of large-scale use of lignin for both human and animal food by the 1990's are promising. Non-consumptive uses of the timber resource for a wide range of recreation activities and aesthetic enjoyment will expand in the future, undoubtedly, along with a greater application of integrated "environmental" forest management intended to optimize benefits from all forest resources. Conflicts, such as those concerning the impact of log processing plants on estuarine areas on the Island's east coast; the future of the Tsitika-Schoen area, the largest remaining unlogged watershed on the Island that is now removed from a logging moratorium; and the prolonged negotiations between industry and the provincial and federal governments concerning the addition of forest land to the southern section of the Pacific Rim National Park, are likely to intensify in the absence of objective and realistic mechanisms for their solution. It remains to be seen whether or not the new Forest Act, passed by the provincial Legislature in June 1978, will provide those mechanisms. The shifting balance between traditional forestry practices and a newer socio-environmental forestry, and all that this implies in the way of changes in in management, industrial, political and public attitudes, will have a profound, but unquantifiable, impact on Vancouver Island's future forest industry.

REFERENCES

1. Canada, *Manufacturing Industry of Canada: Sub-provincial Areas, 1974*. Ottawa: Statistics Canada, 1974. The Vancouver Island-Coast figure includes production from the Powell River mill complex on the mainland.

2. PEARSE, P.H. *Timber Rights and Forest Policy in British Columbia*. Victoria: Royal Commission on Forest Resources, Vols. 1 and 2, 1975.

3. SLOAN, G.M. *Report of the Commissioner Relating to the Forest Resources of British Columbia, 1945*. Victoria: King's Printer, 1945; and *idem.*, 1957.

4. The Esquimalt and Nanaimo Railway Company was acquired by Canadian Pacific in 1905.

5. The Vancouver Forest District includes Vancouver Island with the adjacent mainland east to the Lillooet valley and northwest to Seymour Inlet.

6. These tenures are discussed in British Columbia, *Forest Tenures in British Columbia*. Victoria: Task Force on Crown Timber Disposal, 1974; and PEARSE, P.H., *op. cit.*, Vol. 2, Appendix A.

7. A cunit equals 2.83 cubic metres (100 cubic feet) of wood, and is the standard measure of log volume in British Columbia. Board foot is the standard measure of lumber, equal to the volume of a board measuring 30x30x2.5 centimetres (12x12x1 inch). One cunit approximates 600 board feet.

8. Steam donkeys were steam-powered engines equipped with drums and cables used to move logs. "High-lead" refers to a system of dragging felled logs to central assembly areas. Cables were strung to large trees and a carriage moving along the cables dragged logs over the ground. The environmental impacts of this technique were severe.

9. HARDWICK, W.G. "Geography of the Forest Industry of Coastal British Columbia," *Occasional Papers in Geography.* Vancouver: Canadian Association of Geographers, British Columbia Division, No. 5, 1963, p. 15; and HAIG-BROWN, R.L. *The Living Land.* Toronto: MacMillan, 1961, p. 73.

10. HAIG-BROWN, R.L., *op. cit.*, p. 62.

11. FULTON, F.J. *Final Report of the Royal Commission of Inquiry on Timber and Forestry, 1909-1910.* Victoria: King's Printer, 1910.

12. Address by MANNING, E.C., Chief Forester, to the Forestry Committee of the British Columbia Legislature, November 15, 1938.

13. MULLHOLLAND, F.D. *Forest Resources of British Columbia.* Victoria: British Columbia Forest Service, 1937.

14. SLOAN, G.M., *op. cit.*, 1945.

15. *Ibid.*, p. 40.

16. The 1978 Forest Act extends this period to twenty-five years.

17. Three of these TFLs extend onto the mainland or the Queen Charlotte Islands.

18. These cutting rights in Strathcona Park were granted to the company as a trade for cutting rights previously held at Cape Scott before that area was declared a provincial park. Other cutting rights, on old timber leases in the southeastern portion of Strathcona Park, are held by MacMillan Bloedel.

19. For a review of the forest industry's role in the Province's economy see British Columbia, *The British Columbia Forest Industry: Its Direct and Indirect Impact on the Economy.* Victoria: British Columbia Forest Service, 1975 (Prepared by F.L.C. Reed and Associates, Vancouver).

20. *The "ABC" British Columbia Lumber Directory.* Vancouver: Progress Publishing, 1973.

137

21. Canada, *Industries: Industry Divisions by Sex, for Canada, Provinces, and Census Divisions, 1975.* Ottawa: Statistics Canada, 1975.

22. *Ibid.*

23. *Ibid.*

24. British Columbia, *The British Columbia Forest Industry: Its Direct and Indirect Impact on the Economy, op. cit.,* p. 56.

25. *Ibid.,* p. 57.

26. *Ibid.,* p. 25.

27. *Ibid.*

28. *Ibid.,* p. 53.

29. See PEARSE, P.H., *op. cit.,* Vol. 1, Chap. 1, for a concise statement of trends in the forest industry.

30. *Ibid.,* Chaps. 17 and 18.

31. British Columbia; *Opportunities for the Expansion of Pulp Production in Southern British Columbia.* Victoria: British Columbia Forest Service, Special Studies Division, 1976, p. 50.

32. *Ibid.,* p. 31.

33. This reduction is referred to as "fall-down."

34. British Columbia, *Five-year Growth Response of Douglas fir to Fertilization in the Sayward Forest, Vancouver Island.* Victoria: British Columbia Forest Service, Research Division, Research Note No. 77, 1976.

35. The new Forest Act (1978) does contain provisions for non-commercial treatment and intensive silvicultural management, although those provisions are couched in very general terms.

36. Personal Communication, B. Devitt, Chief Forester, Pacific Logging Company, 1978.

37. *Ibid.*

38. For a discussion of the advantages and disadvantages of current harvest regulations and their role in maintaining regional economic stability see PEARSE, P.H., *op. cit.*, Vol. 1, Chap. 17.

39. PEARSE, P.H., *op. cit.*, Vol. 1, p. 232.

40. British Columbia, *Opportunities for the Expansion of Pulp Production in Southern British Columbia, op. cit.*, p. 92.

41. TIMMIS, D.W., "What is the Future of the Forest Industry?" Address to the Vancouver Board of Trade by the President, MacMillan Bloedel, September 12, 1975.

42. The industry has long been characterized by a paradoxical high level of capital investment in the face of low rates of return, perhaps due to deep-rooted feelings of certainty and optimism. See PEARSE, P.H., *op. cit.*, Vol. 1, pp. 8-9 and 50-51.

43. In the thermo-mechanical process, sawdust and chips are pre-steamed under pressure to soften the lignin before passing it through a pressurized refiner. The quality of the resulting fibre is almost equivalent to that of chemical pulp.

44. See Chapter 10 of this volume for a discussion of industrial and environmental conflicts in the Cowichan estuary.

45. British Columbia, *Opportunities for the Expansion of Pulp Production in Southern British Columbia, op. cit.*, p. 74.

PLATE 13   Mineral extraction, Utah mines.   *N. Bateman Photo* ▶

7 MINING

C.H. Howatson

Mining on Vancouver Island has not been as spectacular as on the mainland of British Columbia, but coal mining sustained the local economy for a long period and drew the attention of global shipping interests to the region, while lode mining has provided bursts of economic activity. Coal was the first mineral resource to be mined in British Columbia, the first production coming from seams outcropping along the beach at the Hudson's Bay trading post at Fort Rupert. More profitable seams were opened up at Nanaimo and later pits were established in the Comox field at Cumberland. The gold rush of 1858 to the Fraser River and later the Cariboo area bypassed Vancouver Island, but Victoria was used as a convenient supply base. There was a brief flurry of placer gold mining in the Victoria area in the 1860's, however, the deposits were small and widely scattered, and when no lode gold was forthcoming interest in the area quickly waned. Lode deposit mining has been small in scale, short-lived, and of local importance only, with the exception of the present operations at Rupert Inlet and Buttle Lake which are the only working mines on Vancouver Island today. There seems to be a rather diverse accumulation of mineral wealth on the Island, but much of it is too low grade or, if high grade, too limited in amount, and all of it is bound up in a complex geological mold.

GENERAL GEOLOGY

Vancouver Island and the Queen Charlotte Islands make up the Insular Mountains which, with the St. Elias Mountains, form the Outer Mountain area, the most westerly tectonic subdivision of the Canadian Cordillera. The main bulk of the Insular Mountains is made up of three igneous rock types, the Karmutsen Formation, the Island Intrusives and the Bonanza Group, with the Karmutsen underlying about one-half of the Island (Figure 1,7).

141

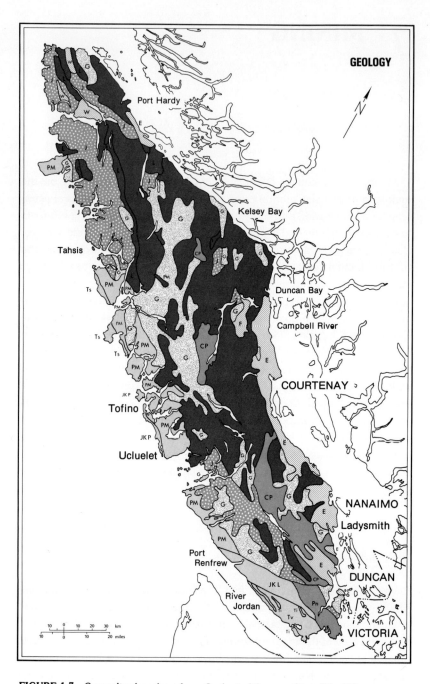

FIGURE 1,7 Generalized geology from Geological Survey, Open File 463.

142

	SEQUENTIAL LAYERED ROCKS			COMPLEXES - POORLY DEFINED AGE	
TERTIARY	Ts	CARMANAH FORMATION	Sediments	Ti	Sooke Intrusives
	Tv	METCHOSIN FORMATION	Volcanics	JKL	Leech River Formation
CRETACEOUS	E	NANAIMO GROUP	Sediments		
	W	QUEEN CHARLOTTE GROUP	Sediments		
JURASSIC		BONANZA GROUP	Volcanics	JKP	Pacific Rim Complex
				G	Island Intrusives
				PM	West Coast Complex
TRIASSIC		VANCOUVER GROUP	Quatsino-Parson Bay Formation / Karmutsen Formation		
PERMS PENN.	CP	SICKER GROUP	Volcanics and Sediments	Pn	Wark, Colquitz gneisses

The oldest known rocks on Vancouver Island, the Wark-Colquitz gneissic complex, have been tentatively dated as Devonian or earlier. The Sicker Group, known to be of Permian age, or older, has been subdivided into three formations, a lower volcanic, a middle clastic sediment, and an upper limestone. This group is thought to represent a mid-Paleozoic volcanic arc and after cessation of the vulcanism clastic and carbonate sediments were deposited.

The oldest Mesozoic rocks are of Mid-Triassic age and are represented by the lowest member of the Vancouver Group, a thin-bedded argillite. The Jurassic period is represented by: the Bonanza Group; the West Coast Complex and the Island Intrusives, all of which seem to be magmatically related; an unnamed upper Jurassic sedimentary series; the Pacific Rim Complex; and the Leech River formation. The Bonanza Group is made up of a series of lavas and intercalated beds of argillite and greywacke. The stratigraphy varies considerably, as the group represents

143

several centres of volcanic activity, one main centre being in the north-west and another in the southwest. The West Coast Complex is a heter-ogeneous mixture of gneiss, amphibolite and quartz diorite, which under-lies a fairly large portion of the central west coast.

> ...the complex is considered to be derived from
> Sicker and Vancouver Group rocks, magmatized in
> Early Jurassic time. Its mobilized granitoid part is
> considered to be the source of Island Intrusives and,
> indirectly, Bonanza volcanics.[1]

The Island Intrusives, which occur in both large and small bodies, under-lie about one-quarter of the Island. They are predominantly granitic in character and are thought to be co-magmatic with the Bonanza volcanics. This igneous activity represents a plutonic arc in which the vulcanism ceased in the middle of the Jurassic, and the Upper Jurassic sediments were deposited on the eroded igneous complex.

The Nanaimo Group of late Cretaceous age, which outcrops only on the east side of the Island, consists of five "cyclical, upward fining sequences of conglomerate, sandstone, and shale, and coal of non-marine or near shore deltaic origin, succeeded by marine sandstone, shale and thin-bedded graded shale-siltstone sequences."[2] Economic coal seams were found in the lowest cycle of the Comox basin and in the second cycle of the Nanaimo basin. This group represents deposition in a basin between the Coastal Plutonic Belt, which in Late Cretaceous time was an active volcanic area, and the Insular Mountains.

The Carmanah and Escalante Formations are clastic sediments of Eocene and Oligocene age which were deposited on an eroded surface that includes the Leech River formation and other Insular Mountain rocks. These sedimentary formations occur on the continental shelf, as well as on a narrow strip along the west coast. The youngest Tertiary rocks are the Miocene-Early Pliocene clastic sediments of the Sooke Bay Forma-tion, which occur as pockets in the erosion surface of the Metchosin volcanics-Sooke Intrusives, and some small occurrences south of Port McNeill of late Tertiary basalts, with poorly consolidated tuffs, brecias and volcanic boulder conglomerate.

Many rivers, lakes and fiords on Vancouver Island are associated with fault zones. Most of the faults are steep and only those associated with Pennsylvanian and Jura-Cretaceous sediments show isoclinal shear folding. There seem to be three predominant sets of faults; one a northerly and westerly set associated with rifting during the outflow of Karmutsen

144

lavas (Late Triassic); a northwesterly trending set created by southwest-ward and northeastward tilting in the Late Mesozoic-Early Tertiary; and a northeasterly set. Examples of the northerly set are Tahsis Inlet-Tahsis River-Woss Lake, Nimpkish Lake, and Bonanza Lake-lower Kokish River, and of the westerly set are Holberg Inlet-Rupert Inlet, Great Central Lake and Sproat Lake. Northwest faults are illustrated by Neroutsos Inlet, Alice Lake-Benson River and upper Nimpkish River-upper Oktwanch River. Trevor Channel and Nitinat Lake are examples of water bodies associated with northeasterly trending faults. The San Juan Fault followed by the San Juan River and Clapp Creek, and the Leech River Fault are thought by Muller to be of Late Mesozoic and Early Tertiary times, respectively, and may be structures that are associated with subduction zones.

COAL

Coal at Fort Rupert (Suquash coal basin) was first reported to the Hudson's Bay Company in 1835, but mining did not commence until 1846 when sixty-two tons of coal were put aboard H.M.S. Cormorant in exchange for clothing and other goods. As in the early days of coal mining at Nanaimo, the coal was picked mainly by Indians from the seams outcropping along the shore and transshipped via canoe. Miners, under contract, were brought out from Great Britain and among them was Robert Dunsmuir, originally foreman at Fort Rupert who later became the most noted coal entrepreneur on the Pacific coast. The coal seams in the Suquash basin are thin and faulted and could not compete with the thicker, more regular seams found in similar geological formations around Nanaimo. It has been estimated that 10,000 tons of coal were mined for steamship bunker fuel during the period from 1849 to 1854 when the Company gave up mining at this northern outpost and turned its attention to Nanaimo.[3] There was further mining in the area from 1908 to 1914 when an additional 12,000-16,000 tons were extracted by Pacific Coal Mines. Attempts were made to reactivate the mines after World War 1, but all operations ceased from 1922 until 1952 when a new company, Suquash Collieries, did some exploratory work. Today, British Columbia Hydro and others are showing some interest in the area, but present estimates suggest that the tonnages available are small and that the Suquash Basin will not become a major coal mining centre.[4]

145

The Nanaimo coalfield was first brought to the attention of Hudson's Bay Company officials at Fort Victoria by an Indian chief in 1852. The first coal, 480 barrels hand picked by Indians, was shipped in that year to Fort Victoria on the company schooner Cadboro.[5] In 1854, the arrival of twenty-four miners from Great Britain with their wives and children quadrupled the white population at this new mining venture.

The miners at Nanaimo were successful because the quality of the coal was good, especially for steam, mining of it was relatively easy, and it was the only readily available coal on the west coast of North America. The main market in the early days was San Francisco, with ships of the Royal Navy being a lesser one. Subsequently, the coal requirements of San Francisco and western American railroads were met by western American mines, but the increased steamship traffic in the Pacific area used Vancouver Island as a convenient bunkering station.

Over a period of time a number of mines and mining towns were developed in the Nanaimo and Comox areas. The original mines were situated on the Nanaimo waterfront and on Newcastle Island where the Douglas and Newcastle seams produced the greatest coal values. A rich seam at Wellington was first exploited in 1871 by Robert Dunsmuir, which marked the beginning of his rise to eminence in the coal industry. The coal from Wellington was delivered, at first by wagon, then by tramline and finally by railroad, to docks on the west side of Departure Bay (Figure 2A,7). Operations later expanded along the Wellington coal seam to East Wellington and Extension, with a connecting railroad to Ladysmith on Oyster Bay providing an outlet for the coal from Extension. One of the last coal mining towns to come into being was Cassidy, between Ladysmith and Nanaimo, where operations did not begin until 1917. Until 1888, the Nanaimo field was the only operating coalfield in British Columbia, but in that year the Comox field began production and, in the 1890's, coal mines in the interior began to compete with the coastal mines. Comox coal was shipped from the mines at Union, renamed Cumberland in 1897, by rail to Union Bay, a good deep-sea port at which wharves, bunkers and coke ovens were built (Figure 2B,7).

Coal production increased slowly at first, then spurted ahead during the latter part of the nineteenth century (Table 1,7). Vancouver Island coal production reached its peak in 1922 when output was 1,754,656 tons.[6] This was also Nanaimo's peak year, with 1,387,819 tons, but Comox had reached its peak in 1919 when the output reached 552,196 tons.[7] The maximum number employed at the mines occurred in 1921 when 4,640

146

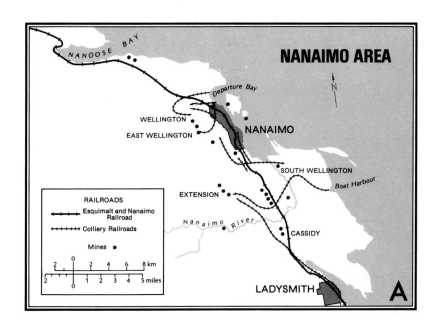

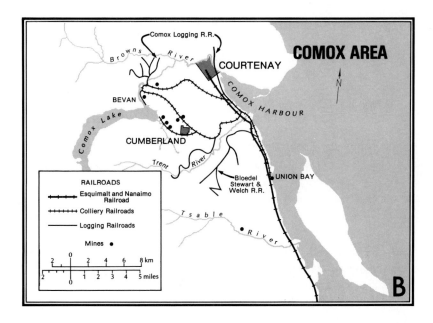

FIGURE 2.7 Coal mines and railroads in the Nanaimo and Comox areas.

147

TABLE 1,7 Coal Mined on Vancouver Island in Tons, 1860-1960

Year	Nanaimo	Comox	Vancouver Island	British Columbia	Vancouver Island as a Percentage of British Columbia
1860	14,246		14,246	14,246	100
1870	29,843		29,843	29,843	100
1880	267,595		267,595	267,595	100
1890	678,140		678,140	678,140	100
1900	1,059,853	323,523	1,383,376	1,439,595	96
1910	1,094,765	518,426	1,613,191	3,139,235	51
1920	1,242,340	455,914	1,698,254	2,696,774	63
1930	744,876	243,929	988,805	1,887,130	52
1940	375,415	357,244	732,659	1,667,827	44
1950	259,587	216,385	575,228	1,756,667	33
1960	2,640	88,764	91,404	884,500	10

SOURCE: British Columbia, Department of Mines and Petroleum Resources, Victoria, Annual Reports.

were on the payrolls (Table 2,7). A high proportion of the miners in the Comox field were Orientals, particularly during the 1920's.

The coal mining towns were badly hurt during the 1930's. Markets were poor, prices were down, the mines were old, production costs were increasing and in many mines the best seams had been worked out. This was the beginning of the end, for in the late 1930's when economic con-

TABLE 2.7 Employment in Coal Mines on Vancouver Island, 1900-1960

Year	Nanaimo				Comox				Vancouver Island
	No. of Mines	Underground White	Underground Oriental	Total at Mines	No. of Mines	Underground White	Underground Oriental	Total at Mines	Total at Mines
1900	10	2,131	0	2,797	3	567	158	904	3,701
1910	14	2,034	11	2,625	4	888	284	1,588	4,213
1920	11	1,884	0	3,079	3	400	428	1,312	4,391
1930	15	1,588	0	2,158	3	309	156	613	2,771
1940	11	N/A	N/A	826	2	N/A	N/A	893	1,719
1950	11	N/A	N/A	369	2	N/A	N/A	558	927
1960		N/A	N/A	14	1	N/A	N/A	248	262

SOURCE: British Columbia, Department of Mines and Petroleum Resources, Victoria, Annual Reports.

ditions were improving the markets for coal were declining, as many users were turning to oil. Ships no longer needed steam coal, the Island coals did not make coke suitable for blast furnaces and British Columbia's coastal copper smelters had closed down.

Mining activity declined markedly at Nanaimo after 1930 where most of the mines had ceased operations by the early 1950's. "As legacy, Nanaimo inherited a collection of abandoned and flooded workings, weed choked railway tracks which led to nowhere and dozens of dilapidated buildings."[8] By 1950, there were still thirteen mines in operation on the Island, but only four produced over 25,000 tons per year and just two mines, number 8 at Cumberland and number 10 at South Wellington, accounted for the bulk of Vancouver Island's production.[9] The Tsable River Mine south of Union Bay was not opened until 1947 and was the only large coal mine to have a name rather than a number. By 1960 all the other large producers had closed down, leaving the Tsable River to carry on until 1966 when it too succumbed. The coal mining industry on the Island had a life span of 112 years, but may be reborn in the near future.

As the mines closed and miners, with their families, moved away, most of the coal mining communities became ghost towns. Mine adits were blasted closed, shafts were filled or covered with concrete slabs, any useful machinery was removed and the remainder was abandoned. At Ladysmith and Union Bay the bunkers and loading wharves were torn down, but at Union Bay the coke ovens remained standing for a long time and were only removed, a bit at a time, when old brick became a fashionable decorating material. Many of the wooden buildings remaining in the communities were bulldozed and those that were not were taken down by people looking for usable building materials. Today, all that remains are concrete loading chutes, covering slabs, and tipple and slag piles, all of which have been so overgrown that it is difficult to find a trace of the former activity, even though a main highway may pass within thirty or forty metres.

A few of the communities have survived the demise of coal mining, Nanaimo being the best example. It not only survived, but thrived as a key transportation and service centre and its economy later was boosted by the forest industry. Ladysmith survived because the Comox Logging Company, working in the hills to the west, established workshops and offices in the town. Extension, Ladysmith's twin in mining, did not have the benefit of a logging operation and died. Almost all of the old mining camps have a few residents remaining, but no longer could they be considered as "towns".

There is renewed interest in coal mining on Vancouver Island. A joint operation by Weldwood of Canada, holders of all the former Canadian Collieries (Dunsmuir) coal mining rights, and Luscar Coal Mining Company is underway to develop three coal seams in the vicinity of Quinsam Lake, approximately sixteen kilometres (ten miles) southwest of Campbell River. It is hoped that the mine will be operating within a few years and the prospectus indicates a production of 1,000,000 tons per year, with a mine life expectancy of approximately eleven years. The coal will be produced partly by open pit and partly by underground workings. It will be trucked from the mines to a processing plant and to the shipping area which, presumably, will be Campbell River. It is hoped that the company will be able to expand and extend its mining operations southeastward along the coal measures, so that coal mining will again take its place as a long term source of economic activity.

PLACER GOLD

Small amounts of gold have been produced on Vancouver Island, mainly from the Leech River area about thirty-two kilometres (twenty miles) west of Victoria. Following the initial discovery by Lieutenant Peter Leech in 1864, several mining camps developed almost overnight, the two most prominent being Leechtown and Boulder City. It has been estimated that there were at least 1,200 "mines" worked by as many as 4,000 "miners."[10] The boom towns boasted of hotels, restaurants and houses, most of which were, in fact, crude log cabins. The gold, in pockets of gravel and in small joints and fissures in the stream bedrock, was quickly removed and the boom short-lived. Prospectors searched for gold bearing gravels in the stream banks similar to those that had been so productive in the Cariboo, and for the 'mother lode' from which the placer gold had come, but the search was in vain and interest in the gold field died in 1865. Subsequently, streams in the area have been worked sporadically with more modern equipment, but very little gold has been recovered. Today it is difficult to find any evidence of the former camps, for the old shanties have rotted away, been burned, scavenged and overgrown by fir and alder.

Some placer gold was recovered in 1899-1900 from black beach sands at Wreck Bay, now part of the Pacific Rim National Park, but there was either not enough gold reported to cause a gold rush, or the means of recovery were so sophisticated as to deter large numbers of individuals from rushing in to stake claims. Some efforts were made, in the early 1900's, to recover gold from gravel beds near the mouth of the Sombrio River, however, the value of the gold available would not cover the cost of removing the overburden. This has been the fate of most placer mining attempts on Vancouver Island — insufficient gold in return for the effort involved.

LODE DEPOSITS

The most important metallic ore deposits on Vancouver Island are:[11]

1. Massive sulphides of zinc, copper, lead, gold and silver in Sicker Volcanics. An example is Western Mines at Buttle Lake (Figure 3,7).

2. Skarn deposits of copper and iron in Quatsino limestone. Examples are Texada and Coast Copper mines.

3. Porphyry copper deposits surrounding and within high level Island Intrusions (Island Copper) or in the Sooke Intrusions (Mt. Washington, Catface).

4. Copper in shearzones in the amphibolized Sooke gabbro (Jordan River).

The copper mines worked in the vicinity of Mt. Sicker from 1897 to 1907 are a good example of the nature of lode mining on Vancouver Island (Figure 3,1). There were three mines on Mt. Sicker and one nearby at Copper Canyon. Activity in the area started in 1885, with the staking of claims which proved to be worthless, but in 1886 there was the discovery of a large outcrop of ore which had been laid bare by a forest fire on the west side of Mt. Sicker. The values revealed in the new showing led to a rush of "prospectors" from the farming areas of the nearby Cowichan valley and within weeks of the discovery the whole area was staked and counterstaked. Although the mines were not far from the Esquimalt and Nanaimo railroad at Westholme, development was difficult because the area was heavily forested and the land very steep, in many places cliffed. At first, transportation was by wagon which was adequate for bringing in supplies, but inadequate for the export of ore. An aerial tramway was built to the Lenora Mine, but even this could not keep up with the increasing ore production. In 1900, construction was started on a narrow

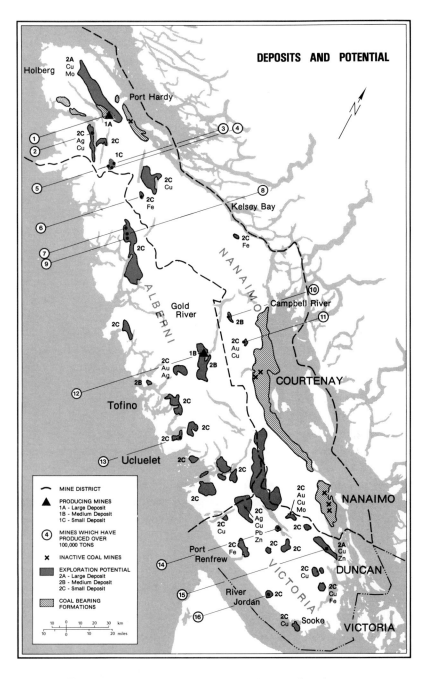

FIGURE 3.7 Mineral deposits, mining districts and potential production areas.

153

gauge railroad from Osborn Bay, now Crofton, to the mine. Although the Lenora and Mt. Sicker Railroad was only eleven miles long:

> ...the LMSRR has been described as being one of the most difficult and dangerous trackways ever laid in the province. Engineers faced a nightmare of 50 degree curves, switchbacks and trestles along the face of sheer cliffs and a grade so steep that it resembled something like a roller coaster ride.[12]

Part of the grade was thirteen percent for nearly one mile. The railroad, in spite of its handicaps, was capable of handling full mine production and delivered ore to a newly built copper smelter on Osborn Bay.

At the same time as the Lenora mine was in operation, two other mines nearby, Tyee and Richard III, were being worked. The Lenora and Tyee mines set up townsites and transportation links and it has been suggested that the mines on Mt. Sicker would have had a much longer life had all parties cooperated in the planning of a common townsite and transport system. A drop in the price of copper and depletion of resources forced the closing of all the mines between 1906 and 1908 (Table 3,7). Attempts have been made, at various times, to reopen the Mt. Sicker mines, but none have been successful and the scene of furious activity for ten years now has been masked by vegetation. The town of Crofton survived and was made more active by the construction of a pulp and paper mill by British Columbia Forest Products in 1958.

The Zeballos area was the scene of a very active mining camp in the 1930's and 1940's, with the successful operation of several gold mines along Spud Creek. The main producer was the Privateer mine, but again, this operation, while longer lived than its neighbours, typified early lode mining on Vancouver Island, with its narrow veins, high grade ore and limited tonnage (Table 3,7). In this camp there was no railroad, all the material being moved in and out by road. Fortunately, the mines were not far from tidewater and were fairly low on the valley walls. Mining activity had all but ceased by 1953 and the town of Zeballos reverted to a small centre for wintering fishermen until iron mining started in the early 1960's. This activity lasted for a short time only and since 1964 there has been very little mining in the area.

There was a flurry of mining activity in various parts of the Island during the 1950's and 1960's when several iron and copper mines were in operation. The main iron mineral was magnetite, but again, the tonnage of ore was relatively small and the operations short-lived. Five of the

154

TABLE 3,7 Metallic Lode Deposit Production on Vancouver Island*

Mine Common Name	Dates of Operation	Tons Mined	Major Product	Minor Product
1. Island Copper	1971-	—	Cu	Au, Mo
2. Yreka	1902-1904	273,534	Cu	Ag, Au
3. Coast Copper-Old Sport	1962-1972	2,200,000	Cu, Fe	Au, Ag
4. Coast Copper-Bensen Lake	1968-1971	660,000	Cu	
5. Kingfisher-Raven	1957-1967	3,716,809	Fe	
6. Nimpkish Iron	1959-1963	2,398,294	Fe	
7. El (Ford)	1962-1969	1,887,598	Fe	
8. Privateer	1934-1948	285,771	Au, Ag	Cu, Pb
9. Roper, Goldfield Spur	1936-1942	210,271	Au, Ag	Cu, Pb
10. Argonaut	1951-1957	4,029,821	Fe	
11. Mt. Washington	1961-1967	420,835	Cu	Au, Ag
12. Western Mines	1967-	—	Zn, Pb, Cu	Cd, Au, Ag
13. Brynnor	1962-1968	4,439,391	Fe	
14. Blue Grouse	1917-1954, 1960	274,804	Cu	Ag
15. Mt. Sicker	1989-1909	300,382	Cu	Ag, Au, Pb, Zn, Cd
16. Sunro	1962-1968	1,465,017	Cu	Ag, Au

*Mines that produced less than 100,000 tons are omitted. Locations of mines are indicated by number on Figure 3,7.

SOURCE: British Columbia, Ministry of Mines and Resources, Economics and Planning Division, Victoria.

larger iron mines were the Argonaut near Campbell River, El (Ford) near Zeballos, Brynnor near Kennedy Lake, Nimpkish Iron south of Nimpkish Lake, and Kingfisher-Raven southeast of Port Alice (Figure 3,7 and Table 3,7). Each of these mines produced at least 1,000,000 tons of ore, two even reaching 4,000,000, which on Vancouver Island was considered a large tonnage (Table 3,7). However, reserves of a sufficiently high grade to meet the cost of shipment to Japan were limited, and all the iron mines were closed by 1970. At about the same time there were four copper camps: Coast Copper southeast of Port Alice, Mt. Washington northwest of Courtenay, Blue Grouse at Cowichan Lake, an area that had been worked from 1917 to 1919 and again from 1954 to 1960, and Sunro at Jordan River (Table 3,7). The latter mine was operated from 1962 to 1968, but was flooded when the underground workings came too close to the bed of the Jordan River. The cost of plugging the hole and de-watering the mine proved to be too high to warrant further operations and the mine closed down. Higher copper prices spurred an attempt to reactivate the mine in 1972 which was successful, but the continued cost of operation could not be borne by the low grade of the remaining ore and it closed within two years.

The only mines in operation at present are Western Mines at Buttle Lake and Island Copper at Rupert Inlet. Western Mines produces about 3,000,000 tons of ore per year from underground workings, which yield zinc, lead, copper, cadmium, gold and silver. The Island Copper Mine, in addition to copper, produces molybdenum and gold from a large scale (12,000,000 tons per year), low grade (0.52 percent copper, 0.029 percent molybdenum) open pit operation, with a total estimated reserve of 280,000,000 tons. To date, the mine has managed to remain in operation while other copper producers of the same age on the mainland have had to close down. Both mines have been the cause of much discussion concerning land use conflicts and pollution. Western Mines is situated within Strathcona Provincial Park and has been accused of negligence in operations which have led to a loss of aesthetic values and pollution of the lake from improper handling of poisonous waste. Island Copper has had environmental problems also, in this case from the disposal of waste into the tidal waters of Rupert Inlet. There have been claims of damage to the marine environment through the dispersion of finely ground waste from the mill and from the concentration of poisonous materials in the waste. At the moment, there does not seem to be sufficient environmental deterioration to warrant any changes in either of these mining operations.

STRUCTURAL MATERIALS

Within this category only limestone, sand, gravel and clay have major significance on Vancouver Island. There are extensive limestone deposits, but many of them are so very narrow relative to their width that they cannot be shown easily on a generalized geology map (Figure 1,7). There is an abundance of sand, gravel and clay, the sand and gravel mainly from glaciofluvial deposits and the clay from glacial clays deposited in the sea.

Only those limestone deposits which are easily accessible have been exploited, mainly for use in cement plants, but some have been worked for material to be used in agriculture and in paint and brick manufacture. At Tod Inlet, on the east side of Saanich Inlet near Victoria, the Vancouver Portland Cement Company built a plant in 1904 on a limestone deposit. A decade or so later it amalgamated with the Associated Cement Company, which had been operating at Bamberton on the other side of Saanich Inlet, to form the British Columbia Cement Company. Resource depletion by 1921 prompted the new company to close down the Tod Inlet quarries and transfer all cement production to Bamberton. One of the abandoned quarries was planted with ornamental shrubs as a hanging garden and has become part of the famous Butchart's Gardens. A second quarry was used as a reservoir, while the third, adjacent to the old cement plant, is flooded. The Bamberton limestone deposits were quarried for cement manufacture for several decades until depletion forced the use of more distant supplies to keep the plant operating. The cement was shipped by freighter or special barge to markets around the Gulf of Georgia, mainly in the Vancouver area. With increasing costs of transportation for limestone, fuel and cement, the Bamberton plant soon will be closed and Ocean Cement, the British Columbia cement successor, will supply its market with a new, more economic plant on the mainland. Quarrying of limestone for agricultural applications has been carried on at Cobble Hill, intermittently, since 1886, and for use in paint manufacture at Malahat Station in the 1940's. In the Victoria area the Atkins Road quarry was worked for a few years after 1907 to provide the lime used in a sand-lime brick plant and a lime quarry and kilns were operated for a number of years before World War I at Rosebank near Esquimalt Harbour.

Vancouver Island is so well supplied with sand and gravel deposits, with a wide range of material sizes, that almost any user can get an easily accessible supply. Many municipalities and logging companies have their own pits, as well as the Ministry of Highways, mainly for road building and maintenance. Most of the larger pits are commercial operations providing basic materials for ready-mix concrete and a variety of screened material for other construction purposes. The dominant use of sand and gravel for construction in urban areas is reflected in the value of these products in the three mining districts (Figure 2,7). In 1976 Victoria produced material worth approximately 7,400,000 dollars, Nanaimo 2,700,000 and Alberni 700,000.

At the present time there are no clay deposits being worked, except, perhaps, some small pits to provide local potters with material. At one time or another bricks and tiles have been made at Nanaimo, from glacial and interglacial clays and the grey shales of the Nanaimo Series at East Wellington;[13] at Duncan, from glacial clays and Upper Cretaceous shale near Hillbank; at Sidney (Bazan Bay), from glacial and interglacial clays obtained at the north end of the Saanich Peninsula, as well as on James and Sidney islands; and at Victoria, from glacial clays dug from pits where Mayfair Shopping Centre now stands. Other deposits suitable for making common brick and tile are available, when needed, at Courtenay, Union Bay and Port Alberni.

CONCLUSION

Over the years mining has produced a relatively continuous, though modest, income for the Island; first with coal mining, then with periods of activity in lode mining for copper, lead, zinc, iron and gold, and latterly with a long term copper deposit, a reasonably steady and substantial production of structural materials, and now a renewed interest in coal mining. It is expected that mining, in the near future, will maintain its position in the economic life of Vancouver Island.

REFERENCES

1. MULLER, J.E., Geological Survey of Canada, marginal notes on map of Geology of Vancouver Island, Sheet 3 of 3, Open File 463, 1977.

2. *Ibid.*

3. British Columbia, *Annual Report of the Minister of Mines*. Victoria: Department of Mines, 1896, p. 501.

4. Personal Communication, Ministry of Mines and Petroleum Resources, Victoria. The 1952 estimate of 27,410,000 tons is still considered reasonably valid.

5. PATERSON, T.W., *Ghost Town Trails on Vancouver Island*. Langley, British Columbia: Stagecoach Publishing, 1975, p. 78.

6. British Columbia, *op. cit.*, 1922, p. 285.

7. *Ibid.*, 1919, p. 320.

8. PATERSON, T.W., *ibid.*, p. 81.

9. British Columbia, *op. cit.*, 1950, p. 244.

10. PATERSON, T.W., *ibid.*, p. 23.

11. MULLER, J.E., *op. cit.*

12. TURNER, R.D. *Vancouver Island Railroads*. San Marino, California: Golden West Books, 1973, p. 36.

13. McCAMMON, S. and CUMMINGS, J.M. *Clay and Shale Deposits of B.C.* Victoria: Department of Mines and Petroleum Resources, Bulletin No. 30, 1952.

PLATE 14 Scenic agriculture, Saanich Peninsula. *I.H. Norie Photo* ▶

8 AGRICULTURE

Colin J.B. Wood

The presence of a rugged, mountainous terrain, with a general absence of extensive lowland, is a major deterrent to the widespread development of agriculture on Vancouver Island. Only 1.5 percent of the total land area is held as farmland, of which half is improved, while a minuscule 0.25 percent of the area is used for forage and cash crops.[1] Compared with the forest products industry and tourism, which generate sales of about 400,000,000 and 100,000,000 dollars, respectively, agriculture's total contribution to the Island's economy is a mere 15,000,000 dollars per annum.[2]

Nevertheless, according to the 1971 census, 7,300 people are classed as having an agricultural occupation or residence and they contribute in several ways to the personality and landscape of the Island. The agricultural community is that sector of the population most closely identified with the land, as owners, resource managers and landscape architects. Managers of a renewable resource which requires care, attention and not a little love, farmers contribute a strong thread of stability to the fabric of a regional economy which in several ways is still a resource frontier. In this chapter the general characteristics of the farming environment are outlined, regional variations are identified and attention is focused on specific farming operations, as well as on some of the recent changes and issues currently facing the community who work the land.

Development of Agriculture

The selection of the location of Fort Victoria in 1843 was partly influenced by the perceived agricultural potential of the southern part of the Island. The open, oak-forested landscape interspersed with grass ''prairies'' of the Victoria region seemed ideal for the quick realization of a supply of food to feed the fledgling settlement. Company farms were established to supply the immigrants, but it was not until the 1860's that the pace of colonization and land settlement increased, spurred on by discoveries of gold and coal and the expansion of the lumber industry. The frontier of settlement gradually spread up the east coast of the Island,

161

from the core areas of Victoria, Duncan, Nanaimo and Courtenay, but its progress inland, with the exception of the Cowichan and Alberni Valleys was checked, both by the arduous task of clearing the forest and by the mountains.[3] The pattern of concentration of agriculture on the narrow eastern coastal plain has remained basically unchanged to the present day (Figure 1,8). However, a significant restructuring has taken place as farming has evolved from the pioneer phase, while changing economic and political influences continue to create a climate of uncertainty for the farmer.

Physical Setting

Vancouver Island's temperate climate is characterized by the longest growing season in Canada, that is, from early March until late November (Figure 1,8). An additional advantage is the high frequency of bright sunshine hours in the Victoria region. However, these attractions are offset by the moderate nature of the summer temperatures which limit the degree-day totals and reduce the range of crops which may be grown, and by the occurrence of low summer precipitation, which can result in drought conditions.[4] While the first cut of hay may be relatively early, the weather can make curing difficult, hence requiring ensilage. To ensure sufficient summer forage and crop production irrigation is necessary.

Irrigation requirements have been estimated in millimetres (inches in parentheses) as follows: Sidney 259 (10.2), Duncan 246 (9.7), Nanaimo 218 (8.6), Parksville 229 (9.0), Courtenay 196 (7.7), Alberni 145 (5.7). Both inland and northward from the southeastern coastal plain the rapid increase in total precipitation and decrease in annual total of degree days are constraints on arable farming. From the climatic standpoint, the eastern coastal plain is suited to most types of temperate region farming activity, with localized variations compatible with the regional climatic subdivisions: cool Mediterannean (Victoria-Saanich), Transitional (Duncan to Parksville) and Maritime (west coast and north of Courtenay).

The soils of the main farming areas are derived principally from glacial deposits, in some areas reworked by marine and fluvial action, that were laid down over interglacial sands and gravels. Together with the temperate climate and forest cover of fir and hemlock, this has produced soils which generally are Brown Podzolics. The great variation in topography and drainage can produce marked variations of soil type over relatively short distances, for example, from compact, stoney till, to well drained, sandy soil or heavy, poorly drained clays.[6] To the farmers this means that some of their fields or parts of them dry out much quicker than others and that some fields have to be almost as regularly cropped of their stones as of their produce (Table 1,8). In response to climatic variation, leaching

162

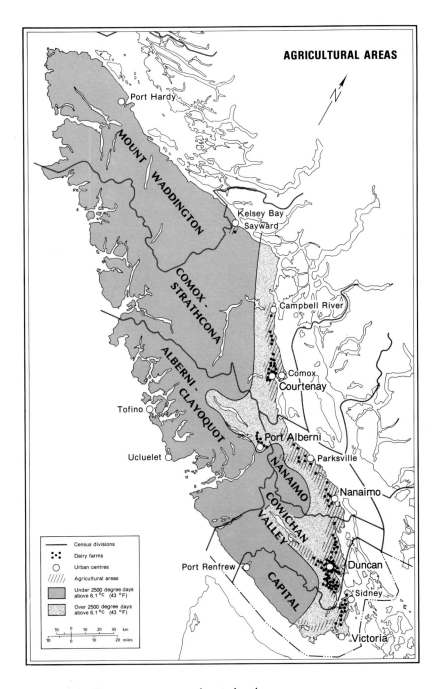

FIGURE 1,8 The growing season and agricultural areas.

163

Soil Qualities and Representative Types on Southeastern Vancouver Island

	Quality		Representative Soil		Comment
Class	Hectares	Percent	Type	Percent of Class	
I	33,400	11.6	Fairbridge silt loam	42	Suitable for general farming; high organic content; well drained.
II	35,000	12.2	Cowichan clay loam	29	Lower moisture holding; higher acidity; less fertile.
III	102,400	35.6	Shawnigan gravelly sandy loam	31	Lower moisture holding; low fertility; poor drainage.
IV	82,000	28.7	Qualicum gravelly sandy loam	37	Rough topography; very stoney.
Other	34,000	11.9	Tidal flats		
Total		100.0			

SOURCE: DAY, J.H. *et. al.*, *op. cit.*, 1959.

and podzolization increase northward, while water deficiency increases southward. In terms of soil preparation, a light dressing of lime is required in all areas, with the exception of the Saanich Peninsula where, on unirrigated soils, only nitrogen fertilizers are necessary. The local variability of the physical terrain, coupled with the arduous task of land clearing, has resulted in an interesting patchwork of fields, often small in size and sometimes irregular in shape, bounded with a variety of fencing materials. It presents an attractive foreground to the backdrop of mountains (Figure 2,8).

Economic and Political Setting

The farmers' decision making environment is comprised of economic and political, as well as physical, variables. Belonging to an Island community ensures that a certain measure of protection from other producers is enjoyed, but the costs of imported inputs into the farming operation, naturally, are going to be higher. A comparison of approximate costs of

FIGURE 2,8   A high quality agricultural area on the Saanich Peninsula.
B.C. Government Photo ▶

inputs in British Columbia and neighbouring territories indicates that the Province is a relatively high cost agricultural area (Table 2,8). Within British Columbia, Vancouver Island faces the extra burden of freight and ferry costs.[7] Additionally, the physical constraints described above prohibit economies of scale in crop production. Thus, agricultural producers on the Island need to specialize either in high weight-bulk or perishable produce for local consumption, or low weight, high value produce for a larger market.

The set of economic factors is connected inevitably with a political dimension, since federal and provincial governments regulate the agricultural industry in many ways.[8] Vancouver Island's long growing season is an advantage only in an east-west or Canadian context. If agricultural produce moved freely across the international border from even milder southern regions this physical advantage would be eliminated. To protect farmers the federal government imposes varying tariffs on imported agricultural produce. On vegetables, for example, a tariff exists for the period April to December on imported produce, but not for the winter months when local output diminishes. Despite the tariff, British Columbia producers have complained of dumping by Americans when harvests south of the border have been abundant, as occurred recently with potatoes.[9]

Excessive price fluctuations in agricultural produce are to a certain extent mitigated for farmers by the federal Agricultural Stabilization Act and the provincial Farm Income Assurance Program. Other major areas of government intervention are the numerous marketing boards and the agricultural land use controls under the Land Commission Act. Dairy and egg producers are strictly regulated by a production quota system. This stabilizes supply and ensures that returns to producers are reasonably fair, but it is at the expense of the consumer. The system has been criticized both by consumer groups and some farmers who feel that they are carrying inefficient producers. Nevertheless, it ensures the long term survival of the industry, an asset which has been brought sharply into focus by the droughts which have affected agricultural output in California.

Consequently, the overall decision making environment facing the Vancouver Island farmer is similar to that in most developed countries. Technology has reduced much of the impact of natural hazards and increased production, but not without considerable capital outlay, while government policies have preserved existence, but virtually eliminated independence.

TABLE 2,8   Farming Input Costs, 1976-1977

Inputs	British Columbia	Alberta	Washington
Land: dollars per acre	6000	400-500	1000-5000
Interest: percent per annum	9-10	5-9	8
Labour: dollars per hour	4-6	3-4	2-3
Fuel: cents per gallon	49	38	47
Fertilizer (11-48-0): dollars per ton	231	205	215
Dairy Supplies: dollars per ton	175	165	146
Poultry Concentrates: dollars per ton	250	218	226

SOURCE: *Country Life*. October, 1977, p. 4.

Pattern of Farming

An overall picture of farming activity on the Island can be portrayed through the use of census statistics (Table 3,8). The value of agricultural livestock and produce for the Province in 1971 was 128,000,000 dollars and Vancouver Island accounted for seven percent of this total. In terms of value, the provincial agricultural economy is dominated by livestock, followed by dairying and fruit and vegetable production. On Vancouver Island the livestock emphasis is less pronounced, but dairying is of greater importance, being double the provincial average. Tree fruit production is relatively insignificant, while greenhouse and nursery output also averages twice the level of the Province. A measure of the intensity of farming activity can be obtained by comparing the value of product per fertilized acre (Table 4,8). The intensity of farming on the Island is close to double the provincial average, and in the Capital Division it is nearly triple. The physical constraints that greatly limit agricultural land, the positive attributes of lengthy growing season and high sunshine hours, and the proximity of an urban area help to explain the

TABLE 3,8 Value of Agricultural Production in Percentage

Type	Census Division					Vancouver Island	British Columbia
	Alberni	Capital	Courtenay	Cowichan	Nanaimo		
Livestock	35	34	48	44	44	41	55
Dairy	55	11	41	41	35	37	18
Eggs	4	13	3	10	6	7	7
Greenhouses and Nurseries	2	24	2	1	10	8	4
Potatoes and Vegetables	2	12	5	3	3	5	5
Tree Fruits	1	5	0	0	0	1	8
Forage	1	1	1	1	1	1	1
Grain	0	0	0	0	0	0	2
Totals	100	100	100	100	100	100	100

TABLE 4,8 Value of Product Per Fertilized Acre in Dollars, 1971

Census Division					Vancouver Island	British Columbia
Alberni	Capital	Courtenay	Cowichan	Nanaimo		
1,900	2,300	740	1,200	1,400	1,508	860

emphasis on intensive operations. As a result, there are few large farms and a large proportion of small holdings (Table 5,8).

The agricultural sector of Vancouver Island, therefore, is made up of a core of commercial farmers who are mainly dairymen or livestock producers, with a few large vegetable growers and horticulturists. In addition to the main commercial enterprises, there are a large number of part-time, retired and hobby farmers who produce a range of products: these include soft and tree fruits, holly, flowers, seeds, vegetables, livestock and wool. Both the commercial and part-time farmers cater to the local market primarily, although a few producers who specialize in livestock breeding, bulbs, daffodils and holly participate in the national and international markets. In short, the agricultural sector concentrates on perishable, high bulk products, such as milk, vegetables and those which take advantage of the climate. Only in this way can the high cost of inputs characteristic of the region be countered. A certain amount of variation in farming occurs among the five census divisions which make up Vancouver Island (Tables 3,8 and 6,8).

Recent Trends

An overview of recent trends in the industry, especially through a comparison of 1951 and 1971 figures, brings out dynamic qualities that are not visible in the returns for a single census. The number of people classed as farm population has decreased from 12,252 in 1951 to 7,362 in 1971, yet, the total area of cropped land has remained virtually unchanged at approximately 11,330 hectares (27,996 acres). This reflects both the replacement of labour by mechanization and the improvement of new land in some areas which has compensated for loss of acreage to urbanization in others. As the number of farms has dropped from 2,739 to 1,770 in the period, some consolidation of holdings has occurred.

Other changes since 1951 have been a switch of 1,619 hectares (4,000 acres) from small grain to hay production and an increase in livestock from 16,000 to 25,000 cattle, a trend which appears to have occurred in

TABLE 5,8 Farm Size Distribution by Census Division

Census Division	Under 10 Acres	10-69	70-239	240-1,119	Over 1,120
Alberni	23	26	21	3	0
Capital	313	253	80	31	6
Comox	44	115	108	26	1
Cowichan	81	207	115	20	0
Mt. Waddington	1	7	3	1	0
Nanaimo	46	150	73	16	1
Vancouver Island	508	758	400	97	8
British Columbia	4,500	6,765	3,186	2,965	784

SOURCE: *Census of Canada*, 1971.

all census districts except Nanaimo. The Island farmer has shifted away from grain to grass and hay production almost exclusively. Despite the decrease from 10,000 to 8,600 milk cows, the output of milk has increased, because yields per cow have risen considerably. Of course, not all dairy herds equal the national record production of the Frueh herd at Cobble Hill of over 9,091 kilograms (20,000 pounds) per cow, per annum.[10] This reflects the general improvements in farm husbandry and breeding, the increasing use of the high milk producing breed of Holsteins, and the influence of the provincial Department of Agriculture and its field agents. The artificial insemination records give an indication of the current popularity of the major milk and beef breeds (Table 7,8).[11]

The trend toward more intensive production of feed for livestock, mainly ensilage, is shown by the growth of irrigation from 345 to 3,037 hectares (853 to 7,501 acres), 1951-1971, and a parallel decrease in

TABLE 6,8 Number of Farms by Type and Greenhouse Area, 1971

| Type | Census Division | | | | | Vancouver Island | |
	Alberni	Capital	Comox	Cowichan	Nanaimo	Total	Change 1966-1971
Livestock	9	46	33	22	29	139	+ 55
Dairy	7	22	25	79	25	158	−37
Poultry	2	38	8	19	7	74	−41
Fruit and Vegetables	2	51	3	5	3	64	+ 1
Greenhouses (square metres)	12,500	1,283,600	38,400	18,500	144,600	1,498,000	

TABLE 7,8 Artificial Inseminations on
Vancouver Island by Breed, 1976-1977

Dairy Cattle		Beef Cattle	
Holstein	2,948	Hereford	553
Jersey	136	Angus	399
Ayrshire	79	Simmental	148
Guernsey	14	Other	16
Total	3,177		1,116

SOURCE: *Country Life*, February, 1977.

pasture of 2,024 hectares (5,000 acres). Extensive grazing has given way
to intensive livestock husbandry, in some instances virtually approximat-
ing a feed-lot style of operation. This is a reflection of labour costs, mechanization and modern production methods. The dairy operations are the
backbone of the Island's farming and, like most other agricultural enterprises, are faced with problems of soaring input costs, high capital investment, scarcity of suitable labour, controlled production quotas and pressures of vertical integration from retail food chains. Under such pressures, many farmers near urban areas have, understandably, taken the
opportunity to subdivide and sell their land.

The loss of farmland through urbanization has been an acute problem
because much of the best agricultural land is close to the larger towns and
cities. However, in December 1972, the Provincial government froze land
sales of parcels greater than two hectares (five acres) and in the following
year passed the Land Commission Act. This legislation instituted Agricultural Land Reserves, in effect, a form of zoning which restricted the
use of agricultural land solely to agricultural purposes. For example, the
agricultural areas of the Saanich Peninsula, which have some of the best
soil and climatic conditions in the Province for farming, were experiencing pressure from the growth of Victoria and its dormitory villages of

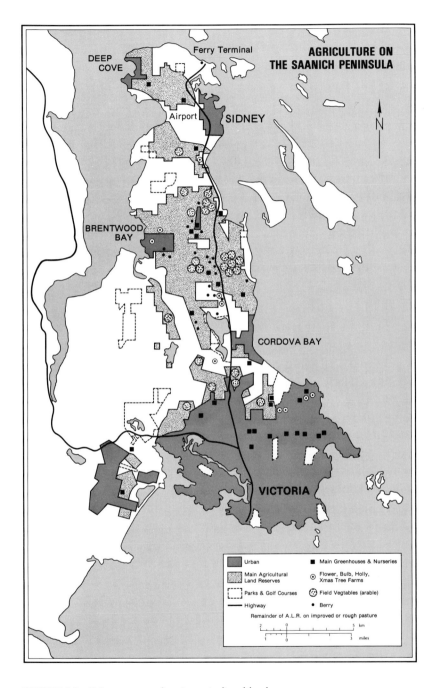

FIGURE 3,8 Urban areas and main agricultural land reserves.

173

Brentwood and Sidney (Figure 3,8). The reaction by farmers to this legislation was mixed, since many who stood to gain from subdividing felt cheated of their potential retirement funds, whereas others farther away from built-up areas gave it support.[12] In view of the recent population growth rates of Victoria, Duncan, Nanaimo and Courtenay, and their coincidence with the best farming areas, the inception of the Land Commission Act could not have been more timely for the survival of agriculture.

In conclusion, the continued existence of farming on Vancouver Island seems assured by the presence of a growing local market and the diversity of agricultural activity that is physically possible, reinforced by the Island's isolation and the protective legislation of British Columbia. The future prosperity of the family farm is a more intangible consideration in an age of rising input costs, controlled production and agri-business. British Columbia imports more than half of its food, as a result of its seasonality of production and the cheaper input costs and longer growing season south of the border.[13] While there are many advantages to regional specialization in economic activity, an over-dependence on foreign producers can pose a problem. It would seem that only a cooperative effort by the industry, government and labour can improve agriculture's present condition and reduce some of that imported total. Yet, agriculture is not all money and politics. The numerous family farms of several generations give continuity and empathy to the man-land relationship that has survived crises in the past. The rising attendance at the annual agricultural fairs, for example, the Saanichton Fair which has been in existence for 110 years has an attendance of over 40,000, suggests that the city dweller is as much interested in the prosperity of the farm as the farmer, and second, that such fairs represent a measure of the aesthetic value of farming to the Island landscape.

REFERENCES

1. Canada, *Census of Canada*, 1971.

2. British Columbia, *Vancouver Island Bulletin Area*. Victoria: British Columbia Lands Service, Area Bulletin No. 4, 1974, p. 19.

3. *Ibid.*, p. 8.

4. DAY, J.H., FARSTAD, L. and LAIRD, D.G. *Soil Survey of South East Vancouver Island and Gulf Islands*. Ottawa: Department of Agriculture, British Columbia Soil Survey Report No. 6, 1959, p. 9.

5. *Ibid.*, p. 19.

6. *Ibid.*, pp. 23-76.

7. For a detailed cost return evaluation of farming in the Cowichan Valley which can be taken as representative of the Island dairy industry see British Columbia, *Pasture, Hay and Haylage Production*. Victoria: Department of Agriculture, Farm Economics Branch, January, 1976, 16 pp.

8. A discussion of the extent, complexities and value of government intervention in agriculture is beyond the scope of this chapter. The *Canada Yearbook* summarizes concisely the legislation pertaining to and government involvement in the industry.

9. *Country Life*, December 1976, p. 10.

10. *Country Life*, July 1976, p. 17.

11. Cattle are not the only livestock. Although no large commercial flocks exist, there are over 11,000 sheep, with several prize flocks, and there has been a recent revival in keeping them. Pigs number about 5,000. After a serious decline in the late 1950's and early 1960's horses are coming back, mainly for pleasure riding, and now number over 2,000.

12. Canada, *Impact Analysis of the British Columbia Land Reserve Act*. Ottawa: Lands Directorate, Environment Canada (no date, preliminary report).

13. *Country Life*, August 1977, p. 2.

PLATE 15   The Island's fleet.   *B.C. Government Photo* ▶

9 FISHERIES

William M. Ross

From the initial habitation of Vancouver Island, the fisheries, especially salmon, have been an essential element in the economic and social lives of the people. For the earliest inhabitants salmon was the chief source of marine food, although consumption of herring roe, clams, and other seafoods was not uncommon. As the fishery became more commercialized in the latter part of the nineteenth century salmon remained the most important species.

Much of the early commercial salmon industry was organized from Victoria, and while the majority of commercial establishments were situated on the mainland, Alert Bay and Clayoquot Sound were early salmon cannery locations on Vancouver Island. After the turn of the century the role of Victoria as an entrepôt largely disappeared. The number of canneries and other fish handling facilities on the Island increased until the 1920's, but since then these facilities have tended to concentrate in Prince Rupert and Vancouver.

Since 1950 the Vancouver Island fisheries have become more recreation oriented and some centres, such as Cowichan Bay and Campbell River, have emerged as important sport fishery locations. In addition, the Island has become a prime centre for fisheries research, with facilities at Victoria and Nanaimo.

HISTORICAL BACKGROUND

The wide variety of species frequenting the waters surrounding Vancouver Island were central to the culture of the native Indians. The major runs of salmon that migrate along the west coast of Vancouver Island, through the Strait of Juan de Fuca, around the northern end of the Island, and through Johnstone Strait to the Fraser, were especially important. All of the major Indian groups on the Island, the Kwakiutls, Nootka and Coast Salish, developed a seacoast culture, made the products of sea and rivers their prime food source, traveled by water and lived remarkably close to the coast.[1] All groups were salmon fishermen, and it is estimated that individual Indians consumed 700 pounds of fresh fish per year.[2]

Most fish were for individual consumption and there was little trade among villages or groups, but there was regional differentiation in consumption among the groups. The Nootkas, on the west coast of Vancouver Island, depended greatly on chum salmon and then, in order, herring and codfish as their staples. The Kwakiutls, at the northern end of the Island, relied on all species of salmon, halibut and eulachon.[3] The Salish, residing mainly south of Campbell River on the east coast and merging with the Nootka in the vicinity of Sooke and River Jordan, utilized sockeye as their most important species, although herring and shellfish were also important in their diet.[4]

A fishery trade was initiated after the arrival of Cook on the west coast of Vancouver Island in the 1770's. The Nootka exchanged sea otter skins for various knick-knacks. This trade, involving a few ships per year, continued until 1820 when the harvest of sea otter pelts had fallen to such low levels that even small scale trading was not feasible. The Indians successfully spurned intensive white contact until Fort Victoria was established in 1843. After that time the Indians were increasingly drawn into a commercial fishery organized from Europe and other parts of North America. In the 1850's the Nootkas developed trade in dogfish oil with sawmill owners in the Puget Sound area. Fur seal hunting became an important occupation in the 1880's when many worked under contract to white schoonermen. Between 1870 and 1890 all the Indian groups on Vancouver Island became linked in some way with the commercial salmon industry. Many worked as fishermen for the canneries and some even migrated, in season, to work in the Fraser River canneries.

Early commercialization of the fishery centred on the salting of salmon and herring for export to Europe and the Orient. It was not until the early 1870's that salmon canning commenced in British Columbia on the Fraser River. During this period the industry consisted largely of small, independent firms situated at specific resource sites. It was characterized by low levels of plant concentration and a high degree of local proprietorship and financing. Much interest was shown in the infant industry by Victoria merchants, who sought greater financial returns than those possible from gold mining, which was on the decline. Typical of these merchants was J.H. Todd who operated a wholesale grocery business in Victoria and financed early canneries at Esquimalt and Steveston. In addition to

178

financing the industry, Victoria was its entrepôt and much of the manufacturing equipment used in the industry was made locally by the Albion Iron Works.[5]

Between 1890 and 1930 the emergence of limited companies brought a semblance of order and stability. No longer was the fishing business based solely on shaky financial foundations and dependence on Victoria merchants and brokers.[6] Large corporations with outside capital began to dominate the industry. The Anglo-British Columbia Packing Company had its headquarters in the United Kingdom, the Victoria Canning Company was financed by the Welch and Rithet interests of San Francisco and the British Columbia Packers Association was backed by a group of eastern Canadian and United States financial interests. These companies anticipated large profits from the industry and sought to restrict competition by establishing fishing plants in all areas along the coast.[7] Moreover, most of them had their headquarters in Vancouver which by 1900 had displaced Victoria as the preeminent financial and distribution center for the industry.

The one area which remained financially linked to Victoria was Vancouver Island. Victoria was a source of capital for such small companies as West Coast Packing, Capital City Canning and Padock Brothers. They built and operated plants, respectively, at Nootka Sound, Victoria and Quathiaski Cove. During this period, other canneries were operated periodically at Quatsino Sound, Clayoquot Sound, Alberni Inlet, Nitinat, Port Renfrew, Sidney, Nanaimo, Lasqueti Island and Alert Bay.[8] The number of canneries fluctuated considerably, but there were never more than ten plants operating in any one season and it was only after 1930 that the majority of canneries on Vancouver Island were operated by the limited companies headquartered in Vancouver. Salmon remained the dominant species. Halibut were caught off the northern part of the Island, but were sold in a largely domestic market. There was also some processing of pilchards, herring and whales, mainly on the west coast, and at times the reduction plants were associated with salmon canneries. The provincial production of dry, salted herring was concentrated mainly on Vancouver Island in the vicinity of Nanaimo, Clayoquot Sound and Barkley Sound, and the Orient, particularly China, was the herring market. By the 1960's, however, the Island was no longer a major processing area.

THE COMMERCIAL FISHERY IN THE 1970's

The present day commercial fishery off the shores of Vancouver Island is based primarily on species which do not use the rivers and streams of the Island. In terms of numbers of fish caught and landed value, the predominant pattern has been to catch species, such as halibut, whose life cycle is entirely at sea, or salmon destined for the mainland rivers, particularly the Fraser. There are exceptions, however, including the major spawning grounds for herring on the west coast of the Island, the significant shellfish fishery on the eastern shores, and the large salmon runs in certain major waterways, such as the Campbell, Qualicum and Cowichan rivers and Nitinat Lake.

Salmon which spawn in the rivers of British Columbia range over large areas of the Pacific Ocean. The migration patterns of coho salmon as they approach the coast may be used as an example (Figure 1,9). Other species differ in terms of range and direction, but this migration pattern typifies the approach of salmon to Vancouver Island. Fish entering Johnstone Strait off northeastern Vancouver Island spawn in local rivers and in many of the Fraser tributaries. Salmon migrating through the Strait of Juan de Fuca are bound either for Washington State rivers or for the Fraser River and its tributaries. In both instances the Fraser is the dominant spawning river.

There is considerable mixing and overlapping of stock bound for southeastern Alaska, Washington and British Columbia (Figure 1,9).[9] It is particularly serious in the Juan de Fuca area where there is intense competition between the United States and Canadian fishermen. United States fishermen catch sockeye and pink salmon that spawn in the Fraser and Canadian fishermen intercept coho bound for Washington rivers. As a result, the International Pacific Salmon Commission was formed to protect and jointly manage the runs. However, it is restricted to managing pink and sockeye salmon and there remains considerable disagreement over the fifty-fifty catch allocation between Canadian and American fishermen.

The migration patterns also have particular significance for the commercial salmon fishery. The commercial catch off the shores of Vancouver Island is concentrated in four statistical areas (Figure 2,9). These waters account for forty-two percent of the total catch of the Province (Table 1,9). Two are at the northern end of the Island (areas 12 and 27) and the others are on the west coast between Sooke and Ucluelet (areas 20 and 23). The Johnstone Strait fishery focuses on pinks and chums, while the west coast fishery dominates the spring, sockeye and coho catches.

These migration patterns also have important ramifications for onshore communities. Many of the small communities on the west coast, such as Tofino, Ucluelet, Bamfield and Sooke, provide services for the gillnet,

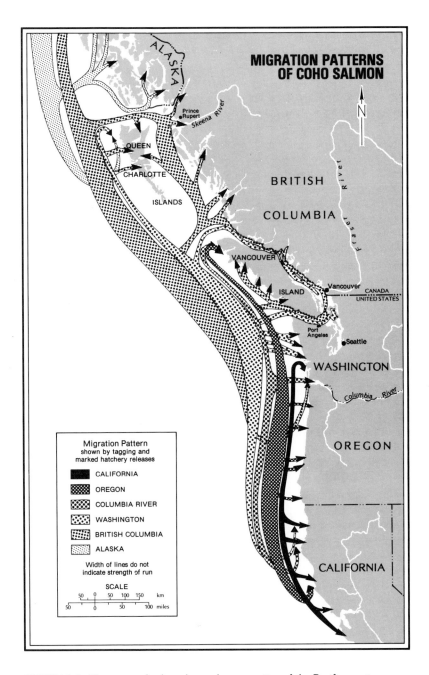

FIGURE 1,9 The range of coho salmon along a portion of the Pacific coast.

181

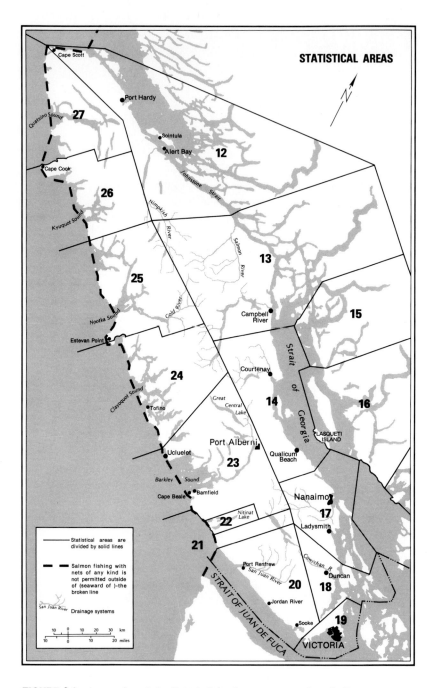

STATISTICAL AREAS

Cape Scott

Port Hardy

27

Quatsino Sound

Sointula

Alert Bay

12

Cape Cook

26

Kyuquot Sound

Johnstone Strait

Nimpkish River

Salmon River

13

25

Nootka Sound

Cold River

Campbell River

15

Estevan Point

24

Courtenay

Strait of Georgia

Clayoquot Sound

Tofino

Great Central Lake

14

16

Ucluelet

Port Alberni

23

Qualicum Beach

LASQUETI ISLAND

Barkley Sound

Cape Beale

Bamfield

Nanaimo

17

22

Nitinat Lake

Ladysmith

21

Cowichan R.

Statistical areas are divided by solid lines

Salmon fishing with nets of any kind is not permitted outside of (seaward of)-the broken line

San Juan River   Drainage systems

Port Renfrew

San Juan River

20

Duncan

18

Jordan River

Sooke

19

10   0   10   20   30   km

10   0   10   20   miles

STRAIT OF JUAN DE FUCA

VICTORIA

FIGURE 2,9   Areas of catch for British Columbia waters, southern half.

TABLE 1.9 Total Salmon Catch From 1972 to 1976*

Statistical Area**	Springs	Sockeye	Coho	Pinks	Chums	Steelhead	Total
12	268 (4)†	2,305 (9)	746 (4)	8,123 (19)	2,702 (15)	6 (10)	14,150 (13)
13	181 (2)	549 (2)	225 (1)	1,117 (3)	2,373 (14)	1 (2)	4,446 (4)
14	207 (3)	2 (-)	313 (2)	3 (-)	450 (3)	- (-)	975 (1)
17	334 (5)	225 (1)	47 (-)	54 (-)	141 (1)	- (-)	801 (1)
18	31 (-)	194 (1)	18 (-)	60 (-)	76 (-)	- (-)	379 (-)
19	- (-)	- (-)	- (-)	- (-)	- (-)	- (-)	- (-)
20	222 (3)	3,954 (15)	1,749 (11)	2,039 (5)	610 (3)	5 (8.5)	8,579 (8)
21	203 (3)	9 (-)	452 (3)	51 (-)	1 (-)	- (-)	716 (1)
22	1 (-)	- (-)	3 (-)	- (-)	1,465 (8)	- (-)	1,469 (1)
23	2,016 (27)	1,750 (7)	2,737 (16)	451 (1)	148 (1)	5 (8.5)	7,107 (7)
24	479 (6)	281 (1)	1,470 (9)	330 (1)	105 (1)	- (-)	2,665 (2)
25	96 (1)	176 (1)	457 (3)	204 (-)	494 (3)	- (-)	1,427 (1)
26	189 (3)	110 (-)	754 (5)	205 (-)	146 (1)	- (-)	1,404 (1)
27	147 (2)	673 (3)	841 (5)	649 (2)	72 (-)	- (-)	2,382 (2)
Total Vancouver Island	4,374 (59)	10,228 (40)	9,812 (59)	13,286 (31)	8,783 (50)	17 (29)	46,500 (42)
Total British Columbia	7,396	25,482	16,643	43,093	17,557	59	110,230

*Totals are rounded to the nearest thousand.
**Statistical areas are illustrated in Figure 1.9.
†Figures in parentheses are percentages of the British Columbia total by species.
Discrepancies in percentage totals are due to rounding.

SOURCE: Canada, *Annual Summary of British Columbia Catch Statistics, 1972-1976*. Vancouver: Department of Environment and Fisheries and Environment Canada, 1973-1977.

183

seine and troll fleets. In some of the communities there are small fish processing plants and cold storage warehouses. Virtually all are focused on the commercial fishery. The same may be said for the communities on the northeastern shores of the Island, such as Port Hardy, Sointula and Alert Bay.[10] In most of these locations gas, food and ice are available to the fishermen.

Communities on the east coast of Vancouver Island south of Campbell River are quite different. In these locations the sport fishery and the shellfish industry provide a measure of industrial diversification. There are canneries at Brentwood Bay, Cowichan Bay, Nanaimo and Quadra Island that cater to sport fishermen and custom-can their catches. In almost every settlement there are companies which provide sport fishing guides and/or boats for sport fishing. Particularly noteworthy is the concentration in Campbell River. Shellfish harvesting on the east coast of the Island is centered in the Courtenay-Comox, Union Bay, Ladysmith and Qualicum Beach areas.[11]

There were four canneries operating on Vancouver Island, which utilized commercially caught salmon. Situated at Victoria, Nanaimo, Quadra Island and Port Hardy, none of these plants had the capacity of the large plants in Prince Rupert, Vancouver and Steveston. They produced special packs, such as sample gift packages, or ran a low scale commercial operation.[12] Thus, Vancouver Island, once the financial and processing center for the industry and an area rich in offshore fish, has lost its preeminence in the commercial fishery. Although fish are still abundant off its shores, the industrial concerns which remain are small and increasingly oriented toward the sport fishery.

SPORT FISHERY

The sport fishery on Vancouver Island has never been studied in great detail and attempts to place a value on its contribution to the province are at best educated guesses. Nevertheless, it is known that since World War II the number of sport fishermen, the value of the fishery, and the competition between commercial and sport fishermen have increased.[13]

Estimates have placed the number of sport fishermen, both salt and fresh water, at between 150,000 and 250,000. The value of the sport fishery is between 200,000,000 and 400,000,000 dollars. Most of the sport fishing has been concentrated on the southeastern coast of the Island between Campbell River and Sooke, chiefly in large bays and at the mouths of major rivers. These include the Campbell, Cowichan and Qualicum rivers and Saanich Inlet.

Major conflicts have arisen between commercial and sport fishermen over fish supply. Most sport fishermen contend that the federal fisheries department favours commercial fishermen and that they are being "ripped-off".[14]

In some cases, however, special sport fishing reserves have been set aside. The largest, established on July 1, 1967, is a sixty-four kilometre (forty mile) long area which stretches around the southern tip of Vancouver Island from Sheringham Point on the west coast to Curteis Point at the end of the Saanich Peninsula (Statistical Area 19).

Perhaps the major impact of the sport fishery has been on the tourist industry. Campbell River is a good example of this linkage. This area, considered to be one of the prime fishing locations, has a resident population of less than 15,000, but has an influx of approximately 300,000 visitors every summer.[15] Most of these are sport fishermen and the majority come from Alberta and the states of Washington, Oregon and California. Washington alone accounts for over fifty percent of the out-of-country sport fishermen.[16] There has been considerable public complaint over the impact that non-residents, especially Americans, have had on the sport fishery. Residents contend that non-residents are catching fish illegally, selling them commercially and crowding local facilities. In addition, there is considerable tension between sport and commercial fishermen, since both blame non-residents and each other for depletion of salmon runs. As a result, there has been considerable pressure from both groups for exclusion of non-residents from the fishery and for increased investment in research and artificial propagation.

RESEARCH AND SALMON ENHANCEMENT

The federal Department of Fisheries and the Environment has major research stations on Vancouver Island at Patricia Bay, near Victoria International Airport, and at Nanaimo. The Institute of Ocean Sciences at Patricia Bay centres its studies on the physics and chemistry of the ocean environment in the Pacific and the Western Arctic. There are some biological studies of organisms, but these are largely confined to organisms which are not able to swim freely. Many of the studies undertaken by the Institute are intended to provide a broader understanding of offshore waters. In addition, the Institute has a major responsibility for conducting hydrographic surveys and preparing sailing guides and tide and current tables which are heavily used by commercial and sport fishermen.

The Pacific Biological Station at Nanaimo concentrates more specifically on fisheries research. Organized into three major sections, Fish Populations, Aquaculture and Fish Health, and Fisheries Ecology and Salmon Enhancement, the station attempts to provide improved information for culture, development and best use of Pacific coast living marine and anadromous resources. Specific studies focus on the size, distribution and sustainable yield of major west coast stocks, refinement of the biological parameters which are essential to successful salmon enhancement, the development of safeguards against proliferation of fish diseases and man's impact on fish habitat.

While many of the investigations at Nanaimo centre on basic fisheries research, the Department of Fisheries and Environment has a number of artificial propagation projects and has announced plans to significantly increase salmon levels. Prior to 1977 there were two hatcheries, the Quinsam at Campbell River and the Big Qualicum at Qualicum, and two major spawning channels, at Robertson Creek near Port Alberni and on the Puntledge River.

In 1977 the Canadian government announced a fifteen year, 400,000,000 dollar salmonoid enhancement program. The first stage involves expenditures of 43,400,000 dollars, of which 17,600,000 is to be spent on projects on Vancouver Island. Most of the capital projects are designed to expand populations of chum, steelhead, coho and chinook salmon. The largest project on the Island is a 3,400,000 dollar coho, chinook and steelhead hatchery on the Puntledge River which was scheduled to be completed in 1978. Other projects include a chum salmon maternity channel and a coho rearing pond on the Big Qualicum, a spawning channel for chums on the Little Qualicum, incubation boxes for chum on the Little Qualicum, incubation boxes for chum on the Nitinat, Toquart and Tlupana river systems, a chinook rearing pond on the San Juan River and pink salmon incubation boxes on Courtenay's Wolf Lake system.

Some of the lakes and rivers of the Island are to be used for experimental purposes. Great Canal, Henderson, and Kennedy lakes on the west coast were used in 1977 and will be used in 1978 for experimental programs which are to produce 500,000 to 1,500,000 sockeye salmon within four years. In addition, the degraded habitats of many small streams are to be improved. Various measures are planned, ranging from boulder and log jam removal to bypass channels.

Studies by the federal government suggest that in the Sooke to Victoria area there will be an increase in all species of 63,000 for sport fishermen and 1,943,000 for commercial fishermen. Catches in this area now average 75,500 and 2,200,600 for sport and commercial fishermen, respectively. In Georgia Strait sport fishermen are expected to gain an even greater share of salmon from the enhancement program. The average catch for the sport fishermen is expected to increase some 495,500 on an existing base of 324,100. Commercial fishermen would more than double their catch from 486,000 to 1,235,000 salmon.[17]

CONCLUSION

The fisheries of Vancouver Island and their changing role over time mirror well the changing nature of Vancouver Island. In colonial times and in the early period after Confederation when Vancouver Island was at the centre of the economic, administrative and cultural life of the Province, the fisheries played a leading role. The Island was the financial centre for the industry, much of the equipment used in the industry was manufactured there and almost all of the marketing of fish products was done through Victoria. The executives of the industry were among those who dominated the early social and cultural life of the Province.

As Victoria lost its preeminent position to Vancouver, as Vancouver Island no longer dominated the financial life of the Province and as other industries began to contribute more to the provincial economy, the value of the commercial fishery declined, at least in relative terms. The species which frequented waters adjacent to the Island continue to follow the life cycles which they have done for centuries, but their role on the Island has changed. They are no longer at the heart of a large localized industry, but now form a critical element in the recreation and tourist industry, which is second only to forestry in the Island economy. The new role of the fisheries on the Island is unlikely to change markedly over the next few years.

REFERENCES

1. DRUCKER, P. *The Northern and Central Nootkan Tribes.* Washington: Smithsonian Institution, Bureau of American Ethnology, Bulletin 144, 1951, p. 9.

2. BENNETT, M.G. *Indian Fishing and Its Cultural Importance in the Fraser River System.* Vancouver: Department of Environment, Pacific Region, Fisheries Service and the Union of British Columbia Indian Chiefs, 1973, p. 8.

3. BOAS, F. *Kwakiutl Ethnography.* Chicago: University of Chicago Press, republished and edited by CODERE, H., 1966, p. 8.

4. BARNETT, H.G. *The Coast Salish of British Columbia.* Eugene: University of Oregon Press, 1955, pp. 78-82.

5. RALSTON, K. "Patterns of Trade and Investment on the Pacific Coast, 1867-1892: The Case of the British Columbia Canning Industry," *B.C. Studies,* 1 (1968-1969), pp. 37-45.

6. ROSS, W.M. *Salmon Canning Distribution on the Nass and Skeena Rivers of British Columbia 1877-1926. Vancouver: University of* British Columbia, Department of Geography, unpublished graduating essay, 1967, pp. 55-73.

7. REID, D.J. *The Development of the Fraser Canning Industry.* Vancouver: Department of the Environment, Pacific Region, Northern Operations Branch, Economics and Sociology Unit, 1973, pp. 2 and 3.

8. STRONG, G.G. *The Salmon Canning Industry in British Columbia.* Vancouver: University of British Columbia, Department of Economics, unpublished graduating essay, 1934, pp. 19-21.

9. Figure 1 is adapted from United States, "Report by the United States Section," *Reports by the United States and Canada on the Status, Ocean Migrations and Exploitation of Northeast Pacific Stocks of Chinook and Coho Salmon to 1964.* Washington: Informal Committee on Chinook and Coho, Vol. 1, 1969, p. 82.

10. SINCLAIR, W.F. *The Importance of the Commercial Fishing Industry to Selected Remote Coastal Communities of British Columbia*. Vancouver: Department of the Environment, Fisheries Service, Pacific Region, 1971.

11. Personal Communication, J. Kemp, Fish and Wildlife Branch, Victoria, June 1977.

12. *Ibid*.

13. CRUTCHFIELD, J.A. "The Fishery: Economic Maximization", in ELLIS, D.V. (ed.) *Pacific Salmon Management for People*. Victoria: University of Victoria, Department of Geography, Western Geographical Series, Vol. 13, 1977, pp. 1-33.

14. MERRIMAN, A. "Are 300,000 B.C. Sport Salmon Fishermen Being Ripped Off?" *B.C. Outdoors*, 30, No. 3 (1974), p. 34.

15. SINCLAIR, W.F. and REID, D.J. "Conflicts Among Recreational Resource Users – The Case of Non-Canadian Participation in the Regional Sport Fisheries of British Columbia and the Yukon," *Annals of Regional Science*, 8, No. 2 (1974), pp. 38 and 39.

16. British Columbia, *The Value of Non-Resident Sport Fishing in British Columbia*. Victoria: Prepared for the Fish and Wildlife Branch by Pearse Bowden Economic Consultants, 1972.

17. Personal Communication, G. Robinson, Environment and Land Use Committee Secretariat, Victoria, June 14, 1977; and MERRIMAN, A. "$43.4 Million Soon For Salmon Rivers," *Victoria Colonist*, Sunday, January 9, 1977, pp. 27-28.

PLATE 16   Sawmill complex, Chemainus.   *I.H. Norie Photo* ▶

WATER, ENERGY
AND TRANSPORTATION

INTRODUCTION

The topics grouped in Section 4 are related in the sense that they can be looked upon as utilities, although water, for example, is a many-faceted resource used for a variety of purposes other than as a domestic and industrial water supply. Perhaps it is appropriate that the water chapter is placed between fisheries, for obvious reasons, and energy because hydro power still is the major energy source. As may be expected, most of the water management problems occur in the densely populated coastal plain which is also the main area of energy demand. The interior acts as a great watershed, feeding the lakes and rivers and providing water resources for power generation and other uses of benefit to the eastern lowland. The pattern of transportation emphasizes the contrast between east and west coasts. Only during the last twenty-five years have roads penetrated the interior to reach the west coast and, even today, a continuous, multi-modal transportation system exists only along the east coast.

In Chapter 10 attention is focused on present problems in water management, such as waste disposal, water quality, water supply, recreational use and problems involving multiple use conflicts. Two case studies are investigated more fully, in order to illustrate the nature and complexity of the issues that arise. One is concerned with a water supply problem, while the other pertains to a conflict situation in a multi-use estuary. The difficulties encountered in meeting the present and projected energy needs of the Island are explained in Chapter 11. The mounting demands are matched against the existing and potential supplies, and alternative strategies for achieving increased energy delivery are assessed. An environmental controversy that was precipitated by one of the energy expansion proposals is explored. The evolution of the transportation system is traced in Chapter 12, using a chronological approach. The changing significance of railway, highway, water and air transportation is indicated, as well as the relative importance of transport nodes, such as ports or air traffic destinations.

PLATE 17   Pipe laying, Saanich Peninsula.   *Alex Barta Photo* ▶

PLATE 18   The Cowichan Estuary.   *I.H. Norie Photo* ▶

194

10 WATER MANAGEMENT

W.R. Derrick Sewell

Water management on Vancouver Island is at an adolescent stage of development. While no longer totally of the "frontier" type with a minimum of control and planning, it has yet to reach the levels of sophistication attained in other parts of North America.[1] Dominantly, it is characterized by a single purpose, single means, locally focused approach to water problems. The emphasis is on controlling the resource, rather than on encouraging alterations in human behaviour. There is considerable fragmentation in the administration of the Island's water resources. The public plays a minor role in planning and policy-making.

There are good reasons for the present approach. The Island is very well endowed with water resources. Much of its area receives more than 850 millimetres (33.5 inches) of precipitation per annum, and its hundreds of rivers and lakes offer opportunities for a wide range of uses (Figure 1,10). Variations in the temporal and areal distribution of precipitation give rise to problems of flooding and water deficiency in some areas, but only in a few cases have they reached a crisis stage where drastic action has been required. As a consequence, reliance has tended to be placed on a traditional approach to water management. For the most part, water problems have rated very low on the agendas of most local authorities on the Island or in the activities of provincial or federal agencies. Typically, an *ad hoc* approach has been taken in dealing with issues and no comprehensive river basin plans or other guidelines for action have been drawn up.

There are indications, however, that a move toward a higher level of sophistication now is needed. In some areas, such as the greater Victoria region, water demands are mounting rapidly, and new sources of supply are being sought farther and farther afield. It is clear that these will be very expensive, and the traditional "extensive" approach to water scarcity problems is being challenged by those who favor more efficient use of existing supplies.[2]

Elsewhere there are growing conflicts in water use. To some extent these conflicts are economic in nature, as in the case of commercial

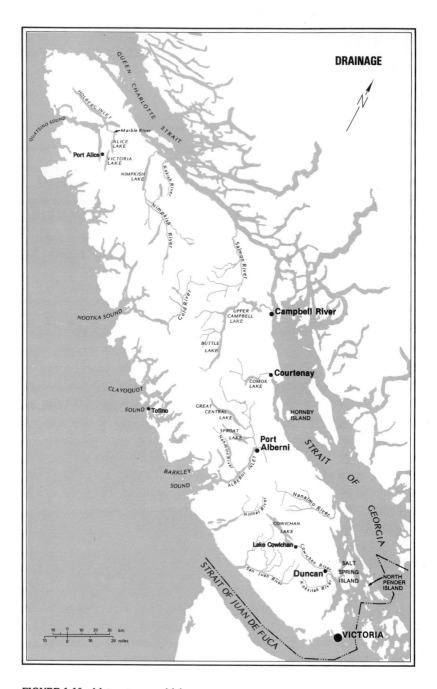

FIGURE 1,10 Major rivers and lakes.

fishermen battling with mining or forestry interests for the use of certain rivers and estuaries.[3] But to an increasing degree overall environmental quality and the preservation of habitats are being much more seriously considered in decisions relating to water management on the Island. This has forced a much more vigorous effort to identify a wider range of options for dealing with water problems and a weighing of the implications of adopting each of them. It has indicated the importance of consulting the views of the public at large during, rather than at the end of, the decision-making process. And it has emphasized the need for cooperative efforts on the part of the federal and provincial governments in dealing with some of the Island's major water problems.

PRESENT PROBLEMS

It is not possible within the confines of this chapter to review all water related problems in detail, but a number of them will be touched upon in general terms. Several areas face supply problems. There is water scarcity on the Saanich Peninsula, resulting from rapidly growing population, increasing per capita usage, and greater emphasis on irrigated agriculture. Other communities on the Island, such as Nanaimo, also are facing mounting demands for domestic and industrial water supplies, but these have not yet reached crisis proportions. There are difficulties on some of the Gulf Islands, resulting from the major expansion of population that has occurred in the past two decades. Increasing attention is being paid to water availability in the granting of permits for subdivision development, particularly as a result of the adverse experiences on Salt Spring, Hornby and North Pender islands where over-pumping resulted in contamination of groundwater supplies, either from septic tanks or from salt water intrusion.

There are also important problems of waste disposal from both domestic and industrial sources. These have become particularly acute in Victoria and Nanaimo, and are of growing significance in some of the more isolated industrial communities, such as Port Alberni, Port Alice and Tofino, and on the Gulf Islands.[4] Formerly, there was almost complete reliance upon septic tanks and direct discharge of untreated effluent into rivers, lakes or estuaries. The passage of the British Columbia Pollution Control Act in 1967, the establishment of the Pollution Control Branch, the introduction and implementation of standards for waste discharge, and the more rigorous application of federal water pollution control legislation has encouraged and facilitated a more sophisticated approach to water quality management in the Province. Dischargers now must apply for permits to dispose of wastes into water bodies. Attempts are being made to raise progressively the quality of particular rivers and lakes. Both the federal and provincial governments are developing extensive networks to monitor water quality. At the same time, efforts are being made to link water management to land use planning. In the case of the Gulf Islands, for example, the imposition of a ten acre minimum lot size, undoubtedly, has assisted in arresting water supply and sewage disposal problems.

There remain criticisms, however, of the present approach to water quality management in British Columbia. Some observers have questioned the effectiveness of the permit system, both in principle and in practice. They note the huge backlog in dealing with permit applications, and the failure to prosecute those who exceed the conditions set out in the permits.[5] Others have suggested that a more efficient and equitable approach would be to make the polluter pay according to the volume and nature of his discharge, as is done in several European countries.[6] Unfortunately, data are collected at a limited number of locations and on a few parameters only, although a more extensive monitoring system is being introduced. As a consequence, it is difficult to determine what improvements, if any, have been made in the quality of particular water bodies.

For Vancouver Island as a whole, floods are a relatively minor problem. The largest city, Victoria, does not have a riverine location, and any flooding that does occur is small in scale and short in duration. It causes relatively little damage. There are a few places, however, which occasionally sustain important losses from floods, notably Port Alberni, Campbell River, Courtenay, Duncan, Lake Cowichan and Shawnigan Lake (Figure 1,10). Studies have been undertaken to assess the significance of these flood problems, and in some instances proposals have been put forward for corrective action. Particular attention has been given to the problem in the Cowichan region.[7] Benefit-cost analyses of the various alternatives, however, have failed to demonstrate the economic feasibility of any of the strategies proposed so far. In the case of the Cowichan River, effective flood control might be attained only at the expense of the salmon fishery.[8]

Water based recreation is growing rapidly in popularity on Vancouver Island, both within and beyond the major urban areas. Occasionally, this results in major conflicts in water use. Although Victoria has several ocean beaches which are heavily patronized, there is a considerable demand for recreation on lakes close to the city, notably Elk, Beaver,[9] and Thetis. This demand comes in part from Victoria residents, but also to an increasing extent from tourists.[10] A wide variety of recreation experiences is sought, ranging from motorboating and sailing to swimming and sunbathing. Increasingly, the various activities are coming into conflict, particularly motorboating and other pursuits. Several solutions have been suggested, including area zoning with ropes or buoys, rotating use schedules by time of day, week or season, and the opening up of lakes within the watersheds managed by the Greater Victoria Water District. The approach so far has been to ban power boats on some lakes, such a Thetis, and restrict their use to specified areas on others, such as Elk, Beaver and Prospect (Figure 2,10). The Greater Victoria Water District does not permit recreation on its reservoirs, claiming that the costs of maintenance and additional water treatment would be too great and that, in any case, there are sufficient opportunities elsewhere in the region.

The foregoing is but a brief overview of the major types of water management problems that are emerging on the Island. It serves to indicate, however, that while most of these issues can be handled within the existing institutional framework, some may require important alterations in laws, policies, and administrative arrangements if they are to be solved satisfactorily. Two case studies have been selected to identify the types of modification that may be required. One concerns the provision of additional water to satisfy the growing demands on the Saanich Peninsula. The other relates to a multi-conflict situation in the Cowichan Estuary.

SAANICH PENINSULA WATER SUPPLY

Greater Victoria possesses a highly efficient water system, furnishing the city with water at an average cost of less than thirty cents per 1,000 gallons. Administered by the Greater Victoria Water District, the system now is capable of supplying 45,000,000 gallons per day, a volume sufficient to satisfy the needs of the city's population at least until the end of the present century.[11]

In contrast, the Saanich Peninsula is experiencing considerable difficulties in obtaining sufficient water. The peninsula covers an area of some ninety-five square kilometres (thirty-seven square miles), and includes the municipalities of Central Saanich and North Saanich, and

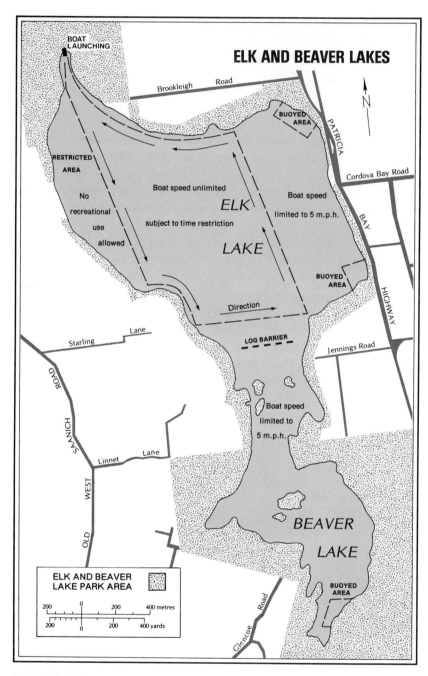

FIGURE 2,10 Space allocation for recreational uses.

the town of Sidney (Figure 3,10). It is basically an agricultural area, with a large part of its land now protected by the Agricultural Land Reserve. Berry crops, vegetables, flowers and bulbs thrive there. The gently rolling terrain, with spectacular views of the ocean in places, has considerable aesthetic appeal. These features, together with the high land prices and high taxes in the city, have brought increasing pressure to open up the peninsula to further residential, and perhaps some industrial, development. Water availability is a major restricting factor.

The present system is capable of supplying some 3,000,000 gallons per day during the summer months. Basically, it consists of Elk Lake, a series of small reservoirs, and a number of wells at various points on the peninsula (Figure 3,10). A thirty-one centimetre (twelve inch) pipeline constructed in 1940 from Elk Lake to the airport, and subsequently extended to Swartz Bay, is used mainly to supply Central Saanich and the ferry system, as well as the needs of North Saanich and Sidney in the summer months. There are also approximately 3,000 wells serving private owners. A temporary additional supply was obtained in 1977 from a 3,659 metre (12,000 foot) pipe connecting the peninsula to the Greater Victoria Water District. In the summer of 1977 this furnished an additional 400,000 gallons per day for the peninsula.

Overall demands on the municipal systems during the summer months of 1977 reached 3,500,000 gallons per day. There have been occasional droughts, and even though the summer peak exceeds the minimum monthly consumption by a factor of six, the occasional restriction of use has not resulted in major inconvenience or large losses of income. In the past few years, however, a number of factors have begun to alter this situation, the foremost of which has been the rapid increase in population (Table 1,10). At the same time, per capita usage has expanded, resulting from increased affluence and the shift of the area toward a more urban life style. In addition, there has been a gradual shift in the types of crops grown, from berries to vegetables, thus increasing the volumes of water required for irrigation. If present trends continue, consultants have estimated, water demands on the peninsula will have reached 10,000,000 gallons per day by 1996.[12]

Meanwhile, present sources have begun to diminish either in quality or quantity. Elk Lake, the major source, is being used increasingly as a recreational facility, and it is important to maintain its level during the summer months for this purpose. The discharge of effluents from septic tanks and fertilizers from farms surrounding the lake has led to increasing problems of eutrophication and a decline in quality for drinking water.

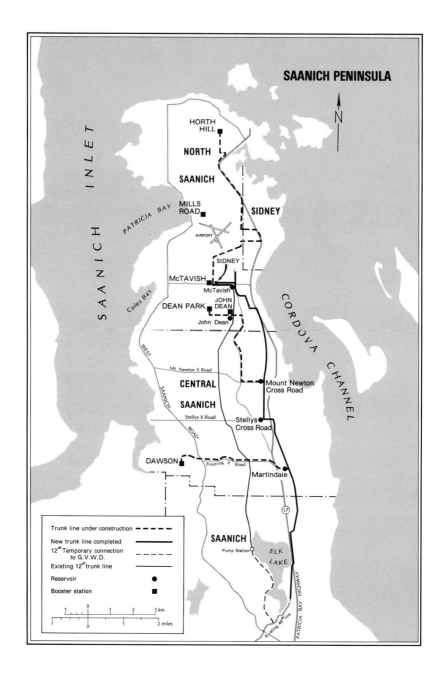

FIGURE 3,10 The water supply system, 1978.

202

TABLE 1,10   Population Growth on the Saanich Peninsula, 1951-1976

1951	5,964
1961	7,835
1966	9,696
1971	13,600
1976	18,842

SOURCE: *Census of Canada, 1951-1976.*

In the summer of 1977 it was decided not to use the lake for the latter purpose, and a temporary alternative source was obtained from a connection to the Greater Victoria Water District supply. The volume of water available from some of the peninsula's major wells has fallen in recent years, in some cases to less than half the original production.

The need to solve the water problem has been recognized for some time, but progress has been hampered by fragmentation of jurisdiction. There are two water improvement districts (Deep Cove and Brentwood Bay), three municipal bodies, the Capital Regional District, the British Columbia Land Commission, and the provincial and federal departments of Agriculture, each with a different view of what the region's economic and environmental future should be, and each with a different opinion as to who should foot the bill for the provision of additional water supplies.

In an attempt to deal with this problem, the Minister of Municipal Affairs established the Saanich Peninsula Water Commission in January, 1977. It is composed of eleven members, drawn from the municipalities, the waterworks committees and the Capital Regional District Board. Its responsibilities are to examine the water supply situation, consider alternative solutions to the emerging problems, and initiate the necessary actions to deal with them. The Commission will perform a role similar to that of the Greater Victoria Water District, acting as a bulk wholesaler for the region.

The Commission has examined a variety of possible means of obtaining additional water, based largely on studies undertaken by engineering consultants.[13] The majority of the alternatives included, as an integral part, the construction of a major trunk line to connect with the Greater Victoria Water District's system at Haliburton Road, and this is now under development (Figure 3,10). The trunk line and associated facilities, which will supply up to 9,500,000 gallons per day, will cost approximately 9,000,000 dollars.[14] It has been suggested by the Minister for Housing and Urban Affairs that the cost will be about $1.22 per 1,000 gallons. While this figure would not be an undue burden on the average householder, it would be a major challenge to the heavy water users, that is, those whose monthly consumption is in excess of 10,000 gallons. Presently they pay only thirty-five cents per 1,000 gallons. A quadrupling in price would certainly preclude use by most agriculturalists.

Cognizant of the likelihood that farmers will be unable to pay such high prices, the Water Investigations Branch has been examining ways in which irrigation demands might be satisfied. Specifically, they have been considering a dual system, whereby residential users would draw upon the trunk line, while agricultural users would depend upon ground water supplies and, possibly, water from Elk Lake. Where necessary, farmers would install water purification facilities for domestic uses. The advantage of this scheme is that its costs would be borne largely by the senior governments. Under the Agricultural and Rural Development Act the federal and provincial governments jointly would pay seventy-five percent of the capital cost, and the farmers would pay the rest as a charge against their land.[15]

The trunk line is due to be completed by the end of 1979, but many are unhappy with this solution. Members of the Saanich Peninsula Water Commission have balked at the proposal that they should pay a fee amounting to twelve cents per 1,000 gallons to join their system to that of the Greater Victoria Water District. They feel that citizens of the peninsula should pay no more for water from Victoria than the citizens of the latter. Moreover, they argue that the Agricultural Land Reserve provides a green belt service for the city, while restricting economic development on the peninsula. Considered in this light, the payment of the proposed fee is regarded as even more inequitable. Negotiations on this matter continue. There have also been suggestions that the line will have much more capacity than is required. These views are based on the belief that the population projections underlying the estimates were unduly optimistic, and that farmers will be unwilling to pay such high prices for the water.

A major theme in the search for more sophistication on water management is that of widening the range of choice. So far, the approach on the

Saanich Peninsula has been "extensive" in nature, the search for water being progressively farther afield as local sources have been exploited.[16] Relatively little attention has been given to possibilities of demand management, in which consumers are encouraged to make more efficient use of existing supplies, rather than purchasing additional water at progressively higher costs.[17] There are many ways in which efficiency might be improved. The introduction of crop varieties which use less water, the repair of leaks in water mains, and the use of much smaller tanks for toilets are but a few of the potential means.[18] Another which has considerable value for the peninsula would be an alteration in the pricing schedule. At present, water use above the first 1,000 gallons costs only one-quarter as much as the initial 1,000 gallons, which amounts to an incentive to consume. If water for essential uses were provided at a reasonable rate, followed by steps in which each additional 1,000 gallons cost progressively more, there would be a much needed incentive to conserve. This would be particularly so if the price increased dramatically with successive steps. Rationing might also be combined with price increases. In Marin County, California consumption is allowed to reach a certain level, after which the supply is cut off and a high fee is charged for re-connection.

Finally, much could be attained through consumer education. In recent years local newspapers and other media have helped to encourage conservation by explaining inefficiencies that result from excessive sprinkling or dripping faucets.[19] School teachers made a major contribution toward this end during the Goldstream crisis in 1970 when they explained the need for reductions in use in order to save salmon runs.[20] The result was a reduction in consumption in greater Victoria of 1,000,000 gallons per day.[21]

MULTI-CONFLICT RESOLUTION IN THE COWICHAN ESTUARY

Another theme in modern water management is the development of institutions for the resolution of conflicts.[22] This is especially important in those instances where there are conflicts between uses that are mutually exclusive, and where jurisdiction is divided among several levels of administration. Various mechanisms have been introduced in Canada, the United States and elsewhere to deal with such matters, in an effort to encourage a more comprehensive and rational approach to water development.[23] The Water Commission, the River Basin Commission,

205

the federal-provincial Water Investigation Board and the *ad hoc* Task Force are among the devices that have been used in this connection. There has been no in-depth study of experience with the various mechanisms, but there is evidence that some have been extremely successful, particularly at the planning stage, while others have failed.[24] The cooperative efforts of the federal and provincial governments in the case of the Okanagan Basin Study are an illustration of the former.[25] The experience with the resolution of the conflicts in the Cowichan Estuary seems to be an example of the latter.

The Cowichan and Koksilah rivers are highly important as chinook, coho, and chum salmon spawning streams (Figure 4,10). The annual values of the commercial and recreational histories of these rivers has been estimated at 2,200,000 dollars and 2,400,000, respectively. The Indian food fishery harvests more than 5,000 salmon annually.[26] The estuary also provides a valuable habitat for a wide variety of waterfowl and other bird species and is an important waterfowl hunting area.

The early economic development of the Cowichan valley focused on farming and on the forest industry. Small dairy, beef and horticultural farms still thrive in the area, principally in the estuary and valley bottom lands. Full development of the potential of the agricultural lands of the region, however, is hampered by the problems of floods. The forest industry became established in the 1880's and has been an important part of the region's economy since that time. The sheltered Cowichan Bay has attracted considerable attention in recent years for further developments in this industry. A large sawmill has been built by Domans on reclaimed land in the estuary and the bay acts as a major log booming ground, with logs supplied partly from the local area and partly from other locations.

In 1974 the provincial government established the British Columbia Development Corporation to foster economic expansion in the Province. The Cowichan Estuary, offering the important advantages of a tidewater location, a considerable amount of flat land and railway links, attracted its attention. It was recognized, however, that the estuary is environmentally a highly sensitive area, hence, the Environment and Land Use Committee of the provincial government requested its Secretariat to coordinate a Task Force which would evaluate the likely impact of four types of development.[27]

1. Agricultural and recreational dedication.
2. Status quo.
3. Limited economic expansion.
4. Industrial-commercial development.

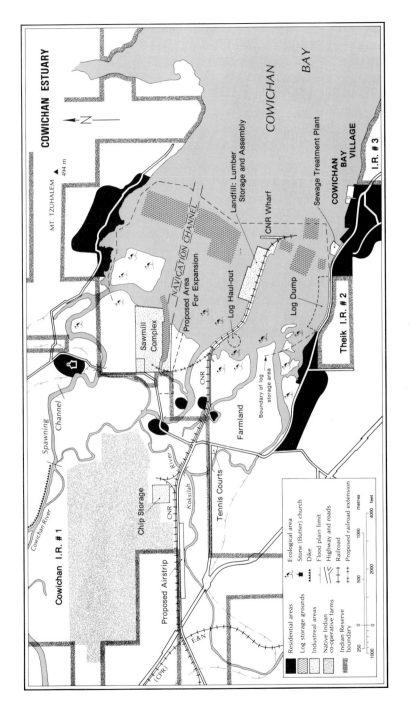

FIGURE 4.10 Potential developments in the Cowichan Estuary.

207

The Task Force was composed of representatives of thirteen government agencies. Its report showed that the estuary possesses fisheries and wildlife of considerable economic and aesthetic value and it found that these would suffer considerable damage if major industrial development were to take place. At the same time, an investigation by the Canadian Wildlife Service indicated that a considerable portion of the habitat of the wildfowl and migratory birds would be lost.[28] The overall conclusion was that the development of the area's agricultural and recreational potential constituted the most desirable course of action.[29] The Cowichan Bay planners appeared to endorse that viewpoint and went even further in suggesting that some of the existing development in the estuary eventually should be phased out.[30]

In recent months, however, there has been a dramatic alteration in viewpoint of some of the agencies responsible for the management of the estuary's resources. The Cowichan Valley Regional Board, in particular, has decided to review its no-growth policy in the light of the present heavy unemployment in the region and proposals for industrial expansion.[31] There have been several proposals for the estuary area, including the extension of the present sawmill, the construction of a pelletizing plant, the development of a shake mill, the installation of a log-haul-out and the construction of a pulp mill.[32] Each of these would have differential impacts on the region's ecology, economy, and social relationships.

Although proponents of such expansion have claimed that it would be a boon to the region, others have vigorously opposed the various proposals. As a response to the diverging viewpoints, another Task Force composed of representatives of federal, provincial, regional and municipal agencies, and members of the Cowichan Indian Band, was established in January 1978. With a membership of twenty-one, the Task Force faces a major challenge in reaching agreement on anything. Inevitably, members' views will reflect their agencies' responsibilities, as well as their own professional backgrounds. A common viewpoint would be difficult enough to achieve within a single level of administration, but the Task Force encompasses three of them. Officials of the federal Department of Fisheries and Environment fear that bark from the log booms, toxic materials from decomposing wood chips, and effluents that would be discharged from a pulp and paper mill would adversely affect the salmon runs of the Cowichan and Koksilah rivers. Those in the provincial Department of Recreation and Conservation are cognizant of the fact that the area has considerable potential for various recreational pursuits and probably will resist proposals which would impair the realization of that potential. On the other hand, the Department of Economic Development officials are anxious to ensure that the most favourable opportunities for industrial expansion are utilized. Meanwhile, the members of the Cowichan Valley Regional Board appear sharply divided on the issue.

The problem is further complicated by the fact that there is considerable pressure to produce a broadly acceptable solution to the conflict within a few months. Those working on the Task Force are critically aware of the need to examine the potential economic, social, and environmental effects of each of the proposed developments, but are hampered by the lack of information on many of these impacts. In some instances this difficulty can be overcome by rapid surveys or comparisons with situations elsewhere. In others the problem is much more difficult. It is not known, for example, how various scales of industrial development would affect particular fish runs. Is there a threshold beyond which survival is impossible? In addition, there is no broadly accepted measure that could be used in trading off the gains to those who would benefit from the expansion of the forest industry against the losses to those who would prefer to catch fish or enjoy the waterfowl of the wetlands and the beauties of the landscape. Even more important, there is no way of measuring the cost of destroying an irreplaceable asset, such as an estuary.

The experience in the Cowichan Estuary case highlights the weakness of the *ad hoc* approach to water management. Thus, the various aspects, such as flood control, water supply, recreation, and estuarine management, have been dealt with in isolation. Sometimes this has resulted in important conflicts in the policies of the various agencies. The *ad hoc* approach also has precluded the development of a long term plan for the water resources of the region. And it has tended to place the various interests in adversary positions, rather than fostering a spirit of cooperation. Task forces have tended to be staffed exclusively by agency personnel, and hearings usually have been held in camera, rather than in open forum. Seldom has there been a statement of which views have been taken into account and which factors have been weighed in arriving at recommendations. It is not surprising that the resulting reports often have been ignored.

CONCLUSIONS

Water management on Vancouver Island has reached an important checkpoint in its evolution. Hitherto, the problems that have emerged have been small in scope and isolated in occurrence. Existing laws, policies, and administrative arrangements have been adequate to meet the challenges placed before them. In the past few years, however, mounting water scarcities and various conflicts in water use have indicated that some major changes in these institutions may be required. Particularly important is the need to coordinate the responsibilities of the various levels of government and to ensure that planning becomes an ongoing process, rather than an *ad hoc* activity.

REFERENCES

1. WHITE, G.F. *Strategies of American Water Management*. Ann Arbor: University of Michigan Press, 1969.

2. SEWELL, W.R.D. "The New York Water Crisis," *Journal of Geography*, (November, 1966), pp. 384-389.

3. FERGUSON, A. *Institutional Aspects of the Coastal Zone: the Case of Estuarine Management on Vancouver Island*. Victoria: University of Victoria, Department of Geography, unpublished M.A. thesis, 1977.

4. ELLIS, D. "Sewage Disposal to the Sea" in Foster, H.D. (ed.) *Victoria: Physical Environment and Development*. Victoria: University of Victoria, Department of Geography, Western Geographical Series, Vol. 12, 1976, pp. 289-332; and Neate, F. *The Gorge Waterway: Selkirk Water to Portage Inlet*. Victoria: Corporation of the District of Saanich, March, 1970.

5. CROOK, C.S. *Environment and Land Use Policies and Practices*, Victoria: British Columbia Institute for Economic Policy Analysis, 1975.

6. JOHNSON, R.W. and BROWN, G.M. *Cleaning Up Europe's Waters*. New York: Praeger, 1976.

7. WESTER, J. *Cowichan and Koksilah Preliminary Flood Control Proposals*. Victoria: Department of Lands, Forests and Water Resources, Water Investigations Branch, 1967.

8. LILL, A.F. *et al. Conservation of Fish and Wildlife of the Cowichan-Koksilah Flood Plain*. Vancouver: Environment Canada, Fisheries and Marine Service, 1975.

9. STROYAN, P. *Recreation Possibilities of Elk-Beaver Lake*. Victoria: Corporation of the District of Saanich, 1968.

10. Capital Regional District, *Regional Park User Survey*. Victoria: Capital Regional District Board, 1974.

11. BANCROFT, C.G. *Strategies for Solving Urban Water Supply Shortages*. Victoria: University of Victoria, Department of Geography, unpublished M.A. thesis, 1974.

12. Capital Regional District, *Saanich Peninsula Water Supply Study*. Victoria: Report prepared for Capital Regional District Board by Underwood, McLellan and Associates, 1977.

13. *Ibid.*

14. "Water Line Cost Set at $8 million," *Victoria Times*, March 16, 1978.

15. *Victoria Times*, July 30, 1977.

16. SEWELL, W.R.D., *op. cit.*, p. 384.

17. DAVIS, R.K. and HANKE, S.H. "Conventional and Unconventional Alternatives for Water Supply Management," *Water Resources Research*, 9, No. 4, (August, 1973), pp. 861-870.

18. BAUMANN, D., *et al. Planning Alternatives for Municipal Water Systems*, Indianapolis: Butte University, Holcomb Research Institute, 1976.

19. BEASTALL, J. "You Can S-a-v-e on Water Bills," *Victoria Times*, June 16, 1973; and BEASTALL, J. "Watering Restrictions No Real Disaster," *Victoria Times*, June 25, 1977.

20. SEWELL, W.R.D. and WOOD, C.J.B. "Environmental Decision-Making and Environmental Stress: The Goldstream Controversy," a paper presented at the Annual Meeting of the Canadian Association of Geographers, Waterloo, Ontario, June 1971.

21. PALMER, D. "The Goldstream Drama: a Water Use Conflict," *Environment Tomorrow*, No. 2, (February 1971), pp. 5-7.

22. WHITE, G.F., *op. cit.*; and MITCHELL, B. (ed.) *Institutional Arrangements for Water Management: Canadian Experiences*. Waterloo, Ontario: University of Waterloo, Department of Geography, Publication Series, No. 5, 1975.

23. SEWELL, W.R.D. "The Administrative Framework for Water Management in Canada: Challenges and Responses," in *The Administration of Water Resources in Canada*. Montreal: Canadian Council of Resource Ministers, September, 1968, pp. 17-26.

24. BELLINGER, D. "Canadian Water Management Policy Instruments: a National Overview," in MITCHELL, B., *ibid.*, pp. 1-42.

25. O'RIORDAN, J. "The Public Involvement Program in the Okanagan Basin Study," in UTTON, A., SEWELL, W.R.D. and O'RIORDAN, T. (eds.) *Natural Resources for a Democratic Society: Public Participation in Decision-Making*. Boulder, Colorado: Westview Press, 1976, pp. 177-196.

26. BELL, L.M. and KALLMAN, R.J. *The Cowichan-Chemainus River Estuaries: Status of Environmental Knowledge to 1975*. Vancouver: Environment Canada, Special Estuary Series No. 4, 1976.

27. British Columbia, *Development Alternatives for the Cowichan and Koksilah Estuaries*. Victoria: Cowichan Estuary Task Force, October 25, 1974.

28. TRETHEWAY, D.E.C. *An Assessment of the Impacts of Wildlife and Wildlife Related Recreation of Four Alternative Development Proposals for the Cowichan River Estuary and Floodplain.* Delta, British Columbia: Canadian Wildlife Service, 1974.

29. British Columbia, *op. cit.*

30. Cowichan Valley Regional District, *Cowichan Bay Official Community Plan.* Duncan, British Columbia: Urban Programme Planners, report prepared for Cowichan Valley Regional District, 1975.

31. TEMPLEMAYR, M. "Jobs or Fish: Can Vancouver Island's Richest Salmon River Survive the Unemployment Crisis?" *Monday Magazine*, February 13, 1978.

32. *Ibid.*

PLATE 19 John Hart Generating Station, Campbell River. *B.C. Hydro Photo* ▶

11 ENERGY RESOURCES AND ENERGY USE

W.R. Derrick Sewell

Vancouver Islanders enjoy a very high standard of living. With a per capita income of over 4,000 dollars per annum, a considerable segment of the population working less than forty hours per week, and a high proportion of the work force engaged in tertiary activities, they have a level of material well-being comparable to that of most other parts of Canada and in excess of that experienced in many other countries. To an important extent this has been made possible by the harnessing and use of vast quantities of energy. Today, the Island's homes, industries and transportation modes use almost 100×10^{12} BTU per annum, or 229×10^9 BTU per capita (Table 1,11). For comparison, the per capita use in Canada as a whole is about $227 \times 10.^9$ The somewhat higher level of energy use on Vancouver Island is a reflection of the mechanization of industry, the use of a wide range of labour saving devices, and the importance of transportation in the Island's economy.

Energy consumption has grown rapidly, particularly in the years since World War II. During that period it has more than doubled every decade, that is, at a rate in excess of seven percent per annum. The demand for particular forms of energy has grown even more spectacularly, notably electricity. In the latter case, consumption expanded at a rate of over ten percent per annum until very recently.

There is now a mounting concern that the Island will face a major energy crisis by the end of the century unless firm steps are taken soon to avert it. It has become clear that local sources of some forms of energy have been used up or are now too expensive to develop. Increasingly, Vancouver Islanders are looking elsewhere for their energy supplies. Proposals for other means of satisfying the growing demands have met with substantial opposition, particularly on grounds of environmental disruption. The possibility of constructing a nuclear power plant near Duncan was mooted by British Columbia Hydro some years ago, but met with a very hostile reception. Presently, a proposal to build a 500 kV DC transmission line from Cheekye on the mainland to Dunsmuir on northern Vancouver Island is being opposed by residents of Lasqueti Island over which it would pass. This dilemma emphasizes the need for a thorough-going review of the Island's energy resources and its future needs, and for the development of a set of guidelines for policy. Without these the prospective crisis will occur inevitably, probably within the next ten years.

In this chapter the emerging energy situation is described and alternative strategies that might be adopted in dealing with it are considered. The Lasqueti Island controversy is used to highlight the various issues that have been raised in the search for a solution to the Island's energy problem.

MOUNTING DEMANDS

Although no precise estimates can be made of the volume of energy used in the different sectors of the economy or in various parts of the Island, it is possible to gain a broad appreciation of the present situation from the data that are available. The largest amount of information that is currently available relates to the residential sector. British Columbia Hydro publishes, annually, the volumes of electrical energy purchased in this sector, while the Energy Commission furnishes estimates of consumption of refined petroleum products and liquefied petroleum gases. Unfortunately, no data are gathered on the use of firewood, which in some parts of the Island is a source of fuel for home heating. Refined petroleum products dominate residential energy consumption, followed by electricity (Tables 1,11 and 2,11). There is a small but significant consumption of liquefied petroleum gases, particularly butane. Most of this is used in the more isolated communities and on the smaller islands.

Consumption in the commercial sector is more difficult to estimate. This sector covers all uses other than those in the home, and in manufacturing, mining, forestry, and transportation. It embraces agriculture, fishing, wholesale and retail trade, and utilities.[1] No data are available relating specifically to the commercial sector on the Island. For the purposes of the present study, it has been assumed that much of the demand in this sector is related to the size of the population. Based on the Island's relative share of the British Columbia population in 1976, 435,841 of a total of 2,515,526, its share of the commercial sector's energy consumption in that year was about 17.4×10^{12}BTU.

TABLE 1,11   Energy Consumption on
Vancouver Island, 1976 in BTU x 10^{12}

Residential*	21.0
Commercial**	17.4
Industrial and Transportation†	58.2
Total	96.6

SOURCES: *British Columbia, *British Columbia's Energy Outlook, 1976-1991*. Victoria: British Columbia Energy Commission, 1976.

**Based on an allocation of commercial demands in British Columbia according to population distribution.

†Personal communication, British Columbia Energy Commission, March 29, 1978.

TABLE 2,11   Energy Consumption in the Residential Sector, 1976

Energy Form	Consumption in BTU x 10^{12} Equivalent	Percentage of Provincial Total
Electricity	4.9	21.5
Refined Petroleum Products	15.3	36.8
Liquefied Petroleum Gases	.8	36.4
	21.0	

SOURCE: Adapted from data in British Columbia, *British Columbia's Energy Outlook, 1976-1991*. Victoria: British Columbia Energy Commission, 1976; and information supplied by British Columbia Hydro and Power Authority.

The remaining consumption is accounted for by the Island's major industries, forestry, mining, and manufacturing, and by transportation. Together, these uses account for about sixty percent of total energy demand (Table 1,11). Unfortunately, no precise breakdown is possible. As other chapters in the volume indicate, however, there are a number of large, integrated and non-integrated forest products operations at various points on the Island, and copper and molybdenum refining operations at Rupert Inlet and Buttle Lake. Manufacturing, other than forest products, is little developed on Vancouver Island and much of it consists of light industries with relatively modest energy requirements.

In the Province as a whole energy demands for transportation are considerable, accounting for about twenty-eight percent of all energy consumption. While it is not possible to determine whether or not a similar proportion prevails on the Island, it is probable that at least twenty-five percent of the total is used in the transport sector. As noted in the chapter on transportation, the resource exploitation industries rely heavily on truck haulage, and there is a substantial fleet of tugboats and ferries connecting various points on Vancouver Island with other islands and the mainland.

While there has been a slowing in the energy demand rate of growth in recent years, it still remains above five percent per annum. No attempt has been made by the various task forces that have studied the situation to predict the overall demands for energy on the Island by the end of the century. This is largely because there is considerable uncertainty about the probable location of future industrial development in the Province, about the future price of petroleum, about the future coal development, and about the lack of firm policies concerning the siting of power stations and transmission lines. However, if demands for energy on the Island continue to grow at the current rate of approximately five percent per annum between now and the end of the century, overall demands will have risen to approximately 311.5×10^{12} BTU per annum. The question arises, how can these growing demands be satisfied?

THE SUPPLY OF ENERGY

Most of the energy consumed on Vancouver Island is imported. This was not always so. In the days before white settlement the Indians used the wood from the Island's magnificent forests, and coal derived from isolated deposits on the west coast. The major developments, however, awaited the advent of the steamship, the railway, and the immigration of skilled miners, notably from the United Kingdom. Coal was discovered at Suquash near Port McNeill in 1835, and a few years later near Nanaimo and Comox. A thriving industry developed, with annual production reaching more than 1,000,000 tons by the turn of the century.[2] Most of this coal was used for heating, either locally or for bunkering ships. Small quantities were carbonized in a plant consisting of 100 beehive ovens which operated until 1922. Economic depression in the 1920's and the 1930's led to a gradual decline in production and by 1962 coal output on Vancouver Island had fallen to less than 82,000 tons a year. Production virtually ceased in 1968.[3] From the time that coal was discovered at Port McNeill until 1962 more than 80,000,000 tons had been mined on the Island, representing well over half the coal extracted in the Province up to that time.

While coal was used dominantly for heating, manufactured gas became increasingly popular for lighting. The Victoria Gas Company was established in 1860, and after some major battles to win public confidence and overcome political barriers, it built a distribution system which covered a large part of the city.[4] Much of it still remains, though it is not used today. Its function was challenged by the electric light that was introduced to the city in 1881 and came into widespread use after the turn of the century. The Gas Company worked feverishly to keep up, and managed to capture a share of the market for heating and cooking. This company eventually was taken over by the British Columbia Electric Company which, itself, was expropriated by the provincial government in 1961. Under the leadership of the British Columbia Electric Company, the distribution system was expanded and gas sales boomed. But, ultimately, gas was succeeded by electricity and petroleum.

Hydroelectric power generation on Vancouver Island began with the construction of a small dam on Bear Creek, which runs into Jordan River. A 3,200 kW unit was installed at the original Jordan River Generating Station in 1911. Three units were added later to bring the total capacity of the plant to 26,400 kW. This plant was in service for sixty years. Since its establishment there have been many other hydroelectric developments on the Island. Some of these have been undertaken by electric power utilities, such as the British Columbia Power Commission and its successor, the British Columbia Hydro and Power Authority. Others have been developed by forest, mining, and fishing companies (Table 3,11). These, however, are extremely small in comparison with those owned by the Hydro and Power Authority. Besides hydroelectric power, there have been some

TABLE 3,11 Electric Power Development on Vancouver Island

Owner	Name of Plant	Location	Type	Installed Capacity in kW
British Columbia	Jordan River	Victoria	Hydro	165,000
Hydro and	John Hart	Campbell River	Hydro	120,000
Power Authority	Strathcona	Campbell River	Hydro	67,500
	Ladore Falls	Campbell River	Hydro	54,000
	Puntledge	Courtenay	Hydro	27,000
	Ash River	Port Alberni	Hydro	25,000
	Georgia	Chemainus	Thermal	75,500
	Keogh	Port Hardy	Thermal	40,500
	Tofino	Tofino	Diesel	400
	Bamfield	Bamfield	Diesel	100
	Zeballos	Zeballos	Diesel	100
McMillan Bloedel		Nanaimo	Steam	33,200
		Port Alberni	Steam	27,000
		Chemainus	Steam	3,750
Rayonier Canada		Port Alice	Gas-Diesel	16,200
		Port Alice	Hydro	2,000
British Columbia		Youbou	Steam	9,300
Forest Products		Victoria	Steam	4,500
Tahsis Company		Tahsis	Steam	8,000
Coast Copper	Raging River	Port Alice	Hydro	1,760

SOURCE: British Columbia, *Power in British Columbia, 1976.*
Victoria: Ministry of Environment, 1976.

significant developments in the thermal electric power field, notably the construction of the 75,500 kW Georgia Station at Chemainus and the 40,500 kW Keogh plant at Port Hardy (Table 3,11).

Faced with the problem of rapidly growing power demands on Vancouver Island, and with high costs of fuel and few remaining opportunities for hydro power development, the Power Commission and, subsequently, the Hydro and Power Authority, have constructed a series of interconnections with the mainland (Table 4,11). These lines, the first of which was installed in 1956, consist of two 138 kV AC circuits and two high voltage circuits which will have a total capacity of 1,044 MW when completed late in 1978 (Figure 1,11).

Electric power loads on Vancouver Island have almost doubled in the past ten years and seem destined to grow at a high rate in the foreseeable future. The peak load on the Hydro system now is 1,120 MW. British Columbia Hydro anticipates that, although demand rates of increase in the residential, commercial and industrial sectors (historically above 8.8 percent per annum) will fall to less than six percent in the years ahead, a peak load of 2,500 MW will occur by 1992. The existing power supply to Vancouver Island will be fully committed by 1982 and additional capacity will be required by October 1983 (Figure 2,11).

A similar pattern of growth is occurring in the consumption of other forms of energy. Consideration is being given to the expansion of oil storage facilities to meet expanding demands for refined petroleum products. There is discussion of the possibility of building a natural gas pipeline from the mainland. In addition, there have been proposals for a nuclear power plant to be built near Duncan, or possibly in a more northerly location. Several of the forestry companies have turned increasingly to hog fuel as a means of avoiding the escalating costs of oil and electricity. Today, approximately 908,000 gravity packed units are used by the industry on Vancouver Island, equivalent to 14.5×10^{12}BTU. The question of future supplies, however, remains a highly contentious one.

Although it is clear that most Vancouver Island residents prize very highly the life style to which they have become accustomed, and while there is an appreciation of the economic importance of finding additional sources of supply, a number of proposals to accomplish the latter have met with substantial public opposition. Two successive premiers of the Province, for example, have stated that they are against the development of nuclear power stations on the Island. There is probably a great deal of public support for this position, even though the issue has not been explored in any depth. Also, there is opposition to proposals for the con-

TABLE 4,11 Undeveloped Power Sites on Vancouver Island

Site	Lake or Stream	Prime Power in kW
Great Central	Great Central Lake	15,700
Sproat	Sproat Lake	7,700
Nahmint-Henderson	Nahmint River	11,900
Port Alice Tunnel	Victoria Lake	28,300
Middle Canyon	Marble River	13,200
Marble Canyon	Marble River	11,600
Kokish	Kokish River	38,000
Nimpkish	Nimpkish River	37,300

SOURCE: Personal Communication, British Columbia Energy Commission, March 28, 1978.

struction of transmission lines, especially where they are likely to alter the character of the rural landscape. The controversy over the Cheekye-Dunsmuir transmission line which would pass over Lasqueti Island provides an excellent illustration of the various dilemmas to be found in planning the future energy supply for Vancouver Island.

LASQUETI ISLAND CONTROVERSY

Cognizant of the continuously mounting demand for electric power on Vancouver Island, the British Columbia Hydro and Power Authority has been exploring alternative strategies for supplying future needs. Basically, the options are of two types:

1. Development of additional generation capacity on the Island.
2. Transmission of electric power from the mainland to the Island.

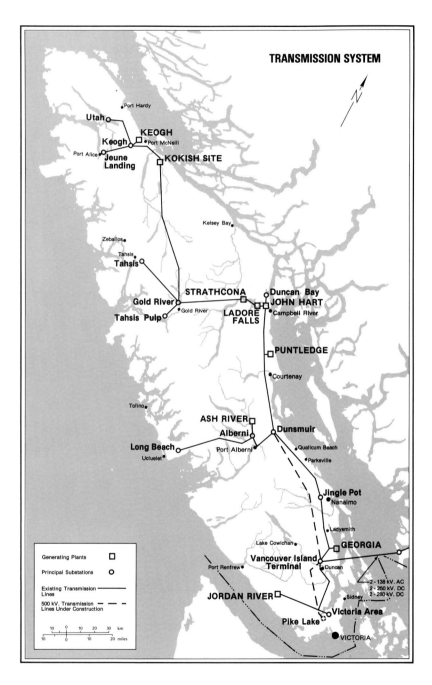

FIGURE 1,11 Generating plants, transmission lines and substations, 1978.

223

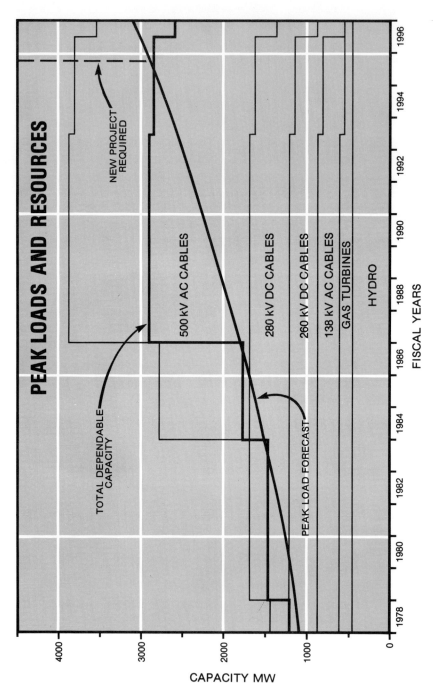

FIGURE 2,11 Electric power resources and peak load forecasts, 1977-1997.

224

The prime generation alternatives include the addition of hydro power capacity from the remaining sites, the construction of thermal power stations and the development of nuclear power. After in-depth studies of these options, the Authority concluded that none of them was as economically attractive as the construction of high voltage transmission lines from the mainland. The remaining undeveloped hydroelectric power sites are small in potential and costly to develop (Table 4,11). Even if all of the possible sites were developed the eventual output would be but a tiny fraction of future requirements. Beyond this, the power from such projects would cost in excess of twenty-six mills per kWh, compared with power from Hat Creek coal which it is estimated would cost less than half that amount.[5] While there are important deposits of coal near Comox and Suquash, preliminary indications are that costs of development for energy would be high (Table 5,11).[6] Concerning the proposed nuclear power station on the Island, British Columbia Hydro officials claim that costs of generation would be lower than from other alternatives, but the provincial government continues to reject the idea. Besides this, the lead time required for the construction of such a station is about thirteen years. Even if development were commenced immediately completion would be too late to avoid the perceived shortfall in capacity to meet demands in the early 1990's. Consideration also has been given to the installation of gas turbines, but operating costs appear to be too high, particularly in view of the rising cost of natural gas.

Attention has now turned to the possibility of constructing transmission lines from the mainland to the Island. As noted earlier, several such lines are already in operation, connecting the substation near Tsawwassen to the Vancouver Island Terminal near Duncan (Figure 3,11). Portions of these lines are submarine cables. It had been proposed that a new line be built parallel to the existing ones. This has been rejected because it is feared that a single accident might result in a total rupture, thus robbing the Island of almost all of its electric power supply. Another set of possibilities is now being studied, consisting of two 500 kV DC lines from Cheekye to Dunsmuir (Figure 1,11). There are important technical problems in building any of these lines. The most difficult of them is the fact that it is not possible at present to obtain and install continuous cable on the ocean floor, capable of carrying 500 kV, for a distance greater than sixteen kilometres (9.92 miles). It is feared that a spliced line would be a weak link in the transmission system. Should a rupture occur the Island would suffer a major blackout, and the damage would be very expensive to repair. The exact route for the transmission line has not been selected,

TABLE 5,11 Major Coal Deposits on Vancouver Island

Coal Field	Mining Method	Proven Reserves		Potential Resources	
		Millions of Short Tons	Gross Heat Value in BTU per pound	Minimum in Millions of Short Tons	Maximum in Millions of Short Tons
Comox— Campbell River	Underground	64	9,550	850	1,250
Suquash	Underground	(not available)	6,990	50	50

SOURCE: British Columbia, *Alternatives 1975 to 1990*. Vancouver: British Columbia Hydro and Power Authority, May 1975.

partly because the technical studies have not been completed and partly because of substantial opposition to the proposed line by residents of Lasqueti Island and citizens elsewhere in the region.

Soon after it became known that British Columbia Hydro was investigating possibilities of constructing a major transmission line to the Island, interest groups on islands along the route began to voice their concerns. The groups included the Lasqueti Island Steering Committee, Pender Harbour and District Ratepayers Association, British Columbia Aviation Council, and the Powell River Regional Board. The reasons for the concern varied from one group to another, but common themes were the environmental disruption it might cause, and a questioning of the real need for the line.

The most active among these groups has been the Lasqueti Island Steering Committee, reflecting, perhaps, the profound concerns that the residents of that island have about the effect of the transmission line on the life style that they have consciously chosen. Lasqueti Island is the only one of the Gulf Island group that has managed to retain the appearance of an undeveloped area. There is no electric power transmission or car ferry service to the Island. The roads are unpaved. Telephone cables have been placed underground. For those who live there it is an idyllic, rural setting where one can pursue an alternative life style away from the pressures of modern urban society. They perceive a large, overhead transmission line not only as an intrusion which will spoil the rural landscape, but also as a threat to their life style. They believe that, once there, the transmission line will invite further intrusions. Beyond this, they resent having to bear the external costs of a development which will benefit others far more than themselves.

226

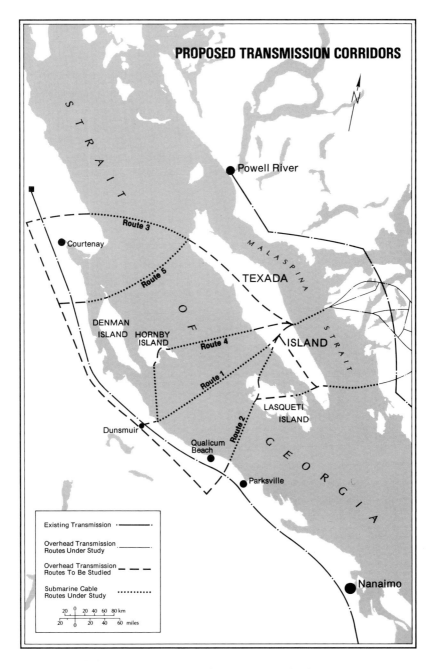

FIGURE 3,11 Route proposals via Texada and Lasqueti islands.

227

The Committee has enjoyed a considerable degree of success in drawing attention to the issue. The group is small, but dedicated, well informed and effectively organized. It is able to call upon expertise from residents who have worked in fields directly related to the development of transmission lines, notably engineering and economics. It has within its ranks several people who are skilled in preparing briefs, writing letters to decision-makers and government officials, and in organizing and distributing a Newsletter. Its efforts have drawn the attention of the media and the group has enjoyed fairly continuous coverage over the past year.

One of the major problems found by the concerned citizen is that of the lack of information. To overcome this difficulty the Committee invited the British Columbia Hydro to hold a public meeting on Lasqueti Island in January 1978. It saw this as an opportunity not only to find out more about the specific details of the proposed transmission line, but also to enable Hydro officials to meet with people who would be affected and to hear their views. The power company agreed to the meeting which took place over two days. There is little doubt that both sides benefited considerably from the interchange. The citizens are now more acutely aware of the problems facing the power company in fulfilling its responsibilities to provide power at the lowest cost, and of its efforts to encourage conservation in energy use. The power company now is better informed about the values sought by the residents of Lasqueti Island, and hopefully will try to accommodate to them in the plans that are being drawn up now. Meanwhile, studies are continuing and the Islanders are anxiously awaiting the outcome.

In a real sense the Lasqueti Island controversy illustrates the present dilemma that faces Vancouver Island. On the one hand, a considerable portion of its citizens have consciously chosen Vancouver Island as a favourable environment in which to live, work and recreate. Many of them have foregone higher economic rewards elsewhere in order to do so. On the other hand, the economic future of the Island hinges upon the provision of increasing amounts of energy, almost all of which must be brought from elsewhere, and whose consumption may result in environmental degradation of various kinds. The challenge is to find more efficient ways of using energy and the means of effectively harnessing renewable energy sources, such as energy from the sun, the winds, and the tides. Little has been done so far to meet this challenge, certainly in terms of government policy. Yet, there are signs that Vancouver Islanders are aware, both of the need and the opportunities. So far, about a dozen houses heated by solar energy have been built or are under construction on the Island, perhaps ten percent of all those built in Canada to date. Several people are experimenting with windmills and others are investigating the possibilities of utilizing biomass for energy production. Realization of these possibilities will enable Vancouver Islanders to continue to enjoy a high level of material well being, while at the same time living in one of Canada's most pleasant environments. The question remains, however, as to whether such actions will take place on a sufficiently large scale to forestall an almost inevitable energy crisis which may be less than a decade away.

REFERENCES

1. British Columbia, *British Columbia's Energy Outlook, 1976-1991.* Vancouver: British Columbia Energy Commission, 1976.

2. British Columbia, *Coal in British Columbia: a Technical Appraisal.* Victoria: Coal Task Force, February, 1976.

3. Personal Communication, British Columbia Ministry of Mines, August 1, 1978.

4. NESBITT, K. *Early Days of the Victoria Gas Company.* Victoria: British Columbia Electric Company, 1960.

5. British Columbia, *Alternatives 1975 to 1990.* Vancouver: British Columbia Hydro and Power Authority, 1975.

6. *Ibid.*

PLATE 20   Victoria: port facilities.   *I.H. Norie Photo* ▶

12 TRANSPORTATION[1]

Charles N. Forward

Vancouver Islanders are a coastal people and water transportation performs the role of commercial lifeline to the mainland, as well as carrier of the logs, lumber and plywood products of the Island industries. Unlike inward-looking Prince Edward Island, its interior is carpeted with mountains and forests rather than farms and crops: it more resembles the wooded, seaward-looking island of Newfoundland, except that its integration with the mainland is far more intimate, especially through its numerous and frequent ferry services. On land, a well developed transportation corridor hugs the east coast of the Island as far north as Kelsey Bay, carrying the highway mode throughout and the railway between Victoria and Courtenay. Laterals, lesser highways and logging roads branch out from the main stem to more remote parts of the Island. Air travel, also, is a boon to Island dwellers and the abundance of lakes and protected inland waterways encourage the use of float planes.

NINETEENTH CENTURY

As the settlement and commercial development of Vancouver Island largely preceded the development of the mainland of British Columbia, transport systems initially radiated from Victoria to up-Island and mainland points. Water transportation was the chief mode, and contact with Great Britain, the mother country, was maintained via the lengthy Cape Horn route. Luxuries and other appurtenances of European society came by sailing ship in colonial times, and even today, antique dealers are fond of describing items of furniture or musical instruments as having come "around the Horn." Regular shipping services were instituted at an early date between Victoria and San Francisco, the nearest major city, and it was through San Francisco that many of the people and supplies flowed that fueled the Fraser gold rush of 1858. It was the gold rush that initiated frequent shipping services between Victoria and New West-

231

minster, as the prospectors scrambled to gather supplies in Victoria and obtain any kind of floating conveyance toward the gold fields. As settlements in other parts of the Island became established, these small communities were served by coastal shipping companies, generally operating out of Victoria. International connections reached a high level of development when the Canadian Pacific Railway Company initiated its Orient services in the late 1880's, adding the famous "Empress" ships in 1891 that called at both Victoria and Vancouver.

Land transportation evolved slowly, owing to rather minimal agricultural development and slow population growth. Local road construction proceeded in the vicinity of Victoria during the 1850's. The narrow wagon road built from Victoria to Sooke at that time was extended to Cowichan Bay by 1861.[2] The water alternative for movement between Island coastal points and the construction difficulties presented by rugged terrain and dense forests were factors that inhibited road building. It was not until the 1870's that a coast road, of sorts, existed between Victoria and Nanaimo.[3] The 1880 map of the southeastern district of Vancouver Island indicates the limited road network of that time (Figure 1,12). The coastal road reached Parksville by 1886 and in that year a road was built between Nanaimo and Port Alberni, replacing an earlier trail.[4] These additions appear on the 1903 map along with isolated stretches of road at Courtenay and Port Hardy.

Uppermost in the minds of British Columbians at the time of Confederation was an insistent demand for a western railway to connect their coastal region to the eastern provinces, in the same manner that the United States west coast had been linked with the east. Such was the obsession with the railway idea that the commitment to build the Canadian Pacific was stated in the terms of union and John A. MacDonald pledged that Esquimalt would be the western terminus. Vancouver Islanders knew that if the railway terminated on the mainland their great port of Victoria would lose its primacy as the gateway to the interior from the broad Pacific and outlet to the world for the riches of western Canada. They wanted the Bute Inlet-Seymour Narrows route followed and the southernmost portion between Esquimalt and Nanaimo built first (Figure 2,12). Although there was an intervening government assertion in 1875 that the Esquimalt and Nanaimo would be built as a local project, with the main railway terminating at Burrard Inlet, MacDonald reiterated his promise in 1879 that Esquimalt would be the terminus of the Canadian Pacific.[5] By 1883 it was clear that the Esquimalt and Nanaimo would be built as a separate, local railway and the British Columbia government

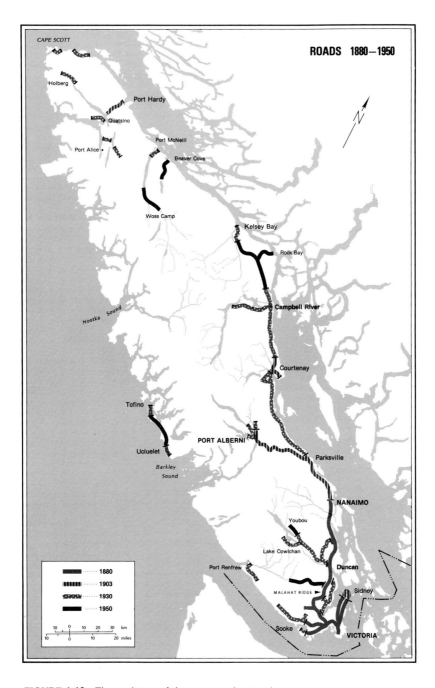

ROADS 1880–1950

CAPE SCOTT

Holberg

Port Hardy

Quatsino

Port McNeill

Port Alice

Beaver Cove

Woss Camp

Kelsey Bay

Rock Bay

Nootka Sound

Campbell River

Courtenay

Tofino

PORT ALBERNI

Ucluelet

Parksville

Barkley Sound

NANAIMO

Youbou

Lake Cowichan

Port Renfrew

Duncan

MALAHAT RIDGE ▶

Sidney

········ 1880
········ 1903
········ 1930
········ 1950

10   0   10   20   30 km
10   0   10   20 miles

Sooke

VICTORIA

FIGURE 1,12   The evolution of the main road network.

gave away 1,902,022 hectares (4,700,000 acres) of land to the entrepreneurs for the construction of 120 kilometres (75 miles) of railway.[6]
About 800,000 hectares (two million acres) were on Vancouver Island,
known as the Esquimalt and Nanaimo Land Grant, and the remainder
were in the Peace River district. The last spike on the Esquimalt and
Nanaimo was driven by John A. MacDonald in 1886, the same year that
the Canadian Pacific Railway reached Burrard Inlet (Figure 2,12). Even
before the Esquimalt and Nanaimo was built there existed a full network
of short, mining railway lines in the Nanaimo coalfields that grew southward as far as Ladysmith, as the mines near Nanaimo became worked out.
Before the end of the century a short railway was built between Victoria
and Sidney, incorporating a ferry link to the mainland lines of the Great
Northern Railway. It was affectionately known as the "Cordwood Limited" because its locomotives consumed huge piles of firewood collected
along its route through the Saanich Peninsula.

TWENTIETH CENTURY TO WORLD WAR II

A feverish period of railway building in western Canada marked the
early decades of the twentieth century and Vancouver Island was included
in many transportation plans, some of which never came to fruition.
Branches of the Esquimalt and Nanaimo were built to Cowichan Lake and
Port Alberni and the main line eventually was extended to Courtenay
(Figure 2,12). The British Columbia Electric Railway Company built a
commuter line on the Saanich Peninsula, paralleling the Victoria and
Sidney that operated for only eleven years, 1913 to 1924.[7] The most
ambitious project was that of the Canadian Northern Pacific Railway
which embarked on a plan to create an extensive network on Vancouver
Island connected by rail-ferry with its new transcontinental line on the
mainland. The plan was to build a line from Victoria northward along an
inland route to Cowichan Lake, Port Alberni, thence north to Campbell
River and west to the Gold River.[8] A short section on the Saanich
Peninsula was to serve as part of the mainland connecting link. Work got
underway in 1911 and the first section completed was the Saanich
Peninsula line opened in 1917, bringing to three the number of competitors on that narrow peninsula.[9] The Victoria and Sidney closed down
its operations two years later, having succumbed to its competitors, while
the Canadian Northern transcontinental system faced bankruptcy and

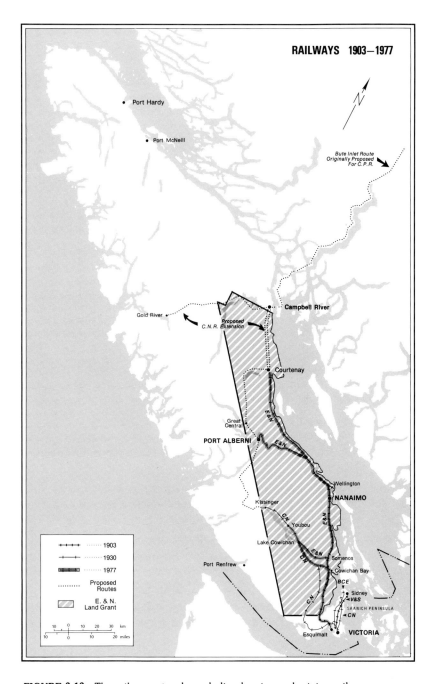

FIGURE 2,12 The railway network, excluding logging and mining railways.

235

became part of the federally-owned Canadian National Railways.[10] Plans for the inland route were not yet abandoned, however, and construction proceeded slowly northward. By 1924 it reached the eastern end of Cowichan Lake and finally was extended to the western end by 1928, which marked the farthest extent reached (Figure 2,12).[11]

Many of the railways of Vancouver Island eventually were doomed by the motor vehicle. As early as 1914 a motor stage service was inaugurated between Victoria and Sidney at lower fares than those of the railways.[12] Passenger business was the first to go, followed eventually by a large part of the general freight. The last of the Saanich Peninsula railways, the Canadian National, managed to survive until the mid-1930's. The road system was upgraded and by 1930 had been greatly extended (Figure 1,12). The circuitous inland route between Victoria and Duncan had been replaced by a more direct coastal route over the rugged Malahat Ridge and one could drive northward from Victoria as far as the vicinity of Campbell River. Beyond that roads existed only as isolated stretches.

Besides the public, common carrier transportation systems, many miles of logging and mining railways were built, as well as logging roads. Railway based, skidder logging was introduced during the first decade of the century and flourished until after World War II when trucks largely superseded the trains.[13] Logging railways in 1945 totalled twenty-one separate valley systems scattered throughout Vancouver Island from Port Renfrew in the south to Port McNeill in the north and amounted to a railway total of 1,027 kilometres (628 miles).

Shipping remained of great importance because many parts of the Island still were inaccessible by land and the ferry services expanded with the growth of population and trade. The Canadian Pacific Railway Company started the triangle run, Vancouver-Victoria-Seattle, in 1909 with the ''Princess'' ships, comfortable passenger ''mini-liners'' that made the crossing from Vancouver to Victoria in about five hours.[14] The port role of Victoria declined relative to that of Vancouver as the twentieth century unfolded, fulfilling the fears of local residents who mourned the loss of the railway terminus function. Nevertheless, a deepsea port facility was built by the federal government at Ogden Point in Victoria during World War I and a grain elevator was added at that location in the late 1920's. Water movement of logs in booms and the extensive use of tug and barge transport served the forest industry efficiently and economically.

Air travel did not assume great significance until after World War II. The first scheduled flights from Victoria to Vancouver began in 1933, but airfields and ancilliary facilities were very primitive.[15] Bush pilots operated small aircraft to many remote points on Vancouver Island. World War II produced a legacy in the form of military airports that could be converted to commercial aviation use, as were those at Port Hardy, Tofino and Patricia Bay near Victoria.

AFTER WORLD WAR II

The recent period witnessed the almost complete triumph of the motor vehicle over the railway, the rise of air travel, even for short haul passenger movement, and the continued viability of water transportation, especially the ferry services.

The road network expanded considerably after 1960, with the greatest elaboration of the network occurring during the past decade (Figure 3,12). By 1950 the only important addition was the extension of the east coast highway to Kelsey Bay (Figure 1,12). During the 1950's most of the logging railways were phased out, to be replaced by upgraded logging roads as the main transport routes through the forests. Public agitation for greater access by car to remote parts of Vancouver Island led to the opening of many private logging roads to public use, usually on a restricted basis, such as weekends and non-working hours during weekdays. Gradually, some of them were removed from the restricted list and eventually transferred to the Department of Highway's jurisdiction, although many important routes still are restricted. In this manner, a large increment in the publicly accessible road network was created during a remarkably short period of time in the late 1960's and early 1970's. Most notable has been the opening up of the northern third of Vancouver Island and the creation of numerous links to west coast points. Bus service now is provided throughout the length of the Island, with frequent service along the heavily populated east coast. As a result, railway passenger patronage has all but disappeared and the need for west coast passenger shipping service to isolated communities has dwindled to a level where only a few small services are left, such as in Barkley and Nootka sounds. Many portions of the older, heavily travelled highways have been rebuilt and widened. The Island Highway from Victoria to Nanaimo now is part of the Trans-Canada Highway, Number 1, and some portions have been widened to four lanes. A large sign in Victoria's Beacon Hill Park near the ocean announces that point as ''Mile 0'' of the Trans-Canada Highway, the other end being in St. John's, Newfoundland.

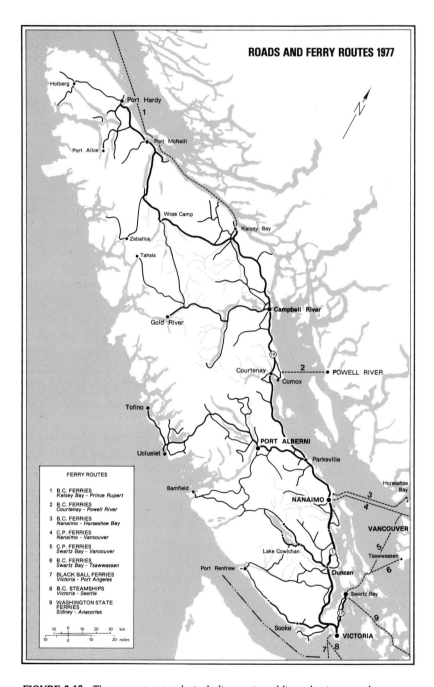

FIGURE 3,12 The present network, including main public and private roads.

238

The virtual disappearance of logging railways has been accompanied by a shrinking of the regular rail system (Figure 2,12). The Canadian National line from Victoria to Duncan lies unused and the portion west of Youbou was sold to a logging company many years ago, leaving only the Youbou-Cowichan Bay section in operation. The Canadian Pacific still operates the Esquimalt and Nanaimo, with its branches to Cowichan Lake and Port Alberni. The company considers the railway still viable as a freight carrier, but claims that the passenger service is a desperate drain on its financial resources. Service has been provided for a number of years by a rail diesel passenger car that makes one return trip per day from Victoria to Courtenay. After refusing earlier requests for discontinuation of the service, the Canadian Transport Commission finally ruled that it could be terminated on January 31, 1978 because it was uneconomic.[16] The public outcry against the abandonment of passenger service was sufficiently strident to result in a delay of the shutdown while the provincial government lodged an appeal. Grounds for the appeal were that the railway was given an unbelievably generous land grant and in return entered into an obligation to maintain its freight and passenger services indefinitely.

The growth of air traffic in the post-war period has been substantial. Scheduled services to many points on Vancouver Island have been operating since the 1950's and there are now approximately twenty airports on the Island. The most important, in order of passenger traffic, are at Victoria, Port Hardy, Campbell River and Comox. Pacific Western Airlines operates regularly scheduled services from all four points, while smaller airlines and numerous charter services operate from these, as well as the other airports. A large portion of the aircraft business is handled by float-equipped planes that can reach most of the populated places on the Island. Frequent scheduled services are operated in this manner by Airwest between Victoria, Seattle, Vancouver and Nanaimo harbours, thereby offering downtown to downtown flights that eliminate time-consuming airport trips. Victoria International Airport is the only point served by Air Canada and is by far the leading traffic centre, with important links to Seattle. By the measure of "arriving and enplaned passengers" it has ranked thirteenth among Canadian airports during most of the past decade.[17]

As indicated by air passenger statistics, Victoria experienced a fourfold growth of domestic traffic during the twelve years from 1963 to 1975 and a doubling of international traffic, almost entirely focused on Seattle

(Table 1,12). In comparison with the other leading airports, it is apparent that Victoria handles seven or eight times the traffic of its nearest Island rival (Table 2,12). While Port Hardy ranks second in passenger traffic, it has experienced little recent growth and is rapidly being overtaken by Campbell River and Comox, whose traffic has more than doubled in six years.

Water transportation remains of utmost importance in integrating the Island with the mainland through regular ferry services and in permitting direct and indirect trading exchanges with coastal and overseas points. Ferry services not only were expanded in the postwar period, but certain routes were altered radically in concept. The major change was the abandonment by the Canadian Pacific in the late 1950's of the mini-liner service from Vancouver Harbour to Victoria Harbour, a long and time-consuming crossing with ships ill-designed for carrying automobiles. The provincial government developed and instituted in 1960 an integrated shuttle service of specially designed vehicle and passenger-carrying ferries between Swartz Bay and Tsawwassen, a far shorter water crossing. New terminals and highway links were built to facilitate rapid loading and unloading and the travel time for vehicles moving between Vancouver and Victoria was cut almost in half. Frequency of service also was increased greatly. A similar service was established between Departure Bay near Nanaimo and Horseshoe Bay near Vancouver, replacing an earlier private company service. Many of the private operations were acquired by the provincial government, but the Canadian Pacific still maintains a vehicle and passenger ferry service between Nanaimo and Vancouver harbours and a freight ferry service between Vancouver and Swartz Bay (Figure 3,12). A new ferry link was established by the provincial government in 1966 between Kelsey Bay and Prince Rupert, a distance of 531 kilometres (330 miles). Other services link the southern end of the Island with Washington state; Victoria—Port Angeles and Sidney—Anacortes being year-round services, while Victoria—Seattle is a summer only connection.

The volume of commodity trade at Vancouver Island ports increased considerably from the 1950's to the early 1970's, although there was a pronounced decline in trade during the mid-1970's, owing to the widespread economic slowdown.[18] Victoria lost its commanding position as by far the leading port in total tonnage handled. While in 1955 Victoria had more than twice the tonnage of any other Vancouver Island port, it was slightly surpassed by Nanaimo in 1970, though in some years, such as 1975, it regained a tenuous supremacy (Figure 4,12). Nanaimo gener-

TABLE 1,12 Air Passenger Origin and Destination Totals,
Victoria International Airport, Selected Years, 1963-1975*

Year	Domestic	International	Total
1963	105,200	41,600	146,800
1965	125,200	51,200	176,400
1967	176,000	64,600	240,600
1969	183,300	60,900	244,200
1971	234,900	69,600	304,500
1973	346,200	89,100	435,300
1975	408,300	87,000	495,300

*Figures rounded to nearest hundred.

SOURCE: Canada, *Airport Activity Statistics*. Ottawa: Statistics Canada, annual
reports, 1963-1975.

ally has occupied the second position during the postwar period, followed
by Campbell River, Port Alberni and Crofton as the other leading ports.
Logs and pulpwood constitute the most widespread and important commodities, the raw materials for the lumber, pulp and newsprint manufacturing centres. The log trade is extensive, using tugs and booms, as
well as self-loading and unloading barges. The tug and barge mode of
transport is highly developed in the protected waters around Vancouver
Island for the movement of such commodities as pulpwood, in the form of
wood chips, lumber, ores, sand and gravel. Large quantities of lumber
are shipped from Port Alberni, Nanaimo, Victoria and Crofton, pulp from
all except Port Alberni, and newsprint from Campbell River, Port Alice,
and Crofton. In variety of commodities handled Victoria consistently has
ranked highest, though by 1975 Nanaimo and Campbell River were not

TABLE 2,12 Air Passenger Origin and Destination Totals
at Leading Vancouver Island Airports, Selected Years, 1969-1975*

	Port Hardy	Campbell River	Comox	Victoria
1969	53,600	16,300	13,800	244,200
1971	48,400	18,100	17,900	304,500
1973	59,400	30,600	27,900	435,300
1975	53,600	34,300	32,000	495,300

*Figures rounded to nearest hundred.

SOURCES: Canada, *Airport Activity Statistics*. Ottawa: Statistics Canada, annual
reports, 1969-1975; and Canada, *Air Passenger Origin and Destination,
Domestic Report*. Ottawa: Statistics Canada, annual reports, 1969-1975;
and *Canada, United States Report*. Ottawa: Statistics Canada, annual
reports, 1969-1975.

far behind. In 1977 a disastrous fire destroyed a major wharf and pulp
storage shed in Victoria, terminating, for a period of time, the handling
of pulp. A new storage shed was built in 1978, with the hope of recaptur-
ing the pulp handling business. Another commodity of historic importance in Victoria is wheat, but the grain elevator was closed in 1976 after
nearly half a century of operation and has been demolished. The loss of
wheat shipments and the uncertainties connected with pulp have damp-
ened further the prospects of the port of Victoria. One saving grace is its
continuing attraction as a port of call for Alaska cruise vessels.

Looking to the future, a number of proposals and prospects may alter
the transportation systems of Vancouver Island and certain trends can be
identified. The highway system is being upgraded all the time, both
through the paving of remote sections of gravel road and the widening to
four lanes of portions of the Island highway. Vehicular traffic continues
its steady growth, as land transportation becomes ever more dominated
by the motor vehicle. In the late 1960's there was even a fanciful proposal
to bridge the water gaps to the mainland from the Saanich Peninsula via

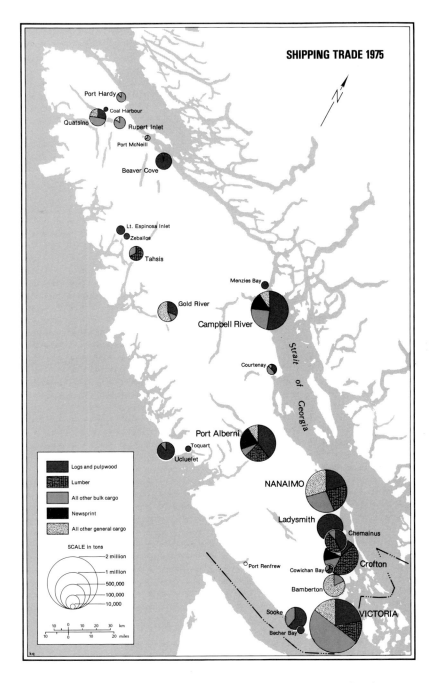

FIGURE 4,12 Total commodities handled in domestic and international trade.

243

the Gulf Islands stepping stones. Such a crossing would be inordinately expensive to construct, especially the twenty-one kilometre (thirteen mile) wide Strait of Georgia section which would have to be designed to allow ocean shipping to pass through freely. The proposal was never seriously considered by government bodies or the public and the likelihood of a crossing being built in the foreseeable future is remote. The railway system seems likely to survive as a freight carrier, but passenger service is on a month to month basis. A worthwhile proposal has been put forward that advocates the establishment of a rail commuter service on the Esquimalt and Nanaimo between Duncan and Victoria, with several stops en route. An early morning train would carry journey to work passengers to Victoria, with the return scheduled in late afternoon. Rather low population densities along the route pose a problem, but any such plan to divert motorists to rail transport has merit. A possible new development in air transportation is the use of the de Havilland Dash 7 short takeoff and landing aircraft between Vancouver and Victoria. The building of short airstrips in the central city areas would be required to gain the obvious advantage of the system: rapid downtown to downtown service. Unlike the existing float plane service by Airwest from harbour to harbour, a short takeoff and landing service would not be restricted to operation in daylight hours. Proposals to speed up the transfer of passengers by water also have been made. An experimental service between Victoria and Seattle was operated recently using a hydrofoil vessel, but evaluations of the experiment did not lead to proposals for early inauguration of such a service. One of the problems encountered was the high incidence of floating logs in the waters traversed. The only certainty is that continuing advances in transportation technology and energy use efficiency will create changes in future.

REFERENCES

1. The research assistance of Diana Hocking who compiled statistics and prepared maps and tables is gratefully acknowledged.

2. JACKMAN, S.W. *Vancouver Island*. Newton Abbot, Devon: David and Charles, 1972, p. 91.

3. *Ibid.*

4. *Ibid.*

5. ROBERTS, J. *The Origins of the Esquimalt and Nanaimo Railway; A Problem of B.C. Politics.* Vancouver: University of British Columbia, unpublished Master of Arts thesis, 1937, p. 51.

6. *Ibid.*, p. 67.

7. HARVEY, R.D. *A History of Saanich Peninsula Railways.* Victoria: Department of Commercial Transport, Railways Branch, 1960, p. 11.

8. TURNER, R.D. *Vancouver Island Railways.* San Marino, California: Golden West Books, 1973, p. 104.

9. HARVEY, R.D., *op. cit.*, p. 13.

10. HEARN, G. and WILKIE, D. *The Cordwood Limited, A History of the Victoria and Sidney Railway.* Victoria: B.C. Railway Historical Association, 4th edition, 1971, p. 71.

11. TURNER, R.D., *op. cit.*, p. 108.

12. HEARN, G. and WILKIE, D., *op. cit.*, p. 63.

13. SWANSON, R.E. *A History of Railroad Logging.* Victoria: Department of Commercial Transport, Railways Branch, 1960, p. 3.

14. JACKMAN, S.W., *op. cit.*, p. 78.

15. *Ibid.*, p. 87.

16. *Victoria Times*, December 17, 1977.

17. Canada, *Airport Activity Statistics.* Ottawa: Statistics Canada, annual reports, 1968-1976.

18. Canada, *Shipping Report, Part II, International Seaborne Shipping by Port*, Ottawa: Statistics Canada, annual reports, 1955-1975; and *Shipping Report, Part III, Coastwise Shipping.* Ottawa: Statistics Canada, annual reports, 1955-1975.

PLATE 21   Port Alberni, forest products centre.   *B.C. Government Photo* ▶

MANUFACTURING, RECREATION AND SOCIAL PATTERNS

INTRODUCTION

Attention is shifted in Section 5 to a number of topics representative of the economic, recreational and social aspects of Vancouver Island. The economic activity of manufacturing is characterized by an overall dominance of the wood industries, although a significant areal differentiation appears between a diversified manufacturing structure in metropolitan Victoria and a highly specialized structure elsewhere. An elaborate park and recreation system has been developed, constituting a valuable asset for the tourist industry, as well as a great attraction for the local residents. Many Vancouver Islanders can be found who have managed to fulfill their vacationing needs without ever having ventured to the mainland. Tourism depends on far more than parks, however, and has been fostered in various ways to become one of the most important contributors to the Island's economy. The basic duality of the Island is exploited admirably in offering visitors a contrasting package of urbane, old world charm in Victoria, along with nearby opportunities for wilderness experience. The contrast between the isolated resource community of the west coast, the epitome of the company town, with the sophisticated, east coast urban centres, particularly the capital, is a noteworthy feature of the Island's cultural geography.

In Chapter 13 the manufacturing industry is compared with that of the whole Province and of the nation, in order to place it in perspective and indicate its distinctive character. A more detailed investigation of the nature of manufacturing in the Capital Regional District is presented, with emphasis placed on the problems of locational disadvantage relative to the lower mainland and the loss of industries. A systems approach is employed in Chapter 14 in viewing the components that make up the recreation resources of Vancouver Island. The various parts of the system are considered separately, including national, provincial, regional and marine parks, as well as forest land, recreation corridors and trails, to isolate the roles they play in the total system, even though they fall under many different jurisdictions. The intimate relationship between tourism and the physical and cultural environments is portrayed in Chapter 15, along with the consequences of this sometimes troubled marriage. The growth of the industry, its implications for the Islander and the areal patterns of facilities spawned to cater to tourists are investigated. Future strategies to deal with the industry's growth are pursued in the conclusion. A three-tiered urban structure is recognized in Chapter 16 as a framework for the exploration of urban social characteristics. The single-enterprise communities at one end of the scale are contrasted with metropolitan Victoria at the other, while the middle tier is described as displaying some characteristics of both extremes. Residential social patterns in greater Victoria are considered under the headings of life level, life cycle and life style. In Chapter 17 a number of photographs have been selected to illustrate the character and diversity of Vancouver Island.

PLATE 22   Pulpmill, Crofton.   *I.H. Norie Photo* ▶

PLATE 23   Shipbuilding in Victoria.   *Jim Ryan Photo* ▶

13 MANUFACTURING

M.A. Micklewright

The manufacturing sector of the Island economy may be characterized by reference to two essential factors; the strong dependence on wood and wood-related industries (Standard Industrial Classification, Division 5, Major Groups 8 and 10) and the concentration of non-wood-related industries in the Capital Regional District. On Vancouver Island the wood and wood-related industries accounted for seventy-five percent of manufacturing employment in 1971, in contrast with forty-six percent in British Columbia as a whole and only twelve percent in Canada (Table 1,13).

The concentration of non-wood-related manufacturing employment may be illustrated by an examination of the employment structure on the Island. In 1971, the latest year in which full census data are available, the Capital Regional District accounted for eighty-eight percent of manufacturing employment in those sectors unrelated to the wood and wood processing industries, although it had only twenty-nine percent of all manufacturing employment. Unless otherwise stated, all statistics quoted in this chapter are from the Census of Canada and the Census of Manufacturing, 1951, 1961 and 1971.

PROVINCIAL AND NATIONAL COMPARISONS

Although the relative importance of the manufacturing sector in the economy of Vancouver Island appears small and highly concentrated in the wood and wood-related industries, a valid appreciation of this situation can be achieved only by comparisons with the whole Province and the nation, not only of labour force, but also of population changes. An examination of the data for the two decades 1951-1971 shows that for the nation as a whole population increased by thirty-one percent between 1951 and 1961, but this rate of growth slowed significantly in the next ten years. In the same period the population of British Columbia increased at a considerably higher rate and, while the rate declined in the second

TABLE 1,13   Labour Force, Vancouver Island, British Columbia and Canada, 1971

	Total Labour Force	Manufacturing Labour Force	Wood-related Industry Labour Force	Percentage of Total Labour Force in Manufacturing	Percentage of Manufacturing Labour Force in Wood-related Industries
Canada	8,631,050	1,707,330	211,555	20	12
British Columbia	930,030	129,308	59,979	14	46
Vancouver Island	155,367	17,999	13,580	12	75
Capital Regional District	80,980	5,280	1,371	7	26

SOURCE: *Census of Canada*, 1971.

decade, this decline was marginal compared with that of the national rate. Thus, over the twenty year period the British Columbia population grew at a substantially higher rate than that of the nation as a whole (Table 2,13).

It is noteworthy that the working age group of the population (15-64) has remained relatively stable in proportion of the total since 1951, but that the dependent groups are composed differently in Victoria, British Columbia and Canada (Table 3,13). While the proportion of children in metropolitan Victoria is considerably lower than in Canada, there is a compensating higher proportion of elderly, resulting in a similar-sized working age group.

When the labour force alone is examined, the differences between the national and provincial rates of change become even more dramatic. In the decade 1951-1961 the labour force of the nation increased by twenty-four percent and from 1961 to 1971 by thirty-two percent; for the Province the comparable rates were thirty-one and fifty-eight, respectively, indicating a consistent and increasing movement of economic activity to the western portion of the country. Vancouver Island shared in this westward movement at a rate of ten percent below the provincial average in the first decade and at the same rate in the second. The Capital Regional District in the first decade experienced a rate of growth in the labour force roughly equivalent to the provincial rate, but in the second decade it was twelve percent below.

TABLE 2,13 Changes in Population, Labour Force and Manufacturing Employment in Canada, British Columbia, Vancouver Island and the Capital Regional District, 1951-1971

	1951	1961	1971
Population			
Canada	14,009,000	18,309,000 (1.31)*	21,568,000 (1.18)
British Columbia	1,165,000	1,629,000 (1.40)	2,185,000 (1.34)
Vancouver Island	215,003	291,700 (1.36)	378,647 (1.30)
Capital Regional District	114,859	155,763 (1.36)	195,800 (1.26)
Labour Force			
Canada	5,277,000	6,521,000 (1.24)	8,631,000 (1.32)
British Columbia	443,860	581,395 (1.31)	920,305 (1.58)
Vancouver Island	82,248	100,631 (1.22)	155,367 (1.58)
Capital Regional District	42,075	55,450 (1.32)	80,980 (1.46)
Employment in Manufacturing			
Canada	1,258,375	1,452,000 (1.15)	1,707,330 (1.18)
British Columbia	93,649	113,019 (1.21)	146,925 (1.30)
Vancouver Island	13,422**	16,308 (1.22)	17,999 (1.10)
Capital Regional District	4,478**	5,899 (1.32)	5,280 (0.90)

*Percentage change in previous decade is shown in parentheses.
**As 1951 figures are not available, these are for 1952.

SOURCE: *Census of Canada, 1951, 1961 and 1971.*

It is when employment in manufacturing is considered that the most significant deviations in trends become apparent. For Canada the increase in manufacturing employment from 1951 to 1961 was significantly less than the increase in population, but the 1961 to 1971 increase was the same as that for population, indicating that changes in manufacturing

TABLE 3,13 Population by Selected Age Groups in Percent, 1951-1971

Age Group	Metropolitan Victoria			British Columbia			Canada		
	1951	1961	1971	1951	1961	1971	1951	1961	1971
0-14	21	28	24	26	31	28	30	34	30
15-64	63	56	61	63	59	63	62	58	62
65 and over	16	16	15	11	10	9	8	8	8

SOURCE: Capital Regional District, *The Challenge: Managing the Capital Region's Economy.* Victoria: Economic Advisory Committee, December 1977, p. 36.

employment had stabilized and were increasing proportionately to the increase in population. During this period, however, employment in manufacturing in British Columbia increased a spectacular fifty-seven percent, twenty-one in the decade 1951-1961 and thirty in 1961-1971. In the first period the growth of manufacturing employment was below both the rate of growth of Canada's and British Columbia's population and of their labour forces, indicating that the national trend of a declining percentage of the labour force engaged in manufacturing also applied to British Columbia, but to a lesser extent. Manufacturing employment on Vancouver Island from 1951 to 1961 followed the trend for the Province as a whole, but in the second period experienced a relatively serious declining deviation. The provincial rate was plus thirty percent, while the Vancouver Island rate was plus ten percent. This deteriorating trend in the industrial employment structure becomes even more serious when the data for the Capital Regional District are examined. In 1951 there were 4,478 jobs in manufacturing in the District, and by 1961 the number had risen to 5,899, an increase of thirty-two percent. By 1971 there had occurred an absolute decline of 619 jobs, a rate of decline of eleven percent. Although the District represented the main concentration of non-wood-related industrial employment on the Island, it is apparent that, even in a period of overall increase in population and labour force, the level of manufacturing employment fell significantly below that of the Province and the nation.

Because of the overwhelming importance of the Capital Regional District as the main centre for non-wood-related manufacturing, and the virtual dependence of the other regional districts on the wood and wood-related industries, which are examined in Chapter 6, the remainder of this chapter is concerned with the Capital Regional District, one of twenty-nine such districts into which the Province is divided (Figure 1,13).

CAPITAL REGIONAL DISTRICT

Population is concentrated in the Victoria Metropolitan Area, but the District embraces the sparsely populated Gulf Islands and the area west of Langford, including Sooke, River Jordan and Port Renfrew. The District consistently has maintained about fifty-three percent of the Island's population since 1951, while its percentage of the labour force has varied between fifty and fifty-five. Employment in manufacturing in the District as a percentage of that on the Island has declined from thirty-three in 1951 to twenty-nine in 1971. As might be expected in a retirement-tourist centre that is also a provincial capital, the leading sectors of the labour force in the Capital Regional District are services, public administration and trade, with manufacturing amounting to only about nine percent (Table 4,13).

The wood industries accounted for almost thirty percent of all manufacturing, even though the Capital Regional District had the great bulk of non-wood-related manufacturing employment (Table 5,13). The only other sectors with significant shares of manufacturing employment were Food and Beverages, Printing and Publishing and Transportation Equipment. However, even in these industries average employment per firm was generally low. The dairying sector, with three establishments, employed a total of 244 persons, while thirty-two bakeries employed only 250. Other sub-sectors of Food and Beverages accounted for sixty-five establishments, employing a total of 462 people. In Printing and Publishing, with twenty-seven establishments, the largest specified group was the "publishing only" sub-sector, accounting for a mere seventeen employees out of a total of 582. The rest are classified as "Other", in which group the publisher of the two daily papers in Victoria accounted for approximately 400 jobs. Transportation Equipment involved fourteen firms, with a total employment of 465. One shipbuilding and repair firm,

255

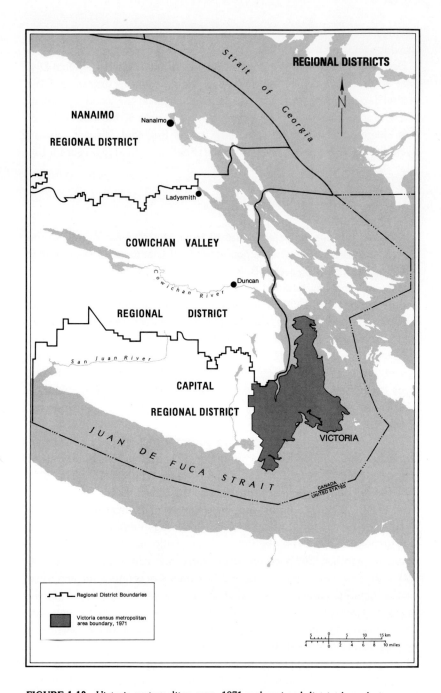

FIGURE 1,13 Victoria metropolitan area, 1971 and regional district boundaries.

256

TABLE 4,13 Labour Force in the Capital Region District, 1971

Occupation	Labour Force	Percent
Agriculture	1,015	1.2
Forestry	1,425	1.7
Fishing and Trapping	490	.6
Mining and Quarrying	165	.2
Manufacturing	7,405	8.8
Construction	5,445	6.5
Transportation, Communication and Other Utilities	5,765	6.8
Trade	13,180	15.6
Finance, Insurance and Real Estate	4,005	4.7
Community and Personal Services	23,590	28.0
Public Administration	15,405	18.3
Unspecified	6,365	7.6
Total	84,195	100.0

SOURCE: *Census of Canada*, 1971.

however, accounted for approximately fifty percent of this number, the average of the other firms being seventeen employees each. The manufacturing sector of the Victoria area, thus, can be characterized as small, both in absolute terms and relative to the size of the sector nationally and provincially, and with a heavy concentration in the wood and wood-related industries.

PLATE 24 Industry on Victoria's waterfront. *B.C. Forest Products Photo* ▶

TABLE 5,13 Manufacturing Employment by
Industrial Sector, Victoria Metropolitan Area, 1971

Industrial Sector	Standard Industrial Classification Major Group	Employment	Percent
Food and Beverage	1	956	20.1
Textile	5	23	.5
Wood	8	1,371	28.8
Furniture and Fixture	9	35	.7
Printing, Publishing and Allied	11	582	12.2
Metal Fabricating	13	315	6.6
Transportation Equipment	15	465	9.8
Non-Metallic Mineral Products	17	135	2.8
Miscellaneous Manufacturing	20	136	2.9
Other Major Groups		742	15.6
Total		4,760	100.0

SOURCE: *Census of Canada*, 1971.

CAPITAL REGION'S ECONOMIC BASE

In the spring of 1976, because of rising unemployment and the closure of a number of manufacturing establishments, the Capital Regional District initiated an inquiry into the economic base of the District, with a view to determining the major generators of income and employment and

TABLE 6.13 Estimated Total 1976 Net Dollar Flow Generated by
Victoria Metropolitan Area Businesses Through Inter-Regional Trade

	Vancouver Island	Vancouver and Lower Mainland	Rest of British Columbia	Rest of Canada	United States	Other	Sub-total	Tourism	Total
Manufacturing	− 40.40	− 6.78	−19.09	+ 17.98	+39.68	+45.04	+ 36.43	+ 8.40	+ 44.83
Construction	+ 55.68	− 6.31	+ 7.88	+ 0.36	− 0.94	—	+ 56.67	+ 8.15	+ 64.82
Transportation, Communication, and Other Utilities	+ 9.16	+ 15.52	+ 3.23	+ 0.40	—	—	+ 28.31	+ 14.72	+ 43.03
Wholesale Trade	+ 54.15	− 19.21	− 7.76	− 31.76	−18.39	− 7.44	− 30.41	+ 20.00	− 10.41
Retail Trade	+ 45.13	−103.22	−24.07	−178.11	−45.55	−42.12	−347.94	+121.78	−226.16
Finance, Insurance and Real Estate	+ 41.04	+ 25.02	+ 7.60	+ 10.65	—	—	+ 61.80	+ 13.16	+ 74.96
Community, Business and Personal Service	+ 48.95	+ 4.16	+15.12	−103.76	+ 1.51	− 0.76	− 34.78	+202.23	+167.45
Total	+213.71	− 90.82	−17.09	−284.24	−23.69	− 5.28	−229.92	+388.44	+158.52

*This table is an expansion of sample statistics to estimate the total economic activity for the entire regional economy.

SOURCE: Capital Regional District, *ibid.*, p. 27.

TABLE 7,13 Estimated 1976 Net Dollar Flow Generated by Sampled Victoria Metropolitan Area Businesses Through Inter-Regional Trade in Millions of Dollars*

	Tourism	Vancouver Island	Vancouver and Lower Mainland	Rest of British Columbia	Rest of Canada	United States	Other	Total (excluding tourism)	Total (including tourism)
Manufacturing	+ 3.31	−15.91	− 2.67	− 7.52	+ 7.08	+15.63	+17.74	+14.35	+17.66
Construction	+ 1.82	+12.44	− 1.41	+ 1.76	+ 0.08	− 0.21	—	+12.66	+14.48
Transportation, Communication and Other Utilities	+ 4.05	+ 2.52	+ 4.27	+ 0.89	+ 0.11	—	—	+ 7.79	+11.84
Wholesale Trade	+ 6.85	+18.55	− 6.58	− 2.66	−10.88	− 6.30	− 2.55	−10.42	− 3.57
Retail Trade	+14.57	+ 5.40	−12.25	− 2.88	−21.31	− 5.45	− 5.04	−41.63	−27.06
Finance, Insurance and Real Estate	+ 1.42	+ 4.43	+ 2.70	+ 0.82	+ 1.15	—	—	+ 6.67	+ 8.09
Community, Business and Personal Service	+10.70	+ 2.59	+ 0.22	+ 0.80	− 5.49	+ 0.08	− 0.04	− 1.84	+ 8.86
Total	+42.72	+30.02	−18.25	− 8.79	−29.26	+ 3.75	+10.11	−12.42	+30.30

*This table is based on a sample of 412 businesses and total activity is not estimated. Purchases from various geographical areas by industry were subtracted from sales to those geographical areas by industry to obtain the net dollar flows for each cell in the table. Purchases consisted of goods purchased for resale plus purchases of raw materials. A plus sign indicates that a particular industry sold more to a given geographical area than it purchased from that geographical area by the dollar amount shown.

SOURCE: Capital Regional District, *Ibid.*, p. 28.

to paving the way for an industrial development program aimed at increasing both employment and income opportunities.[1] It is apparent that the Capital Regional District had a net adverse balance in manufacturing of 66,270,000 dollars in its trading relations with the rest of British Columbia and a positive balance of 102,700,000 dollars with Canada and the rest of the world (Table 6,13). This probably can be attributed to the absolute importance of the wood and wood products industries in the local economy and their dependence on international markets, as well as to the very small size of the rest of the manufacturing sector, necessitating the import of most manufactured goods consumed.

The Economic Advisory Committee examined the local economy in some detail and endeavoured to determine the economic ties of the District with the rest of the Island, the southern mainland, the rest of British Columbia, the rest of Canada and the rest of the world (Tables 6,13 and 7,13). The results of the inquiry established that, among other things, the net income generated by the whole of the manufacturing sector in the District was roughly equivalent to the income generated directly and indirectly by the University of Victoria. The isolation of the Victoria region from the major markets of the world in time-cost terms appears as a strong inhibiting factor for the further development of the manufacturing sector, except for the wood and wood-related industries. The small size of the local market mitigates against achieving the long production runs and consequent economies of scale deemed necessary to the establishment of most viable manufacturing industries. Increasing concentration of industrial ownership has led to a further deterioration of the manufacturing sector and increased its dependence on exogenous factors. Local industrires have been merged with or taken over by national and international corporations which, subsequently, have tended to close local establishments and shift production facilities to the mainland. While the physical isolation has had a deleterious influence on the maintenance and growth of the secondary sector, this same isolation, along with the presence of important amenities related to the physical environment, does exert a positive influence for the attraction of industries whose output is of a high value-low weight nature. Further concentration of effort on those sectors of the economy serving the tourist industry, and a deliberate attempt to attract research establishments and consulting firms, and their related industries, probably will offer a better rate of return on effort expended than government assistance designed to shore up a non-viable manufacturing sector.

The future of manufacturing on Vancouver Island rests largely on the continued success of the forest-based industries. The dichotomy between non-wood-related industries concentrated in the capital region and the wood industries elsewhere seems likely to persist. Manufacturing probably will continue to play an important role in the Island's economy, though further rationalization of the industry seems inevitable.

REFERENCE

1.   Capital Regional District, *The Challenge: Managing the Capital Region's Economy*. Victoria: Economic Advisory Committee, December 1977.

PLATE 25   Forbidden Plateau in Strathcona Park.   *B.C. Government Photo* ▶

14 PARK AND RECREATION SYSTEM

Robert E. Pfister

Vancouver Island's size, physiographic diversity, and favourable climate combine to present residents and visitors alike with ample choice of outdoor recreation opportunities. The beauty and incredible diversity of the Island has led it to be described as "a land of many faces."[1] To understand the "many faces" that comprise the park and recreation system it is necessary, conceptually, to bring together a variety of recreational resources that are not institutionally administered as a "system." The land and water resource units of interest do represent a "system," however, because they constitute a "group of interrelated and interdependent elements which form a collective entity."[2] The application of a systems approach to recreational resources is an outgrowth of the First World Conference of National Parks held in Seattle, Washington in 1962. In a report published by the International Union for The Conservation of Nature and Natural Resources the problem of identifying a park system is described as follows:

> A provincial fish and game agency may control a system of parks to protect, propagate, and maintain the rare or endangered species of animals found in the province; a national park agency may administer a system of natural and cultural areas which protect and interpret features and events of national interest. A municipality may have a system of recreation parks located to permit easy access for each of its residents. Such systems do not represent park systems...(because each)...is based on a single rationale which sets the standards for each individual park in the system and each park is usually con-

265

sidered only in terms of the criteria of its own system. The result is the traditional approach to parks—each one is a separate, discrete unit in space and time and is unrelated to other types of parks which may exist in the same region. Yet every land unit, no matter how large or small, bears some relation to all other land units within some logically defined region around it. . . .Each park within each system bears a relationship to the other parks in other systems and to use patterns of the land in which all the parks are situated.[3]

Thus, by comparing and contrasting the diverse recreational resources which form the many faces of Vancouver Island, a comprehensive perspective of the park and recreation system can be obtained. The recreational resources that supply opportunities within a park and recreation system can be grouped as follows:

1. Parks (national, provincial, and regional);

2. Crown forest land (Public Sustained Yield Unit and Tree Farm Licence areas);

3. Recreational corridors (rivers, trails, and shorelines).

This grouping also highlights the policy, or the absence of policy, which has produced the important decisions that allocate crown resources to public recreation opportunities. It is the purpose of this chapter to examine the role of park areas, forest land, and recreational corridors as resource elements within a park and recreation system and to describe the representative units of these resource elements as found on Vancouver Island today.

THE ROLE OF PARK AREAS

Parks represent a distinctive component of a park and recreation system. Each one has its own legislative history as three levels of government, national, provincial, and regional, are involved with establishing park areas. Representative park areas of each jurisdictional level are described in order to demonstrate the diversity of recreational resource opportunities available on Vancouver Island. Marine parks, however, are considered separately from the terrestrial park areas.

National Parks

Canada and New Zealand have been described as the only countries in the world that have developed national park systems comparable to the system developed in the United States.[4] Since the passage of the Dominion Forest Reserves and Parks Act of 1911, Canada has steadily improved and expanded its national park system. In April of 1970, a formal agreement signed by the governments of Canada and British Columbia provided the basis for the designation of a new addition to the system, Pacific Rim National Park, on the west coast of Vancouver Island. The agreement established boundaries for the Long Beach and Broken Islands park units and a subsequent agreement in 1973 added a third unit known as the West Coast Trail.[5]

Today, the park consists of three physically separate units, each with a distinct character of its own. Unit One, Long Beach, is to be the most intensely developed area, containing the nature centre, campgrounds, and extensive day use facilities. This northern unit's most impressive feature is its hard packed sand beach which is 11.6 kilometres (7.2 miles) long and up to 305 metres (1,000 feet) wide in some places (Figure 1,14). The Broken Islands of Barkley Sound, Unit Two, consists of ninety to ninety-five islands and rocks and will preserve in an undisturbed state the flora, fauna, and sea life associated with the rocky, offshore islands. Studies are under way to determine potential visitor use and its impact on the nature sanctuaries now designated on some of the islands. The West Coast Trail is a seventy-three kilometre (forty-five mile) long unit that is historically renowned as an area where many ships have run aground and it has earned the name "graveyard of the Pacific."[6] As a result of the marine disasters, a wilderness trail was blazed to provide access for rescuers and an escape route for survivors along the Island's spectacular and rugged shoreline. The trail has become a popular focal point of this unit.[7] In total, the Pacific Rim National Park protects ninety-five kilometres (sixty-five miles) of coastline and contains numerous natural and archaeological resources of considerable interest to scientists and visitors alike.[8]

Fort Rodd Hill, a national historic park under the jurisdiction of Parks Canada, is the only other national park on Vancouver Island. Situated in metropolitan Victoria between Esquimalt Harbour and Esquimalt Lagoon, this historic site enjoys the distinction of being the only large fort along Canada's west coast. Adjacent to the fort is Fisgard Lighthouse which has been in operation for over 115 years (Figure 2,14). This park protects

---

FIGURE 1,14   Long Beach in Pacific Rim National Park.   *B.C. Government Photo* ▶

an important cultural resource representative of Canada's heritage and symbolizes the federal effort to identify and manage significant historic sites. Fort Rodd Hill receives a large number of visitors every year, however, there is no provision for camping within the area.

Provincial Parks

Provincial parks represent the most substantial component of the park and recreation system of Vancouver Island, both in number of areas and amount of land. Approximately nine percent of the Island is parkland under the jurisdiction of the Provincial Parks Branch. The fifty-five park areas include eight categories of parkland which range, in the amount of area protected, from a thirty hectare (seventy-four acre) recreation area to a 104,757 hectare (258,860 acre) class "B" park, excluding its nature conservancy areas.

Concurrent with the passage of the Dominion Forest Reserves and Parks Act of 1911 in the Canadian Parliament, the Province of British Columbia established Strathcona Provincial Park by a special act of the Legislature. Strathcona was British Columbia's first provincial park and is the largest on Vancouver Island. Earlier the Legislature had taken action to establish park boards which enabled the Lieutenant-Governor in Council to reserve lands as parks and set fines for damage to them. However, the term "park area" was ill-defined and many resource activities were permitted to occur within them. The British Columbia Forest Service originally was responsible for administering "park areas" and the classification it initiated in the 1940's is still in use.

The parks were divided into three classes. Class "A" parks were reserved from preemption, sale, lease, or licence under the Land Act and certain restrictions were placed upon the holders of mineral claims. Crown timber was reserved from cutting or sale, except when necessary or advantageous for park development and if the criteria of "protecting and preserving the major forest values of the park were met."[9] In the case of Class "B" parks, timber sales which did not impinge upon the recreational values of the park area were permitted, as a basis for obtaining provincial revenue. It was the deputy minister of the Forest Service who made the decision on any timber sale in the Class "B" park areas. Class "C" parks generally were very small areas used as children's playgrounds.[10]

Since the act of 1911 which provided the basis for the creation of the current provincial park system, the agency responsible for provincial

FIGURE 2,14   Fisguard Lighthouse at the entrance to Esquimalt Harbour.
B.C. Government Photo ▶

parks has evolved through several stages. In 1948 an official Parks Division within the Forest Service was created, marking a new recognition of the significance of provincial parks.[11] Ten years later, this division was moved to the new Department of Recreation and Conservation and designated as the Provincial Parks Branch. Since 1957, parks have been separated from the agency responsible for managing the forest resources of the Province and this allowed the Parks Branch the opportunity of defining its responsibilities and policy in the Parks Act of 1965. Through this Act the Branch obtained statutory control over all provincial parks.

At present there are some fifty-five separate parkland areas on Vancouver Island, amounting to more than 270,000 hectares (667,000 acres) (Table 1,14). An additional thirty-one terrestrial park areas lie on the Gulf and adjacent islands of the Strait of Georgia, totalling 2,870 hectares (7,092 acres) and made up almost entirely of Class "A" parks.[12] The spatial distribution of parkland on Vancouver Island and the adjacent islands indicates that most parks are within convenient travel distance from the major population centres (Figure 3,14).

Regional Parks

The regional level is the most recent addition to the park and recreation system of Vancouver Island. The Regional Parks Act of 1965 provided the statutory basis for the twenty-eight regional districts of British Columbia to undertake the function of acquiring land, planning, developing, maintaining, and administering a system of regional parks.

Four of the six regional districts on Vancouver Island have established parks, but only the Capital Regional District centred on Victoria has created a staff complement to plan and develop a park system (Figure 1,13). The other three districts (Alberni-Clayoquot, Comox-Strathcona, Cowichan Valley) have at least one area either acquired or donated under the 1965 act, but planning and development activities have not yet been undertaken by the regional agencies responsible for those areas. The ten regional parks in the Victoria area, totalling 2,427 hectares (5,997 acres), range in size from Cole's Bay Park, approximately 3.7 hectares (9.1 acres) to East Sooke Park, over 1,423 hectares (3,516 acres) (Figure 4,14). During the past ten years there has been frequent discussion of the role of regional parks. At a regional parks conference in 1977, the Associate Deputy Minister of Recreation and Conservation, Mr. R.H. Ahrens, stated that the philosophy behind:

271

TABLE 1,14   Provincial Parkland on Vancouver Island

Type	Number	Area in Hectares
Park Class A	38	44,042
B	2	105,208
C	10	299
Nature Conservancy*	3	122,632
Reserve**	1	Not Available
Recreation Area	1	30
Leased**	1	Not Available
Total	55	272,211

*Areas within Strathcona Park that are not included in Class A or B.

**Areas not established by orders-in-council for which precise boundaries have not been defined.

SOURCES: British Columbia, *Data Handbook*. Victoria: Ministry of Recreation and Conservation, Parks Branch, January 29, 1977, pp. 21-24; and "Schoen Park Preserves 'Unspoiled Wilderness,'" *British Columbia Government News*, November 1977, p. 3.

...regional parks is to provide, in a situation of contiguous municipalities, or neighboring towns... a system of parks based insofar as possible on the natural attractions of significance mainly to the people of that region, and paid for, jointly, by the residents of the whole region from which the park draws most of its users.[13]

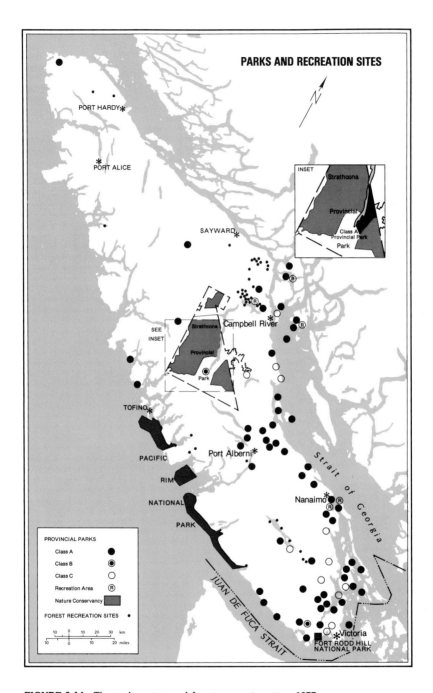

FIGURE 3,14 The park system and forest recreation sites, 1977.

273

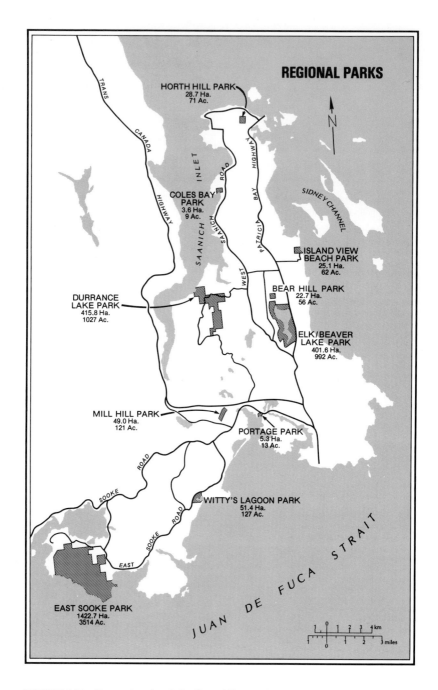

FIGURE 4,14 Regional parks of the Capital Regional District.

274

The concept of the regional park, it seems, is not clearly distinguished from that of the provincial park by the character, size or location of the area, but primarily by the people who use it. As a criterion, it has been suggested that regional parks "be within an hour's drive of most of the metro population which is served."[14] In the case of metropolitan Victoria, it would appear that this criterion has been met (Figure 4,14).

Marine Parks

In recognizing the recreational boating potential of its coastal waters, the provincial government has developed an impressive system of marine parks for the boating public. With the establishment of Sidney Spit Marine Park in 1958, the marine parks became an integral part of the diversified recreation resources of Vancouver Island (Figure 5,14). As the first marine park in the Province, Sidney Spit was designated in recognition of the growing importance of pleasure boating as a recreational activity. Resource protection was not a primary objective in identifying areas suitable for designation. Emphasis was upon managing them as recreation areas.

> Marine parks are those which offer to the boating public, facilities similar to those offered to motorists by wayside parks. They are areas, on waterways, which provide shelter for small boats and opportunities for their operators and crews to go ashore to stretch their legs, to picnic or to rest or to spend a night in camp. Mooring buoys, landing floats and small wharves or docks, campsites with simple fireplaces and, where possible, improved water supply systems are appropriate but outstanding recreational attractions are not essential.[15]

Since 1958, marine recreation has continued to gain in popularity and by 1971, 75,000 Canadian boats and 10,000 American, annually, were cruising in British Columbia's waters.[16] In the southern Gulf Islands, visits to marine parks for which data are available have been increasing steadily in the past six years (Figure 6,14).

The concept of marine parks, however, did not evolve solely in response to the interest in providing wayside opportunities for a pleasure boating public. At the federal level considerable interest was generated as a result of the First World Conference on National Parks which led to the

---

FIGURE 5,14   Sidney Spit on the northern end of Sidney Island.   *I.H. Norie Photo* ▶

adoption of a resolution that "all countries having marine frontiers . . . (should) examine as a matter of urgency the possibility of creating marine parks or reserves to defend underwater areas of special significance from all forms of human interference . . .''[17] In response to this recommendation two federal ministers, the Honourable Jean Chretien and the Honourable Jack Davis, jointly submitted to the Cabinet in 1971 a proposal for the establishment of national marine parks in the Strait of Georgia. This action led to the creation of the Inner Departmental Task Force on National Marine Parks which, in turn, set up a technical working group that had the duty of investigating federal responsibility and jurisdiction with respect to the concept of marine parks.[18] Strategic locations for marine parks were identified and federal-provincial cooperation in the implementation of the marine park concept was established, although no new parks resulting from this joint endeavour have yet been announced.

THE ROLE OF FOREST LAND

Crown forest land consists of a variety of administrative units which contribute substantially to the provision of outdoor recreation opportunities. The administrative prerogative to manage forest land for recreational use varies according to the policies of the public servants responsible for implementing the 1970 amendments to the Forest Act, as well as the types of land tenure established in the Forest Act of 1912 — Tree Farm Licence and Public Sustained Yield Unit. Concerning the actions of public servants, the Chief Forester of the British Columbia Forest Service recently advocated:

> No more forest land should be set aside for parks in
> B.C. Not only can we no longer afford to do so, but
> such a luxury is absolutely unnecessary. We have
> not only 10 million acres in parks already but . . . a
> further 27 million acres in alpine forest and scrub
> timber. These 27 million acres form the greatest
> natural recreational playground imaginable. Do not
> forget there is a further 54 million acres in barren,
> alpine, and swamp. I maintain British Columbia
> already has 91 million acres of wild land that will
> never be touched by logging or industrial activity,
> except possibly a little mining.[19]

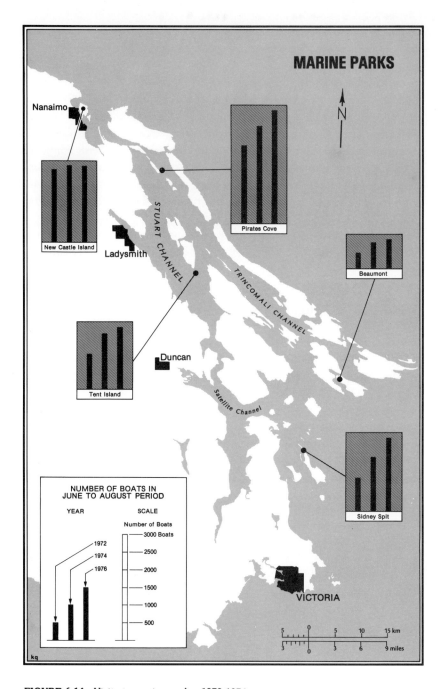

FIGURE 6,14 Visits to marine parks, 1972-1976

This statement generated numerous comments from other public officials responsible for provincial recreation and conservation programs, as well as special interest groups concerned about parkland issues.[20] More importantly, it tends to illustrate how the Forest Service perceives recreational land: if eighty-one million acres of crown forest land are unsuitable for sustained yield forestry they must be highly suitable for recreational use. Obviously, public interest is aroused by the questionable logic contained in that perception.

Tree Farm Licence Areas

Timber firms holding Tree Farm Licences are under no legal obligation to allow public access for enjoyment of the recreational resources within the management units unless they happen to include provincial ecological reserves. However, a park or ecological reserve within a licence area cannot exceed one percent of the total area comprising the unit.[21] Beyond this the provision of a recreation site is entirely the decision of the holder of the licence. There are a few cases where timber companies have taken it upon themselves to initiate pilot recreation projects in the interest of public relations, such as the recreation site developed by MacMillan Bloedel at Nitinat Lake in 1971. It was a joint public-private venture where capital costs were covered by the Forest Service and the operating costs absorbed by the licensee.

Public Sustained Yield Units

Currently, there are approximately fifty recreation sites on Vancouver Island administered by the Forest Service that occur in provincial forests classed as Public Sustained Yield Units. Sayward Forest is an example of such an area (Figure 3,14). It contains campsites, picnic tables, boat launching facilities and restrooms. Almost sixty percent of the recreation sites are in the Campbell River area, with the remainder situated near Duncan (Figure 3,14). When public recreation on forest land became part of the responsibility of the Forest Service in the early 1970's an inventory was undertaken throughout the Province to determine recreation capability of forest land. Today, land classification for recreation has been completed and this data base, combined with inventory work by forest district offices, helps to identify future recreation areas for consideration in the timber folio plans prepared for each Public Sustained Yield Unit.

279

THE ROLE OF RECREATION CORRIDORS

The recreation corridors of Vancouver Island are comprised of rivers and shorelines that provide opportunities for water-related recreational experiences, as well as trails that provide opportunities for hiking and horseback riding. In British Columbia the term "recreation corridor" does not have any official or legal meaning, as it does not appear in either legislation or any policy proclamation. The concept of linear resource areas is not new, however. In the 1960's it was professionally promoted by landscape architects, enacted into federal and state law in the United States and, more recently, incorporated as administrative policy in Ontario.[22]

Rivers

It has been documented through extensive research that, in terms of man's preference, water probably is the greatest of all outdoor recreation attractions. Quite understandably, rivers and the riverine environment are commonly recognized in parts of North America and Europe as major recreational resources, yet they are not so classified in British Columbia. Moreover, they have not been actively identified or inventoried as part of any governmental program, unless within a provincial park or park reserve. In 1972, the British Columbia Wildlife Federation recognized this oversight by public agencies and passed three resolutions calling for government action to protect some of the Province's rivers in a legislated program.[23] Three years later at the First Rocky Mountain-Pacific Rim Park and Forest Recreation Conference the topic of classification and protection of river corridors again received province-wide attention.[24] Concurrently, the Ministry of Recreation and Conservation released its evaluation of the policy alternatives for establishing a recreation corridor system for British Columbia.[25] The most extensive report on this topic was submitted to the provincial government in 1977 by the Outdoor Recreation Council of British Columbia, in cooperation with the Greater Vancouver Regional District and numerous outdoor clubs.[26] This report presents the results of an extensive effort to solicit the opinions of member groups as to their perception and evaluation of trails, rivers, and scenic shorelines of provincial and regional significance. With regard to rivers, in particular, the report identifies eleven provincially significant rivers or segments of rivers on Vancouver Island (Figure 7,14). Each is

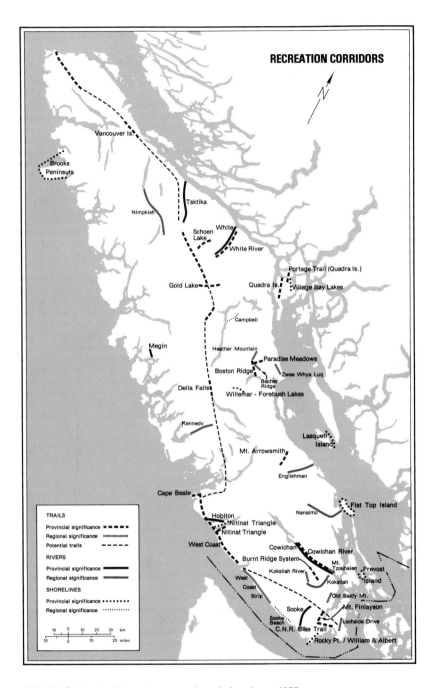

RECREATION CORRIDORS

Vancouver Is.

Brooks
Peninsula

Tsktika

Nimpkish

Schoen
Lake

White

White River

Portage Trail (Quadra Is.)

Gold Lake

Quadra Is.

Village Bay Lakes

Campbell

Megin

Heather Mountain

Paradise Meadows

Boston Ridge

Zwee Whya Luq

Becher
Ridge

Della Falls

Willemar - Forebush Lakes

Kennedy

Lasqueti
Island

Mt. Arrowsmith

Englishman

Cape Beale

Flat Top Island

Nanaimo

TRAILS
Provincial significance
Regional significance
Potential trails

RIVERS
Provincial significance
Regional significance

SHORELINES
Provincial significance
Regional significance

Hobiton
Nitinat Triangle
Nitinat Triangle

West Coast

Cowichan

Cowichan River

Burnt Ridge System

Mt.
Tzouhalen

Prevost

Koksilah River

West
Coast
Strip

Koksilah

Island

Old Baldy Mt.

Sooke

Mt. Finlayson

Sooke
Beach

Lochside Drive

C.N.R. Bike Trail

Rocky Pt. / William & Albert

FIGURE 7,14 Significant rivers, trails and shorelines, 1977.

281

rated as to its significance and the location and length of the segment recommended for protection is described.

In the absence of specific legislation, commercial and non-commercial use of rivers has not been controlled and interested recreationists have increasing amounts of information available to them. Newspapers and periodicals frequently describe fishing opportunities and the availability of commercially guided trips on particular white water rivers.[27] In addition, descriptive guidebooks have been published for those who wish to explore rivers on their own.[28]

Trails

Urban and rural trails provide opportunities for walking, hiking, horseback riding, ski touring, and similar activities. The trails may exist on land that is publicly owned, privately owned, or a combination of the two. There are a number of trail corridors of provincial and regional significance on Vancouver Island, as identified by the Outdoor Recreation Council of British Columbia (Figure 7,14). Detailed hiking trail guides for three different areas of the Island have been prepared by the Trails Information Society.[29]

As is the case with river corridors, British Columbia lacks a policy for planning and management of trails outside provincial parks. Only recently has any attention been given to this question: in 1977, the Parks Branch evaluated alternative proposals for a system of recreational corridors which would recognize not only trails, but also rivers, shorelines, and recreational roadways.[30] Until the government takes some action the trails will receive attention only from the special interest groups that are aware of them.

CONCLUSION

Diversity may be the single most descriptive characteristic of the land and water resources which provide opportunities for outdoor recreation on Vancouver Island. There is diversity in terms of the public institutions involved; national, provincial, and regional; and the types of areas that are under their jurisdiction; parks, forest land and recreational corridors. In the marine environment, the variety of resource units ranges from the long, sand beaches of the Pacific Ocean to the rocky, protected coves of the Gulf Islands. In the terrestrial environment, the life zones vary from the high, alpine habitat of the Vancouver Island Mountains to the low, tranquil habitat of its rivers and estuaries. Thus, the physical variety of the Island and the favourable climate combine to provide a broad spectrum of park and recreation opportunities.

It is suggested that a "systems approach" is a useful technique for viewing the varied recreational resource units, even if they are not administered institutionally as a system. Common issues influence the recreational resources and there is interaction among them in terms of management policy. The identification and elimination of non-conforming activities within the boundaries of the units is a common problem. In the case of Pacific Rim National Park a recent non-conforming use issue arose concerning Wickaninnish Inn.[31] The policy adopted was to exclude privately owned services from the park in favour of the encouragement of such development immediately outside it. In provincial parks, the issue involves the exclusion of hunting, mining, logging, and other activities that constitute consumptive uses of park resources. This management issue is reflected in the classification system for parks which defines circumstances in which consumptive uses are permitted. In the case of river corridors, the production of hydroelectric power is a non-conforming use which directly conflicts with kayaking or rafting on the river and is inconsistent with the protection of fish and wildlife habitat.

The role of park areas and forest land reflects the evolution of legislation and institutional arrangements of the provincial agencies responsible for land management, namely, the former Ministry of Recreation and Conservation and the Ministry of Forests. Within the former ministry, provincial and marine parks constitute a major component of the areas included in the park and recreation system, and this is complemented by the recreation sites designated on forest land by the British Columbia Forest Service. National and regional parks also contribute to the provision of outdoor recreation opportunities, as do the rivers, trails, and shorelines that have been identified as recreationally significant by both private and public institutions.

REFERENCES

1. SMITH, I. *Vancouver Island: Unknown Wilderness*. Seattle: University of Washington Press, 1973, p. 11.

2. MORRIS, W. (ed.) *The American Heritage Dictionary of the English Language*. Boston: Houghton Mifflin, 1970.

3. HART, W.J. *A Systems Approach to Park Planning*. Morges, Switzerland: International Union for the Conservation of Nature and Natural Resources, 1966, pp. 2 and 3.

4. ISE, J. *Our National Park Policy: A Critical History*. Baltimore: Johns Hopkins Press, 1961, p. 658.

5. Canada, *Pacific Rim National Park, Long Beach Unit, Provisional Master Plan*. Ottawa: Department of Indian and Northern Affairs, Parks Canada, July 1973, p. 13.

6. *Ibid.*, p. 15.

7. MORROW, P. "Beachwalking on the Pacific Coast Island," *Canadian Geographical Journal*, 95, No. 3 (1977/78), pp. 44-49; DAVIDSON, M. "Hiking the West Coast Trail," *Pacific Wilderness Journal* (April-May 1974), pp. 8-14; and *The West Coast Trail and Nitinat Lakes*. Vancouver: J.J. Douglas, 1972.

8. HANCOCK, D., HANCOCK, L. and STERLING, D. *Pacific Wilderness*. Saanichton: Hancock House Publishers, 1974.

9. SLOAN, G.M. *Report of the Commissioner Relating to the Forest Resources of British Columbia, 1945*. Victoria: Kings Printer, 1945, p. 185.

10. *Ibid.*

11. British Columbia, *Annual Report of the Forest Service*. Victoria: Department of Lands and Forests, Forest Service, 1947, p. 26.

12. British Columbia, *Data Handbook*. Victoria: Ministry of Recreation and Conservation, Parks Branch, January 29, 1977, pp. 21-24.

13. British Columbia, *Summary of Proceedings of Regional Parks Conference*. Victoria: Ministry of Recreation and Conservation, Recreation and Fitness Branch, March 7-9, 1977, p. 21.

14. Capital Regional District, *Regional Parks*. Victoria: Capital Region Planning Board, August 1969, p. 6.

15. MACMURCHIE, D.L. *Parks Branch Policies*. Victoria: Department of Recreation and Conservation, Parks Branch, unpublished working document, 1963.

16. WOLFERSTAN, W.H. *Marine Recreation in the Desolation Sound Region of B.C.* Vancouver: Simon Fraser University, Department of Geography, unpublished M.A. Thesis, 1971.

17. United States, *First World Conference on National Parks*. Washington: Department of the Interior, National Park Service, 1962, pp. 381 and 382.

18. Canada, *National Marine Parks — Strait of Georgia and Juan de Fuca*. Ottawa: Department of Indian Affairs and Northern Development, Task Force Technical Working Group, 3 vols., 1977.

19. "No More Forest Parks," *Daily Colonist*, March 22, 1978, p. 1; this viewpoint was reported also in "Parks Block 'Out of Tune'," *Victoria Times*, March 22, 1978, p. 2; and "No More Parks in Forest," *Vancouver Province*, March 22, 1978.

20. "Servants Split on Parks," *Daily Colonist*, March 23, 1978; "Ministers at Loggerheads Over Future Use of Forests," *Vancouver Sun*, March 23, 1978; "Who's in Charge Here?" *Victoria Times*, March 25, 1978; and "Sierra Club Raps Flooding of Forests," *Vancouver Sun*, April 6, 1978.

21. Essentially, areas under Tree Farm Licences are managed for timber production, although other uses may be recognized on up to one percent of the area included in "Schedule B" land. For example, see "Land Schedules in the Tskitka Valley," *The Sea Otter*, 1, No. 5 (February 1978), p. 25.

22. LEWIS, P.H., Jr. "Quality Corridors for Wisconsin," *Landscape Architecture*, 54 (January 1964), pp. 100-107; PFISTER, R.E., "Protection of Free-Flowing Rivers," *Water Resources Policy Issues—1975*. Corvallis: Oregon State University, Water Resources Research Institute, Semin WR 020-75, 1975; and Ontario, *Administrative Policies of the Ontario Parks System— Waterway Parks in Ontario*. Toronto: Ministry of Natural Resources, Division of Parks, Second Revised Preliminary Report, April 8, 1975.

23. WARDEN, G. and MANKELOW, E. *A Proposal for Wild, Scenic, and Recreation Rivers in British Columbia*. Vancouver: British Columbia Wildlife Federation, 1972.

24. DOOLING, P. (ed.) *Proceedings of the First Rocky Mountain-Pacific Rim Park and Forest Recreation Conference.* Vancouver: University of British Columbia, 1975.

25. TURNER, R. and DAVIES, E. *A Recreation Corridor System for B.C.* Victoria: Ministry for Recreation and Conservation, Parks Branch, Planning Report No. 7, 1974.

26. *British Columbia's Trails, Rivers, and Shorelines—A Status Report.* Vancouver: Outdoor Recreation Council of British Columbia, 1977.

27. SORENSEN, J. "White-Water," *Daily Colonist*, Sunday, August 21, 1977, pp. 4 and 5.

28. JENKINSON, M. *Wild Rivers of North America*. Vancouver: Clarke, Irwin, 1973; and *British Columbia Canoe Routes*. Vancouver: Nunaga Publishing, 1976.

29. WADDELL, J. (ed.) *Hiking Trails I—Victoria and Vicinity* (1977), *Hiking Trails II—Southeastern Vancouver Island* (1976), and *Hiking Trails III—Central and Northern Vancouver Island* (1975). Victoria: Morriss Printing.

30. LEE, T.E. *Alternative Proposals for a System of Recreational Corridors for B.C.* Victoria: Parks Branch, Long Range Planning, unpublished paper, January 1977.

31. WALLACE, G. "Wipeout at Wickaninnish," *Monday Magazine*, October 10-16, 1977, pp. 16 and 17.

PLATE 26 Sunken Gardens, Butchart Gardens. *B.C. Government Photo* ▶

15 DEVELOPMENT AND POTENTIAL OF TOURISM

Peter E. Murphy

The tourist industry is a hospitality industry and catering for the visitor has become a major business and concern for the residents of Vancouver Island. The Island has experienced considerable growth in its tourism sector. In 1976 its share of the Province's 1,200,000,000 dollar tourist industry was estimated to be 212,000,000 dollars, or eighteen percent of the total, which placed it second only to the lower mainland. Furthermore, the number of visitors that year was estimated at 1,800,000, which was approximately four times Vancouver Island's population.[1] The development of tourism has occurred at a time when other more traditional industries have either stabilized or begun to decline. In 1976 tourism was the Province's third largest revenue earner, after forestry and mining, and ranked third behind manufacturing and construction in terms of wages and salaries.[2]

Tourism has both an economic and visual impact on the Island's way of life. It is now a major factor in the economy and both government and business have become sensitive to anything that could disrupt the industry. The business sector, in particular, is concerned about price competitiveness and the movement of tourists to the Island. Any threat to these brings about substantial political and financial pressure. For example, the financially troubled Princess Marguerite Ferry service operating between Seattle and Victoria was taken over by the provincial government in 1975, mainly as a result of pressure applied by downtown businessmen and the City of Victoria. Likewise, threatened legal action by the Victoria hotel sector over lost revenue was a factor in the settlement of the 1977 British Columbia Ferries strike.

While the Island's business and political community has been concerned with the continued development and growth of the tourist industry, more residents have begun to question the impact of such policies on their physical and social environment. Tourism is one industry where the man in the street is also on the shop floor, whether he likes it or not. The local people and their way of life are part of the area's attraction, but in some cases this same life style is being altered by the tourist activity, leading to the alienation of some residents. The resentment toward the tourist industry has manifested itself in several ways. In Victoria there have been complaints about the congestion around the Inner Harbour, the commercialization of a way of life and the sales techniques of the industry. In the Gulf Islands there is growing concern about excessive subdivision, the development of vacation homes and foreign ownership.

The purpose of this chapter is to examine the manner in which Vancouver Island's tourist industry has developed, the implications of the process and possible future strategies for this important economic sector. In pursuit of these objectives the definition of a tourist and the tourist industry will be treated in a general and comprehensive fashion. The internationally recognized definition of a tourist is "a temporary visitor staying at least twenty-four hours in the country (area) visited and the purpose of whose journey can be classified as leisure."[3] This definition is expanded for the purposes of the present study to include day-trippers, since they form an important element in the tourist business of Victoria and southern Vancouver Island. Although tourism is primarily a service industry, it is "a multi-dimensional phenomenon where many and varied activities each make their own separate and individual contribution to a comprehensive service to tourists."[4] Thus, the tourist industry is viewed as including any activity that can have a bearing on attracting, accommodating and serving the visitor to Vancouver Island.

In British Columbia the tourist industry and related tourism research comes under the authority of the Provincial Secretary who has a dual portfolio including Tourism British Columbia, the new name for the Department of Travel Industry. The province is divided into eight tourist regions and Vancouver Island represents the bulk of Region A. The Island, in turn, is subdivided into the five tourist districts of Greater Victoria, Cowichan Valley, Nanaimo, Alberni-Clayoquot, and Strathcona (Figure 1,15).

GROWTH OF THE INDUSTRY

The growth in Vancouver Island's tourist activity has been considerable in the postwar period, reflecting the international trends in vacation

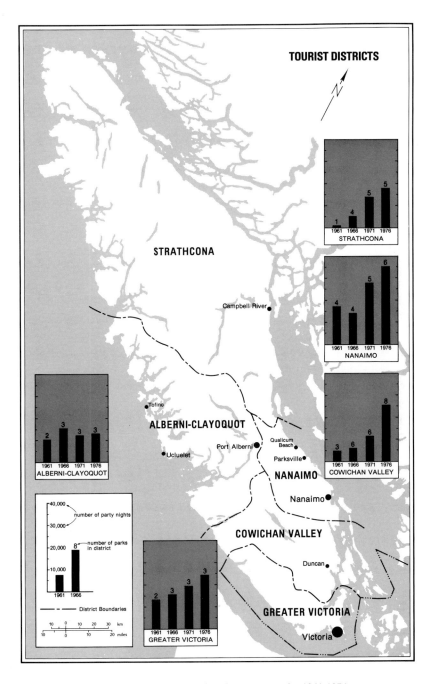

FIGURE 1,15   Party nights in provincial park campgrounds, 1961-1976.

travel brought about by increased discretionary income, more leisure time, higher expectations and lower real travel costs.[5] Growth can be measured in various ways for an activity as diverse as tourism, but the major constraint is one of data availability. Tourism indices have been examined to reflect the supply and demand components of the industry and its overall economic impact. The supply side is represented by the accommodation sector. The demand side is reflected in the number of visitors, including those recorded on the principal ferry routes, and the economic impact is assessed in terms of tourist expenditure estimates.

The growth of the industry is most conspicuous in terms of its accommodation sector. The number of units on the Island increased from 5,875 in 1961 to 13,557 by 1977 (Table 1,15). This represents the doubling of an already substantial base. Furthermore, the figures must be viewed as conservative estimates because they are derived from accommodation directories that require voluntary collaboration and do not include public campgrounds. This growth has not been uniform. The self-catering section has recorded the highest growth rate over the past sixteen years, while the resort section has experienced the lowest growth. The trend to self-catered holidays reflects the international movement toward greater use of holiday apartments, cottages, campers and trailers, but it is basically the camping fraternity which is in the forefront of such vacations on Vancouver Island. In 1961 there were twelve provincial campgrounds which recorded 47,675 party nights and by 1976 this had risen to twenty-five campgrounds and 117,210 party nights (Figure 1,15). Actual campsites available on the Island in 1977 totalled 4,532 commercial and 1,335 provincial.[6]

The evidence concerning the number of visitors is more fragmented, but what data there are point to a substantial growth. Tourism British Columbia has developed an aggregate estimate of 1,800,000 visitors to Vancouver Island in 1976.[7] A rough estimate of 600,000 visitors in 1963 can be calculated from the 1963 summer survey of out-of-province visitors.[8] This amounts to a threefold increase in thirteen years, but it must be emphasized that these are just estimates. Other evidence covering shorter time periods indicates that the growth rate has been uneven. The data on out-of-province vehicles collected each August by British Columbia Ferries on the two major routes to Vancouver Island record little growth between 1972 and 1977 (Table 2,15). These data are conservative indicators in that they do not take into account the British Columbia resident who is on vacation and are limited to a one month period.

TABLE 1,15 Growth of Tourist Accommodation on Vancouver Island

Accommodation Type	1961	1971	1977	Percentage Increase 1961-1977
Hotels and Motels	4,725	6,530	7,475	58
Resorts*	789	1,148	955	21
Self-Catering**	361	3,287	5,127	1,320
Total	5,875	10,965	13,557	131

*Resorts includes lodges, dude ranches, resorts and fishing resorts.

**Self-Catering includes cottages, trailer parks, campsites (private) and camp and trailer parks.

SOURCE: British Columbia, *British Columbia Tourist Accommodation Directory*, Victoria: Department of Travel Industry, 1961, 1971 and 1977.

The economic impact of tourism has long been substantial, but reasonably accurate estimates have been unavailable until the 1970's. It is estimated that Vancouver Island earned 104,000,000 dollars in 1970, 191,000,000 in 1974, and 212,000,000 in 1976.[9] The prime tourist centre, Victoria, was estimated to be earning 137,000,000 dollars from tourism in 1974, which was seventy-two percent of the Island's tourist revenue.[10] The 1977 tourist revenue for Victoria was estimated to be 140,000,000.[11] These figures represent only first round expenditures and if the multiplier effect is taken into account the overall contribution of tourism to the Island's economy is even greater.

PATTERNS OF TOURIST GROWTH

One of the most important aspects of tourism, in general, and its growth on Vancouver Island, in particular, is its diversity. There is no average tourist and there has been no uniform development of the

TABLE 2,15 August Surveys of Out-of-Province Vehicles

Location	1972	1973*	1974	1975	1976**	1977	Percentage Change 1972-1977
Swartz Bay	25,421	18,721	25,254	25,048	—	26,141	2.8
Departure Bay	15,325	12,891	12,978	11,145	—	15,607	1.8

*Data for twenty-six days only, owing to a strike.
**No survey was conducted.

SOURCE: Personal Communication, British Columbia Ferries, January 17, 1978.

industry on Vancouver Island. "Tourism demand does not represent a homogeneous group of people striving to travel pushed by identical motivations. It is a complex of various and sometimes conflicting desires, needs, tastes, likes and dislikes."[12] Therefore, an island that balances a metropolitan capital at one end and a wilderness inaccessible by road at the other, set amid prime fishing and sailing waters, with a climate that permits golf twelve months a year, has given rise to an abundance of tourist demands and activities within a relatively small region.

Just how diverse the tourism demand is on Vancouver Island becomes apparent from the two major provincial surveys conducted in the mid-seventies. The 1974 survey of out-of-province visitors showed that their main activities, in ranked order, were sightseeing, shopping, visiting friends and relatives, fishing and boating.[13] The 1976 activity profile of British Columbia resident tourists was similar, except that the rank order differed.[14] Visiting friends and relatives was the major activity for British Columbia residents travelling within their own Province, followed by shopping, sightseeing, watching sports and theatrical events, boating, fishing and hunting, and camping.

A more detailed examination of the out-of-province visitor data revealed several distinctive features of the Vancouver Island visitor.[15] A classification analysis of 5,402 interviews collected in the 1974 survey yielded five major characteristics that differentiated the Vancouver Island visitors from those who went elsewhere in the Province (Table 3,15). The foremost discriminator was the relative location of the tourists' entry

TABLE 3.15 Significant Classification Analysis Results for
the Vancouver Island Tourist Region, 1974*

	Step 1	Step 2	Step 3	Step 4	Step 5	Step 6
Discriminatory Variables	Entry Point	Number of information sources	Money spent yesterday	Distance from home	Camper	Money spent in British Columbia
Beta Value and (t test)	-0.287 (18.5)	0.168 (10.8)	0.106 (8.5)	0.086 (5.2)	0.008 (5.2)	0.006 (4.5)
						$R^2 = 17.7$

*Level of significance   p = 0.001   N = 3,797

point into British Columbia. The negative relationship indicates that most of the Island's visitors entered the Province via the west coast routes. The route, in conjunction with the fourth variable, a positive relationship to distance travelled from home, confirms the importance of the west coast market to Vancouver Island. It is apparent that the visitors make good use of any available information (second variable). Many tourists would want a clear image of the Island's attractions before committing themselves to such long trips and the extra expenses of the ferries. This last aspect undoubtedly contributed to the "amount of money spent yesterday" and "money spent in British Columbia," along with the general expenses of visiting and staying on the Island. The remaining significant discriminant variable is the presence of the camper. Vancouver Island can be differentiated from other tourist regions in the Province by the large proportion of visitors who bring their own accommodation. For the out-of-province visitor it is a way of offsetting the costs of a long journey and for the Island it has meant an accommodation adjustment, with a substantial rise in the self-catering sector.

To accommodate the variety of tourist demands the industry has developed into an urban-rural dichotomy that maximizes the utilization of the Island's resources. In the urban oriented category fall the southern tourist districts of Greater Victoria, Cowichan and Nanaimo, with Victoria acting as the major magnet. To balance this the northern districts can offer the solitude of wilderness experiences or outdoor recreation activity. Peters' observations seem applicable to Vancouver Island:

> ...some countries are extremely fortunate in that
> they have one asset so outstanding and unique that
> the tourist industry can largely depend on, and be
> promoted by, this feature.[16]

The Island possesses Victoria as its outstanding and unique asset which is complemented by the rural, outdoor recreation emphasis elsewhere. This creates a comprehensive tourist package that can attract many people. It is definitely advantageous to be able to offer something unique in the competitive tourism market of North America and Victoria's island location, plus its strong links with the United Kingdom, have made its "Olde Englande" image a viable and profitable strategy. The industry has capitalized on existing cultural and architectural links with England, like the Empress Hotel high teas and the Legislative Buildings outlined in lights, and supplemented these with replicas, such as the Olde England Inn complex. Such features, along with the numerous shops selling British goods, are a major attraction to the day trip visitors that arrive in downtown Victoria via the Princess Marguerite ferry from Seattle and the Coho from Port Angeles, Washington. In 1977 these vessels brought nearly 500,000 passengers and over 90,000 cars into downtown Victoria during the spring and summer seasons.[17] The majority of the Princess Marguerite passengers are day-trippers who have four hours in which to view the sights. This provides a ready market for numerous tour operators who line the causeway and Inner Harbour selling tours on buses and horse-drawn carriages. Although no exact figures on expenditure are available, it is estimated that in 1977 the Princess Marguerite and Coho summer visitors spent approximately 10,000,000 dollars in Victoria.[18]

The hustle and bustle of the day-tripper traffic, through its great visibility, has created a distorted image of Victoria's tourist industry. In reality it is only one component of the city's tourist business and in economic terms a relatively minor one. The pedestrian and vehicular congestion around the Inner Harbour when the Princess Marguerite and Coho disgorge their passengers leads to temporary blockages in the core and frantic sales pitches from the tour operators along the causeway. But the congestion is limited both in time and space. It is confined to the arrival times of the two downtown ferries and the central attractions that can be visited within a short stay. Furthermore, the recent transfer of the Coho terminal to the south side of the harbour, adjacent to the Princess Marguerite terminal, has rationalized the docking facilities and permitted easier traffic flows past the Legislative Buildings. Other sea borne visitors, those on cruise ships, do not create such congestion or antipathy because they land at the Outer Harbour, are less conspicuous and spend more time and money within greater Victoria. In 1977 there were twenty-eight California-Alaska cruise ship visits which brought more than 30,000 visitors and an estimated 1,000,000 dollars into the Victoria area.[19]

Because the majority of Vancouver Island's visitors come via the British Columbia Ferry routes to Swartz Bay near Victoria, and Departure Bay, Nanaimo, the more urbanized southern districts receive the bulk of the tourist trade. Victoria offers a wide range of attractions and activities for the urban oriented tourist. In addition to the English atmosphere, it displays aspects of its own history in Old Town, Chinatown, and Fort Rodd Hill. The Provincial Museum has outstanding environmental exhibits on native Indian culture and the urban-economic development of British Columbia. Its connection with the sea is ever present, with its marinas, salmon fishing, marine exhibits and float planes descending into the very heart of the city. In addition to these attractions, the capital city provides a full range of accommodation, including camping and trailer spaces within its rural-urban fringe and a wide selection of restaurants and entertainment. It is, in effect, a balanced tourist centre.

The southern districts also possess a major tourist route between the capital city and Nanaimo that is part of the Trans-Canada Highway. Tourists, generally, prefer not to backtrack over their previous route, in order to see as many new things as possible during their visit. Thus, a circular tour linking Victoria, Nanaimo and Vancouver has emerged as a popular option. The city of Nanaimo is actively promoting this mini-tour of the Island and attempting to increase its share of the urban tourist market. It already possesses an historical attraction in its Bastion, plus nearby sport fishing and skiing, but it lacks the overall variety and facilities to match Victoria or be a counter magnet. There is latent tourism potential for cultural and industrial heritage parks, such as Indian village sites and the abandoned coal mines, but such developments have proven more difficult to realize than recognize.[20] A major attraction along the route is the Forest Museum at Duncan. This open-air industrial heritage park shows how information and enjoyment can be combined into an appealing package to attract many people. Other attractions include Goldstream Provincial Park near Victoria, containing a waterfall and salmon stream, and the Malahat Drive which provides outstanding views of the Saanich Peninsula, Gulf Islands and Cascade Range from its 352 metre (1,155 feet) elevation viewpoint.

Elsewhere on the Island the urban tourist centres are small and function as resorts or accommodation centres for surrounding outdoor recreation activities. Parksville and Qualicum Beach base their appeal on the warm, shallow waters on the lee shore of Vancouver Island, which, in conjunction with good beaches, provide an ideal environment for family holidays. Hence, there is a resort atmosphere in these communities, with some fine hotels for their size, many beach cottages, and privately owned and operated summer resorts. Examples of tourist service centres for surrounding hinterlands can be found in Ucluelet and Tofino. Both of these small towns on the west coast have greatly increased their tourism sectors in response to the establishment of the Pacific Rim National Park. Federal regulations prohibit commercial activity within the park itself, but its development creates a tourist magnet that can only be served by adjacent communities. Consequently, new campsites and condominiums have been constructed along the perimeter of the park and the towns themselves have a bustling summer trade.

The remainder of the Island balances the urban orientation of Victoria and other tourism centres. There is an abundance of self-catering accommodation to serve the outdoor recreationist and those wishing to tour the Island (Table 4,15). Many of the camp and trailer facilities serve both urban centres and surrounding hinterlands, whereas the cottages and campsites are oriented toward natural attractions and outdoor recreation activities. Paramount among these activities are fishing, sailing, trekking, skiing and camping itself. Salmon fishing in coastal waters is possible everywhere, but some localities have developed more notable reputations than others and have attracted clusters of fishing resorts and professional guides. Fresh water fishing is reputed to be better the farther north one moves. As the Campbell River area affords excellent salt and fresh water fishing, the city has become the most noted centre for sport fishing on the Island. "About five million dollars comes into the Campbell River area from tourist spending during the 90 day period between June and September."[21] Cruise sailing is popular along the sheltered east coast where the winds are moderate, and the Gulf Islands provide convenient and interesting ports of call. Trekking can take place either along designated trails or in the wilderness areas of the provincial parks. Foremost in these categories are the West Coast Trail and Strathcona Park. The West Coast Trail between Port Renfrew and Bamfield provides a wilderness hiking experience along

TABLE 4,15   Self-Catering Accommodation by Tourist District, 1977

District	Cottage	Trailer	Campsite Private	Campsite Provincial	Camp and Trailer	Total
Greater Victoria	47	36	24	259	1,021	1,387
Cowichan Valley	106	6	78	143	213	546
Nanaimo	240	31	53	395	1,669	2,388
Alberni-Clayoquot	94	0	15	84	615	808
Strathcona	108	230	224	454	317	1,333

SOURCES: British Columbia, *British Columbia Tourist Accommodation Directory*, Victoria: Department of Travel Industry, 1977.
Personal Communication, Ministry of Recreation and Conservation, Parks Branch, Victoria, December 12, 1977.

a stretch of rugged and beautiful coastline (Figure 7,14). Strathcona Park offers outstanding areas of wilderness beauty, alpine meadows, old gold mine workings and environmental education programs. The upland areas of the Nanaimo, Alberni-Clayquot and Strathcona districts contain the Island's three ski resorts. The development of these resorts helps to create a year-round demand for the outdoors, hence, increasing the viability of the tourist infrastructure. Some of the ski resorts are trying to develop an all year capability by including lodges and summer facilities that would appeal to hikers, fishermen and hunters.

The Gulf Islands, where many of the visitors either own or rent summer cottages, offer a distinctive form of rural relaxation. The Islands provide an ideal second home or summer cottage location for both Vancouver Islanders and people from the mainland. They are accessible via regular ferry services from Swartz Bay and Tsawwassen. Many marinas have been built to attract and serve the cruising yachtsmen, as well as the local sailors, and in sheltered areas with good beaches summer resorts have become popular developments. But overall, the atmosphere on the Islands remains quiet and relaxed, since the level of more obvious tourist development does not yet challenge the life style of the permanent resident or long stay visitor.

IMPLICATIONS OF GROWTH

To date the tourist industry has responded vigorously to the desires of the visitors and their varied tastes. But the success of the industry and its continued support on the Island will require an increasing awareness of the social impact and long term economic consequences of the recent growth trends. This implies a move beyond promotion to the consideration of increased regulation and management by government authorities.

Management and coordinated planning policies are required if the Island's tourist industry is to develop its comprehensive tourist package and maintain a sustained yield operation over the long run. In the northern part of the Island the harvesting of natural resources must be integrated with the conservation needs of the tourist industry and future generations. For example, the environmental management of Campbell River and surrounding areas has been suggested because "...the Campbell River area seems to be nearing a dangerous point of environmental overload, beyond which possible irreversible damage to its viability for outdoor recreation could take place."[22] It is not just the resource industries which mar the natural beauty of the Island. Due to its own success the tourist industry itself can overload an ecosystem and destroy the very attraction which is bringing people to the Island. The West Coast Trail, which was reopened in response to the growing demand for wilderness experience and hiking routes, is experiencing such popularity that the wilderness concept could be endangered in certain areas. Since it was reopened the trail is estimated to have had over 50,000 visitors, which means that in the more accessible southern reaches it no longer offers a "wilderness" experience.[23]

The current relaxed atmosphere and pleasant but fragile environment of the Gulf Islands also requires protection, with future developments being carefully controlled. The danger of excessive subdivision for second homes or summer cottages is ever present, such as on Gabriola Island, and can upset the balance between permanent and temporary residents, as well as overload the local ecosystems. A recent survey has indicated that twenty-three percent of the lots on the Gulf Islands are being used for permanent residences and twenty-three percent for seasonal dwellings.[24] Since the remaining fifty-four percent of the lots are undeveloped, this delicate balance could easily shift in favour of the seasonal dwellings and visitors, with an accompanying change in the atmosphere and economy of the Islands.

300

Tourism, being a hospitality industry, needs the support of the local people. The social impact of tourism is a major cause of inhospitality. When tourism creates congestion, develops an artificial and distasteful image of one's home and makes it impossible to lead a normal life people begin to challenge the scale and type of tourism that is being promoted. Tourist congestion and land use in central Victoria has developed to the point of disrupting local life styles, producing some residential alienation. In a letter to the *Victoria Times* a resident described the Inner Harbour scene as:

> The greatest causeway show on earth. All the best of Brighton and Coney Island right here in Victoria. Canadian Tally-Ho, San Francisco trolley car (cum bus), London double-deckers. . . . No need to stress our city was once a pleasant, clean and very different place to visit to get away from all the normal hassle of larger cities everywhere. We were once unique in these respects. Once lost can never be regained.[25]

This is not to say that Victorians have become anti-visitor or that they do not appreciate the economic benefits of such an industry to their city. It means that some are appealing for restraint and balance. Victorians have no complaint about the quality restaurants, gift stores, live theatre and antique shops that depend on tourism to a large extent. It is a problem of management for the tourist industry and local government authorities, for if resident cooperation and the uniqueness of Victoria are to be retained some form of comprehensive planning is needed.

Further development of tourism in the northern districts would, undoubtedly, broaden the economic base of single enterprise communities and could complement the seasonal variations and labour demands of certain resource industries. However, it would be beneficial only if such development were directed toward the upgrading and support of the present outdoor recreation emphasis, rather than toward the duplication of and competition with the facilities and attractions of the southern districts. If tourism development in the northern districts emphasized the multi-purpose potential of the upper Island's forest, mountain and water resources it could take place in conjunction with existing economic activities and in harmony with the environment. Restricting tourist accommodation and support facilities to a few centres would provide a welcome diversity and long term future to settlements and areas pres-

301

ently dependent on the vacillations of the commodity market and exhaustible resources.

One tourism innovation that can broaden the economic base of rural areas without destroying the present life styles and functions of these areas is the farm holiday. In the United Kingdom this type of vacation is being promoted in marginal agricultural areas as a means of supplementing the farming income and maintaining the farm as a viable economic unit. In British Columbia the province has initiated a "Farm Vacation Program," but the scale has been small, with only five Vancouver Island farms being involved out of a total of twenty-four participants in 1977.[26] It would appear that there is considerable potential for the integration of the urban and rural dimensions of Vancouver Island's tourism through farm vacations, with visitors using the farms as bases for more widespread touring.

As with all tourist areas, Vancouver Island's tourist sector experiences seasonal fluctuations that hamper its overall development and acceptance as an employer. A business that experiences highly seasonal demand cannot attract the capital needed to provide high quality facilities and, because it cannot guarantee full-time employment, finds it hard to retain quality staff or develop loyalty and trust among the local community. Nevertheless, Vancouver Island is more fortunate than many other tourist areas, due to its natural environment, local population base and location. It possesses the mildest winter climate in Canada which has helped to make Victoria, not only a retirement centre, but also a refuge for many prairie farmers during the winter months. In addition, certain sports, such as fishing, hunting and skiing, reach their zenith outside the peak summer months and help to extend the tourist season. The diversity of the Island's economy and population produces a considerable pool of local people who can utilize the facilities in the off-season. Some package deals are beginning to encourage more out-of-season business, but to date most of the consumers are local or mainland residents who make use of the weekend specials only.[27] The industry needs to promote the off-season on a more extensive and cooperative basis so that out-of-province people are attracted and more facilities are used.

One area which could be pursued more aggressively in the off-season is the convention business. The convention visitor generally is the highest per capita spender among visitors, comes in the off-season and often returns with his family if favourably impressed. At present the Island can accommodate only the small conventions, with Victoria leading the way. Most of Victoria's conference facilities can handle fewer than 500 delegates, but the city's 1975 total was estimated at 31,000 people who spent approximately 6,500,000 dollars.[28] For larger conventions the choice is restricted to buildings such as sports arenas, many of which could not be considered ideal for regular conventions. What is needed in Victoria is a facility that is centrally situated and convenient to the numerous city hotels. Such a facility should be multi-purpose in design, so that it can be used on a year-round basis by local residents and be an addition to the community facilities, as well as a business operation. A convention centre need not be a large building, for a centre accommodating 1,500-2,000 delegates would be able to compete for ninety percent of the conference business in North America.[29]

FUTURE STRATEGIES

The pattern of tourism development on Vancouver Island has been one of growth through individual enterprise and initiative. This has resulted in a vigorous industry, utilizing the cultural and environmental resources of the Island to produce a wide variety of attractions and facilities. The individualistic nature of the industry, however, has also meant uncoordinated growth, inter-district competition and a lack of regional policy. The Island needs to be considered as a comprehensive tourist package that can be promoted as a whole, rather than as a combination of individual communities and operations. There is the danger that overdevelopment and short term planning by individual companies will ruin the very features that, traditionally, have attracted visitors to the Island. The growing signs of congestion and resident reaction to the tourist industry in certain areas indicates a need to move beyond promotion and marketing to a long-term planning policy that will integrate tourism into the Island's economy and social structure, so that is can provide the sustained yields of a renewable resource.

To move from the short-term horizons of the individual entrepreneurs to long-term comprehensive management of the Island region will require more government supervision of the tourist industry. The provincial government's traditional role as a general promoter of the industry should continue, since the Province had an estimated 400,000,000 dollar travel deficit in 1977.[30] However, the government could play a more active role in the planning and development of the industry to ensure that it developed in the interests of the community as a whole. Regional economic development could be aided by policies designed to foster more

303

interaction between the popular urban centres and surrounding hinterlands, which often pass unnoticed and unappreciated by tourists. To do this the provincial government should underwrite major developments that would become new magnets and subsidize tourist facilities in peripheral areas to encourage the diversification of their economies. But tourists will not visit these areas unless they are informed of the attractions. Therefore, it will be necessary for the government to become a partner with local Chambers of Commerce to develop a system of information centres that are operated under a common logo. In this way, tourists can be lured into new areas and encouraged to stay longer in British Columbia. The longer they stay the more they spend. Within individual communities it is the responsibility of local government to regulate the impact of the tourist industry. As the industry develops into a major business activity, bringing in money and people, local governments will need to ensure that social costs do not outweigh the monetary benefits. The economic situation may be assessed by such techniques as input-output analysis and the social impacts through attitude and perception studies. In general, the tourist sector has initiated most development, while city councils have simply reacted on an *ad hoc* basis to issues as they arise. But there are signs that certain councils are preparing to move beyond the promotional and *ad hoc* management phase to a more comprehensive approach through land use planning, heritage development and zoning. Victoria, essentially, has restricted the tourist activities to the Inner Harbour and along the waterfront of Old Town. This makes economic sense in that it brings diversity and life to the older, depressed area of the core, but it also creates new social and community problems. Following a policy of concentration accentuates the congestion, can create a tourist ghetto and hinders ancillary developments elsewhere in the metropolitan area.

Tourism is big business on the Island and shows every sign of growing larger. A multi-level government program to oversee the management of the industry is inevitable, since it affects so many aspects of daily life and can be a major source of revenue and employment. Only through coordinated management and planning can Vancouver Island's comprehensive tourist package be expanded to attract a large number of visitors, while retaining an image and life style that the permanent residents deem acceptable and appropriate.

REFERENCES

1. British Columbia, *Vancouver Island Tourism Facts Book 1977*. Victoria: Ministry of the Provincial Secretary and Travel Industry, Tourism British Columbia, 1978, p. 1.

2. *Ibid.*, p. 39.

3. PETERS, M. *International Tourism*. London: Hutchinson, 1969, p. 15.

4. ROBINSON, H. *A Geography of Tourism*. London: MacDonald and Evans, 1976, p. xxix.

5. *Ibid.*, pp. 18-28; and McINTOSH, R.W. *Tourism: Principles, Practices, Philosophies*. Columbia, Ohio: Grid Incorporated, Second Edition, 1977, pp. 21-69.

6. British Columbia, *British Columbia Tourist Accommodation Directory*. Victoria: Department of Travel Industry, 1977, pp. 16-31; and Personal Communication, Ministry of Recreation and Conservation, Parks Branch, Victoria, December 12, 1977. "These figures are for the recorded season. Recording season will vary from 2 to 12 months depending on which park and which year is being considered."

7. British Columbia, *Vancouver Island Tourism Facts Book 1977*. *op. cit.*, p. 1.

8. British Columbia, *Visitors '63*. Victoria: Department of Recreation and Conservation, Government Travel Bureau, 1964. The calculation is as follows: there were 943,140 United States and other Canadian provincial visitors in 1963 (p. 6); twenty-five percent of these visited Vancouver Island (p. 8), therefore, the Island received 235,785 visitors. As reported in the *Visitors '74* survey, forty percent of the Island's visitors were from the United States and other Canadian provinces, therefore, in 1963 this proportion would have amounted to 589,463 visitors in total.

9. British Columbia, *Vancouver Island Tourism Facts Book 1977*. *op. cit.*, p. 16.

10. "City Tourism Worth $137 million," *Victoria Times*, May 14, 1975, p. 13.

11. Personal Communication, Don Nixon, Greater Victoria Visitors Information Centre, April 24, 1978.

12. WAHAB, S. *Tourism Management*. London: Tourism International Press, 1975, p. 92.

13. British Columbia, *Visitors '74*, B.C. Research for Department of Travel Industry, p. 70.

14. British Columbia, *British Columbia Resident Tourism Survey 1976*. Vancouver: B.C. Research for Department of Travel Industry, 1977, pp. 71 and 72.

15. MURPHY, P.E. "The Attraction and Potential of British Columbia's Tourist Regions: A Discriminant Analysis," University of Victoria, Department of Geography, (forthcoming).

16. PETERS, M., *op. cit.*, p. 147.

17. Personal Communication, British Columbia Steamship Company, February 27, 1978; and Black Ball Transport, March 31, 1978. The Princess Marguerite had a passenger vehicle ratio of 21:1 in 1977, while the Coho had a 4:1 ratio.

18. This is based on the assumption that most passengers were visitors and that automobile visitors (three to a car) spent thirty dollars a day per capita, because they usually stayed overnight, while day visitors spent twenty dollars a day.

19. Personal Communication, Don Nixon, Greater Victoria Visitors Information Centre, April 24, 1978.

20. Personal Communication, Alice Hutchins, Nanaimo Visitors Information Centre, February 22, 1978.

21. YEOMANS, W.C. *Campbell River Outdoor Recreation and Environment Survey*. Victoria: W.C. Yeomans, Consulting Landscape Architect, 1973, p. 13.

22. *Ibid.*, p. 26.

23. "Trail Nearly Complete," *Victoria Times*, January 12, 1978, p. 41.

24. BARR, L.R. *Land of the Trust Islands: A Review of Subdivision Housing and Ownerships*. Victoria: Islands Trust, 1978, Tables 2 and 8.

25. "The Circus is Here," *Victoria Times*, March 30, 1978, p. 2.

26. British Columbia, *British Columbia's Family Farm Vacations — 1977 Farm Listings*. Victoria: Ministry of Agriculture, Youth Development Branch, 1977.

27. "Packages Called Key to Tourism," *Victoria Times*, November, 1977, p. 9; and "Package Deals Boast Tourism in Off-Season," *Victoria Times*, April 1, 1978, p. 15.

28. NIXON, D. *Victoria's Convention Centre*. Victoria: Greater Victoria Visitor Information Centre, October 1975, p. 3.

29. *Ibid.*, p. 4.

30. Personal Communication, Tourism British Columbia, Victoria, March 1978.

PLATE 27 Relaxation in the Mall, Victoria. *B.C. Government Photo* ▶

16 URBAN SOCIAL GEOGRAPHY

J. Douglas Porteous

Vancouver Island is Canada in microcosm. An isodemographic map would reveal that the population of this wooded wilderness is overwhelmingly urban. Because of the generous census definition of an urban settlement, the Island exhibits a wide array of urban sizes, from many logging and mining communities, with only a little over 1,000 inhabitants, to metropolitan Victoria, with a population of approximately 225,000.

Three tiers of urban settlement are apparent, each with its peculiar social geography. The lowest stratum consists of over a score of small, isolated single-enterprise towns, mostly distributed along the western and northern coasts. The company town is the typical model for these smaller Vancouver Island settlements which tend to be based on forestry, although there are a number of small mining and fishing towns. This tier is illustrated by a consideration of the contrasting towns, Tahsis and Gold River, both owned by the same forest company. At the other extreme lies greater Victoria, sole occupant of the upper tier, with about nine percent of the British Columbia population. Inter-provincial migration flows confirm Victoria's reputation as a retirement centre; its tourist image relies on an apparently British atmosphere. The middle tier of Island towns, all situated on the fragmented eastern coastal plain, comprises fewer than ten settlements of any size, and is dominated by Nanaimo. These middle stratum towns, whether minor regional centres or one-industry settlements, tend to have both company town and Victoria-like characteristics, depending upon size, location and economic base.

SINGLE-ENTERPRISE COMMUNITIES

Tahsis, a sawmilling centre built in the 1940's, represents the traditional company town. Its population of about 1,400 is largely divided between single family houses or duplexes and bunkhouse accommodation.

Until 1971 the town was unincorporated and approachable only by float plane or boat. Gold River is a pulp mill town of over 2,000 population, but is more readily accessible by road from Campbell River, which at eighty kilometres (fifty miles) distance is the nearest significant settlement.[1]

Tahsis displays the traditional company town morphology, with supervisors' residences "on the hill" and those of other workers at lower elevations. With a single major store, one hotel-bar, poor media reception, transportation problems, and almost incessant rain, Tahsis suffers from high labour turnover rates, especially among the bunkhouse population of single men. A sample survey of married workers in 1971 revealed that twenty-eight percent had moved from town to town more than twice in the previous decade, that seventy-two per cent had moved once or twice, and that only fifty-two percent had lived in Tahsis more than two years.[2] The town suffers from a severe population imbalance, with few unmarried women or retired persons.

Gold River was the first town to be built under "Instant Town" legislation, which was specifically developed to provide an alternative to the company town. The 1965 Amendment to the Municipal Act permits the immediate incorporation of a new resource town developed jointly by the provincial government and a private resource company. A varied housing mix is provided, housing may be bought or rented, and non-company private enterprise is promoted.

Gold River was carefully planned as a single neighbourhood, unfortunately divided by the main road. Two areas of single family or duplex houses flank a town core with commercial, recreational, educational, and apartment components. Small parks have been provided, and stands of indigenous trees left as screens and breaks in residential groupings. With a shopping plaza, low density housing, open planning, paved and curvilinear streets with standard lighting, underground cables, and a secondary treatment sewage plant, the town resembles a metropolitan suburb, yet is located in a wilderness forest setting. The "wilderness suburb" model, though deprecated by architects, is strongly favoured by the inhabitants.[3]

Given the contrast between Tahsis and Gold River, differences in attitudes toward isolated urban life might be expected. A survey of the environmental attitudes of residents, indeed, found that Tahsis was considered to be more isolated and to provide more "adventure."[4] Its population imbalance was recognized by eighty-two percent of its residents (Gold River, sixty-two percent). Gold River residents were unanimous in upholding the social equality prevailing in their town, and ninety-eight percent felt that social mixing between blue-collar and white-collar workers was common. Only forty-six percent of the Tahsis respondents agreed with this. Similar sharp contrasts appeared in answers to questions dealing with recreational and other facilities. While all Gold River respondents were satisfied, eight-eight percent of Tahsis residents felt that urban facilities were inadequate. In short, ninety-two percent of Gold River respondents felt that they lived in a "well-planned, model community," whereas eighty percent of the Tahsis respondents disagreed with the statement. Compared with the sawmill town, Gold River residents perceived fewer problems of company interference, housing allocation, and store prices.

On the other hand, residents of both towns felt that diversification of both schooling and job opportunities was necessary. Over two-thirds of respondents in each town agreed that "incorporation is a waste of time." Gold River residents were even more adamant than those of Tahsis in their feelings that, even with home ownership and incorporation, "the town still belongs to the company." When asked if they considered their town to be a company town, an affirmative response was obtained both in Gold River (eight-two percent) and Tahsis (ninety percent).

THE MIDDLE TIER

A series of six nuclei can be distinguished on the eastern coastal plain north of Victoria: Duncan; Ladysmith-Nanaimo; Parksville-Qualicum; Port Alberni; Courtenay-Comox; and Campbell River. These towns exhibit a much more diversified economic base than do the single-enterprise towns, almost all having past or present connections with farming, forestry, the military, railway traffic, port activities, and, more recently, tourism.

The present balance between these activities gives each community its particular social and economic flavour. Port Alberni's preoccupation with forestry endows it with the feeling of a large pseudo-company town. The smaller settlements are most evidently service-oriented centres for minor hinterlands, tourist bases, or residential locales for employees of mine and forestry operations in the vicinity. Nanaimo's large size, its economic diversification, its two-year Malaspina College, and its independent ferry link with Vancouver render the city a commercial and industrial rival of Victoria. Indeed, as an important distribution centre for the Island, Nanaimo has claimed the title of "Hub City."

Even this second largest urban settlement on Vancouver Island, however, was a company town for most of its life. Until World War II Nanaimo was dominated by one or two large coal mining companies. First worked by the Hudson's Bay Company, the coal seams between Lantzville and Ladysmith later were exploited by several companies, the two most powerful organizations being the Vancouver Coal Mining and Land Company (1861) and the Dunsmuir family interests (1871).[5] The Dunsmuirs, buying out their partners in 1883 and finally taking control of their rival in 1928, were the "coal kings" of this Canadian Coketown. After the 1920's the coal industry declined, yet today "the city is very much a 'coal town' in appearance."[6]

The city's radial plan, with streets diverging from the harbour like the spokes of a wheel, was laid down according to a plan created in the Vancouver Coal Company's British headquarters. A series of significant street and district names, such as Selby, Newcastle, Wellington, Jingle Pot, Extension, and Harewood, give the area a distinctive northern English flavour. By the 1920's the scatteration of small mining villages in the Nanaimo hinterland had resulted in a settlement pattern closely resembling those of the Northumberland-Durham and Yorkshire, Derby and Nottinghamshire coalfields.

Indeed, many of the miners were drawn from Scotland and northern England. Like Dunsmuir and other coal owners, the miners imported cultural baggage in the form of a distinctive life style. Mine owners wielded considerable power, which the Dunsmuirs manifested in the series of imposing mansions with which they crowned suitable elevations throughout the district. The Dunsmuirs were later to erect the fanciful Craigdarroch and Hatley mock castles in Victoria, vulgarly symbolizing their *nouveau riche* ascent "from coal mine to castle." Meanwhile, Nanaimo, in common with contemporary boom towns throughout the Americas, was embellished with an opera house in 1890.

Managers and upper-echelon employees were well housed, as, for example, in "seven-roomed houses of a very high class finish built for the official staff."[7] Workers' housing was often of hastier construction and in addition was frequently rented from the company. This proved an important factor during strikes and unionization drives; on occasion the militia were called upon to evict miners from company housing. The Nanaimo district shared the familiar history of mining town occurrences: explosions, flooding, and loss of life; market recessions and layoffs; strikes and lockouts. It retains a general atmosphere of rough-hewn proletarianism which contrasts markedly with the image of gentility assumed by bourgeois Victoria.

Nanaimo has changed character with the decline of coal and the rise of commerce, manufacturing, and the shipment of wood products through an improved port facility. Some remnants of its original Britishness remain, however. Most notable is the lighting of bonfires on November 5; Nanaimo is the only Canadian city which celebrates Bonfire Night. In this connection, the Victoria region is the only Canadian district into which the English skylark has been successfully introduced.

METROPOLITAN VICTORIA

Whereas the occupant of a middle tier town has access to a generous array of services, the isolated resource town resident experiences severe constraints upon his choice of residence, shopping, schooling, and occupation. In contrast, the metropolitan resident is faced with a bewildering array of choices, and constraints are more subtly applied. Urban geographers have tended to use residential location as a convenient yardstick for studying social differences in cities, because buying a dwelling is one of the major economic, social, and psychic investments of one's life.

People appear to establish their residences in areas where they themselves conform to the demographic attributes of existing residents. Parents in the child-rearing stage are keen to find streets replete with potential playmates for their children; they also look for neighbourhoods with good schools and low crime levels. Income constraints result in high land, large lots, and seafront locations being taken by the rich. Finally, racial, cultural, and sub-cultural differences transcend these life cycle and social class factors, resulting in the forced or voluntary segregation of certain groups.

Since techniques for the analysis of residential social patterns were first developed in the 1950's, psychologists,[8] sociologists,[9] and geographers[10] have derived residential segregation patterns for a large number of North American cities. It is assumed that the dwelling reflects the social attributes of the occupant. With data on the social attributes of urban census tracts and using a variety of factor and cluster analyses, clusters of census tracts possessing similar configurations of demographic attributes can be identified. In almost every case the same three variable clusters appear to be the most consistent descriptions of residential patterns at the census tract level. These will be termed:[11]

313

1. Life Level. Also known as social rank or economic status, life level is measured chiefly by education, occupation, and income.

2. Life Cycle. Also known as family status, life cycle stage depends upon household size and the age of household heads and their children, if any.

3. Life Style. As a sub-cultural phenomenon, life style may represent choice, as with Bell's consumerism, familism, careerism trichotomy.[12] Where choice is restricted, life style attributes are commonly associated with ethnic or racial status and related segregation patterns.

Although residential pattern analyses are conducted with aggregate data, it has been suggested that knowledge of an individual's life level, life cycle stage, and life style may provide sufficient data for a fairly good prediction of that individual's choice of residential location, likely behaviour patterns, and attitudes.[13]

In spatial terms the three patterns tend to form wedge-shaped sectors (life level), concentric rings (life cycle), and irregular clusters (life style). The existence of this very simplified triplex pattern was brought out very forcefully by Murdie's analysis of Toronto.[14] A similar factorial ecology of Victoria will not be attempted here, but the triplex model will be used as a framework for discussing the social patterning of the city.

Life Style

Life styles dependent upon choice do not always make a significant impress upon the townscape. Familism is expressed in the growth of suburbs to the north and west of Victoria, and careerism, to some extent, by the development of apartments in the urban core. Between 1952 and 1971 metropolitan Victoria doubled its apartment population every four years, increasingly through the erection of high-rise apartment buildings.[15] By the early 1970's apartment dwelling starts in Victoria were well above both national and provincial averages. Several apartment clusters have emerged. The original cluster, to the southeast of the central business district, has been joined by the redevelopment of much of James Bay, south of the Legislative Buildings. Other nodes appear on major thoroughfares leading from both west and east into the downtown core. It is notable that relatively few apartment buildings have secured waterfront locations; sea front lots normally are occupied by single-family dwellings or remain as open space.

314

Life styles associated with involuntary segregation are not as immediately obvious in Victoria as in larger metropolitan centres. As Lai indicates in an earlier chapter, Victoria has a rich ethnic mix. The most apparent signs of ethnicity are churches, social clubs, restaurants, and festivals. In residential terms there is some clustering of citizens of native Indian, East Indian, and Chinese origin, but only the latter can boast a fully-fledged "quarter," the few blocks of Chinatown north of the central business district.[16] The most obvious ethnic segregation pattern is regional, involving native Indians who occupy small reserves throughout the outer metropolitan district.

The apparent lack of large scale ethnic enclaves is related to the extreme Britishness of Victoria. Of thirty-five inner metropolitan census tracts, only three support a population with less than thirty-five percent British ancestry. These three cluster about the downtown core, from which a gradient of increasing Anglo-Canadianism extends in all directions (Figure 1,16). The whole of Oak Bay municipality, with the adjacent district of Ten Mile Point, boasts British ancestry for at least eighty-two percent of its inhabitants. No other census tract in the region reaches this level, and there is a significant break between those census tracts inside and almost all of those immediately outside the Oak Bay boundary. The data, therefore, confirm the image of extreme Britishness which envelops Oak Bay and culminates in its annual Tea Party. Oak Bay's other major shibboleth, the celebrated "Tweed Curtain," clearly coincides with the municipal boundary.

Within Oak Bay two peaks of extreme Britishness are apparent; in both Uplands and South Oak Bay the population with British ancestry exceeds eighty-six percent. These areas are noted for pseudo-British architectural styles, with an unfortunate tendency toward mock Tudor. Three lesser nodes of Britishness lie outside the Oak Bay-Ten Mile Point ghetto. Cordova Bay and outer Esquimalt reach British ancestry levels of seventy-eight percent and conform in housing quality to non-Uplands sectors of Oak Bay. A third node, of mixed housing quality, appears in the Rockland-Fairfield area.

It is significant that a map of achieved education levels would almost exactly duplicate the British ancestry distribution, with peaks in the Uplands, South Oak Bay, and Rockland areas. However, although equally British and highly educated, the inhabitants of South Oak Bay occupy housing of significantly lower value than those in the Uplands-Ten Mile Point region. Income levels in this area are somewhat lower than farther north, suggesting differences in occupational distribution.[17]

315

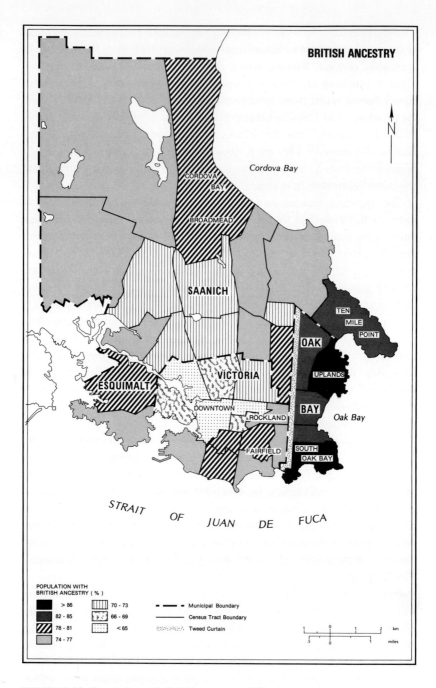

FIGURE 1,16 Population with British ancestry, 1971.

Life styles associated with Oak Bay are quietist in nature; municipal election campaigns are frequently issueless, in contrast with the continuous development debate in Saanich, which has much open land. In Victoria city recent elections have focused on neighbourhood power, and both politicians and developers have had to come to terms with increasingly powerful community groups. The downtown core is now almost wholly surrounded by active community associations rooted in neighbourhood-oriented life styles. Associations, such as those of James Bay, Victoria West, Fairfield, and Fernwood-Springridge, are devoted to neighbourhood upgrading and the prevention of unnecessary house demolition for apartment construction. According to neighbourhood planning theory, all four possess the basic neighbourhood amenities, and all perceive some degree of threat from downtown apartment expansion (Figure 2,16).[18] Rockland, much of which is under a heritage preservation order, remains aloof from this activity; its street pattern emphasizes its elite distinctiveness within the general city grid framework.

Life Level

The implications of social class differences introduced above are explicit in the pattern of housing values, which correlates closely with occupational and income distributions (Figure 3,16). The Victoria townscape clearly reflects the socio-economic differences subsumed in the term life level. From the core of the mid-nineteenth century city, established on the Inner Harbour, suburban expansion proceeded first in James Bay, the original home neighbourhood of the painter Emily Carr. By the early twentieth century the south and east coasts, previously adorned only by beach cottages, were becoming built up. Intra-urban mass transit systems, now long defunct, promoted interior infilling. With mass automobile use the growth trend continued eastward toward Oak Bay, and then turned north, as is evidenced today by the direction of central business district expansion, automobile strips, and subdivision development. The rapid expansion of Greater Victoria has resulted in a larger population in Saanich municipality than in the city of Victoria proper.

Within this matrix the prospective resident encounters a wide variety of residential environments. The downtown core and adjacent tracts of older housing to the east and south, together with industrial-commercial waterfront tracts to the west, exhibit the lowest average dwelling values. Besides modern apartment buildings, this area contains a considerable stock of deteriorated single family dwellings. Concentrations of small dwellings erected by Wartime Housing Limited close to shipyards and

317

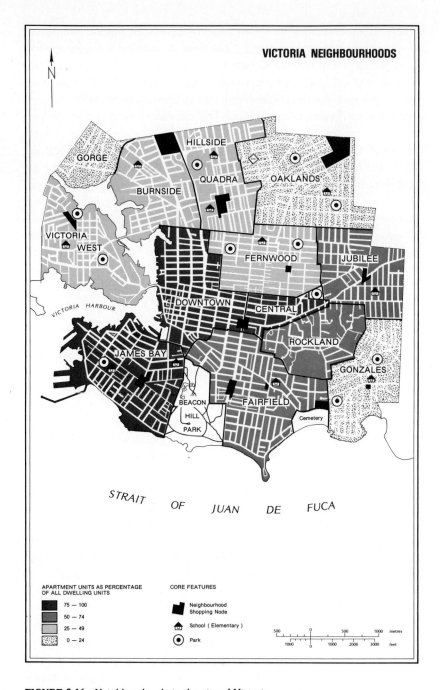

FIGURE 2,16 Neighbourhoods in the city of Victoria.

318

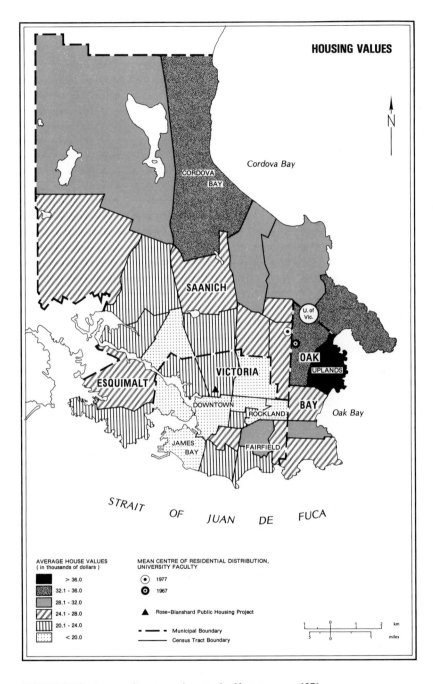

HOUSING VALUES

AVERAGE HOUSE VALUES
(in thousands of dollars)

> 36.0
32.1 - 36.0
28.1 - 32.0
24.1 - 28.0
20.1 - 24.0
< 20.0

MEAN CENTRE OF RESIDENTIAL DISTRIBUTION,
UNIVERSITY FACULTY

1977
1967

Rose-Blanshard Public Housing Project

Municipal Boundary
Census Tract Boundary

FIGURE 3,16 Average housing values in the Victoria area, 1971.

319

the naval dockyard have survived almost intact.[19] In the downtown core residential hotels and rooming houses are common, often located above commercial premises. The number of hotels catering to the independent elderly poor has declined in recent years, however, because of the enforcement of modern fire regulations. North of the central business district the ninety-unit Rose-Blanshard complex is the only significant public housing project in Victoria. This project replaced substandard dwellings, but studies indicate that the occupants of the area's original dwellings did not relocate within the project. Rather, they spread throughout the metropolitan area: "equally as many of the (original) Rose-Blanshard households were living in substandard dwellings after renewal as before."[20]

The housing value gradient largely repeats the Britishness gradient already established, rising in all directions from the core, but most steeply toward the Uplands peak, where average values are approximately double those of the city centre (Figures 1,16 and 3,16). A coastal gradient also is apparent. Moving east and then north from James Bay, almost every census tract is of higher real estate value than the last, until the Uplands peak is reached. Beyond Uplands, the whole northeastern coastal zone exhibits high housing values.

Uplands deserves special attention. Developed after 1909 on garden city lines by the Olmsteds, the Uplands was one of the earliest garden suburbs to be realized. With high ground, a lengthy coastline, Uplands Park, adjacent golf courses, the presence of the Royal Victoria Yacht Club, and, later, the University, the Uplands estate rapidly acquired a social cachet which it retains, almost unchallenged, today. Deed restrictions were followed by special by-laws, and dwelling quality control has ensured that the area, far from suffering decline in favour of newer elite subdivisions, has achieved an impressive longevity if not intimations of immortality.[21] The curved street pattern, irregularly shaped blocks, and abundance of vegetation, together with underground wiring throughout, provide a pleasant residential setting.

Other cores of high quality housing both predate and postdate the Uplands development. The Cordova Bay-Broadmead area has experienced the construction of high value housing tracts since the late 1960's. The Rockland area, a wooded ridge close to the inner city, epitomizes the fashionable street of the late nineteenth century, focusing on the residence of the Lieutenant-Governor. Despite apartment conversions, Rockland stands out as an area of high quality housing wholly surrounded by lower value housing tracts at lower elevations (Figure 3,16). The contrast with Fairfield, to the south, is particularly instructive. Both are very

British in ancestry, but the much lower housing values in Fairfield confirm its position as the most strongly British working class district in the region (Figure 1,16). Fairfield, however, is now undergoing the process of "gentrification," as middle class professionals increasingly invade to renovate its splendidly ornate turn of the century houses.

Images of housing tracts are significantly influenced by realtors. Content analyses of real estate advertisements lead to the conclusion that neighbourhood nomenclature is considered very important by the real estate industry.[22] In some cases, existing neighbourhood names are recognized and invested with supportive characteristics via advertising. Thus, Uplands and adjacent properties frequently are described as "executive," "spacious," "elegant," "exclusive," "prestigious" and the like. The newer, elite Broadmead development is "superb," "successful" and "professional." In contrast, central city housing is described as "cozy," "convenient," "cute," and even "handyman's special." The gentrification of Fairfield is indicated by terms such as "charming," "old-world" and "character."

Realtors go beyond image promotion. In Victoria they are actively engaged in extending the perceived boundaries of prestigious areas. For example, Oak Bay now is flanked by a realtor-generated tract known as "Oak Bay Border," and one may achieve a measure of prestige by relocating to "Uplands Edge." Elsewhere altitudinal terminology is used to distinguish certain sub-tracts from their undistinguished matrix, as with "Dean Heights" and High Quadra."

Similarly, the number of streets, shopping centres, and subdivisions which incorporate "university" into their titles attests to the social cachet of areas surrounding the University of Victoria campus. In this connection, studies of the residential choices of younger university faculty indicate an initial tendency to locate in the southwestern sectors of Victoria, often in apartments, with subsequent moves northeastward toward the campus, thus increasing housing value while lowering transportation costs.[23] Another study traced the residential relocations of fifty-two older faculty members throughout the decade 1967-1977. A campus-oriented agglomeration was characteristic, and during the period the mean centre of residential distribution moved slightly campusward (Figure 3,16). During the decade two-thirds moved to a census tract of similar or higher status. Fully seventy-five percent of the sample relocated after receiving a promotion, and fifty-five percent within two years of being promoted. Of course, the status-linked pattern of northeastward movement is confounded by relocation toward suburban space because of changes in family status.

Life Cycle

The importance of life cycle stage in residential choice in greater Victoria is enhanced by age structure imbalances: Victoria's population is considerably more elderly than that of British Columbia. While child-rearing families are constrained to choose peripheral suburbs, the independent elderly are attracted to the conveniences of the central city (Figure 4,16). The low income elderly inhabit the downtown core, fifty-nine percent of the population of which is over age fifty-five. Those with greater means are found in the apartments of James Bay (forty-four percent) or in the mixture of apartments and houses in Fairfield (forty-eight percent), a further impetus toward Fairfield's gentrification. The five inner-city neighbourhoods, Downtown, James Bay, Fairfield, Central, and Rockland, form an elderly-oriented zone where those over fifty-five account for at least forty percent, and those under twenty for less than twenty percent, of the population. A solid outer ring of family-oriented inner suburbs surrounds this core. Well-balanced Jubilee neighbourhood is anomalous, with a mixture of family-oriented persons and career-oriented young adults related to the adjacent hospitals.

Concern for the elderly in Victoria is reflected in recent geographical research. A study of transportation needs confirmed the value of the subsidized bus system, and found that trips taken by the elderly related mainly to shopping, visiting, and attending organizations.[24] In particular, profiles of elderly suburbanites clearly distinguished between drivers and non-drivers of similar health levels. Compared with non-drivers, drivers were younger, more residentially stable, had higher incomes, lived farther from downtown, tended to have a spouse living with them, rarely used buses or walked, made more trips, and were more satisfied with their transportation. The central city elderly include many non-drivers seeking locational convenience. Certain apartment blocks, notably those adjacent to Beacon Hill Park, have an overwhelmingly elderly tenant age structure. The dependent elderly are found in scattered rest homes and hospitals, in "board and room" complexes in the central city, and in senior citizens' projects throughout the suburbs.[25]

Less research has been devoted to Victoria's youth. Restricted in range by locomotion constraints, teenagers are likely to form gangs whose membership criteria are based upon propinquity. Loose-knit gangs exist throughout inner Victoria, but the gang whose turf comprises the Burnside area has received most attention (Figure 2,16).[26] Cognitive mapping of gang members' subjective social space confirmed the coincidence

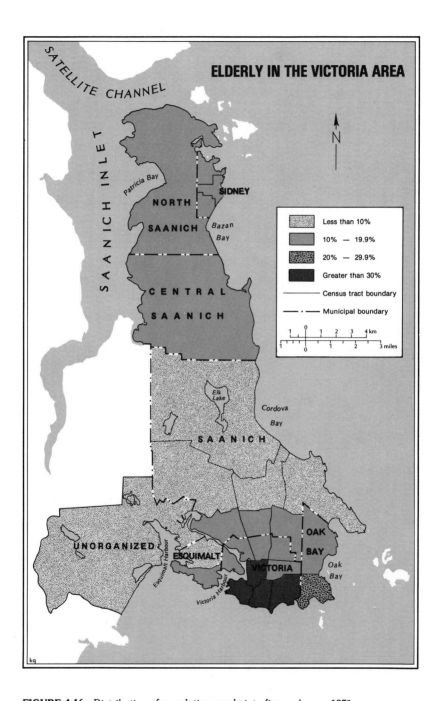

FIGURE 4,16   Distribution of population aged sixty-five and over, 1971.

323

of the perceived turf core with the mean centre of distribution of gang meeting places and activities. During the early 1970's greater Victoria municipalities attempted to reduce delinquency by creating neighbourhood drop-in centres for juveniles. Locational decision-making involved placing the centres either at the core of the gang turf or on the boundary between adjacent gang territories. The relative efficacy of these alternatives has not yet been adequately demonstrated.

CONCLUSION

Sufficient evidence has been presented to confirm that Victoria's residential patterning conforms largely to the North American norm. A tendency toward life cycle-related annular rings, life level sectors, and ethnic clustering is apparent. Whereas such patterns come into being in metropolitan centres through the operation of a wide array of factors, in isolated company towns segregation is frequently promoted through company policies.

Only the main features of the extreme examples of Vancouver Island's urban social geography have been considered. The subtleties of the Island's townscapes, particularly in terms of architecture, social structure, and activity patterns, would require a much longer exposition. The reader is, therefore, encouraged to take to the streets on his or her own urban geographical expedition.

REFERENCES

1. PORTEOUS, J.D. "Gold River: An Instant Town in British Columbia," *Geography*, 55, (1970), pp. 317-322.

2. PORTEOUS, J.D. "Quality of Life in British Columbia Towns: Residents' Attitudes," in Pressman, N. (ed.) *New Communities in Canada*. Waterloo: University of Waterloo, Faculty of Environmental Studies, 1976, pp. 332-346.

3. PORTEOUS, J.D. "Resource Towns in B.C. Opt for Wilderness Suburbs," *Habitat*, 17 (1974), pp. 2-7.

4. PORTEOUS, J.D., *op. cit.*, reference 2.

5. JOHNSON, P.M. *Nanaimo*. Nanaimo: Trendex, 1974, pp. 49-53.

6. *Ibid.*, p. 49.

7. *Ibid.*, p. 62.

8. TRYON, R.C. *Identification of Social Areas by Cluster Analysis*. Berkeley: University of California Press, 1955.

9. SHEVKY, E., and BELL, W. *Social Area Analysis*. Stanford: Stanford University Press, 1955.

10. BERRY, B., "Internal Structure of the City," *Law and Contemporary Problems*, 30 (1965), pp. 111-119.

11. PORTEOUS, J.D. *Environment and Behavior: Planning and Everyday Urban Life*. Reading, Massachusetts: Addison-Wesley, 1977, p. 144.

12. BELL, W. "The City, The Suburb, and a Theory of Social Choice," in Greer, S., *et. al. The New Urbanization*. New York: St. Martin's Press, 1965, pp. 132-168.

13. YEATES, M., and GARNER, B. *The North American City*. New York: Harper, 1971, pp. 286-308.

14. MURDIE, R.A. *Factorial Ecology of Metropolitan Toronto 1951-61*. Chicago: University of Chicago, Department of Geography, Research Paper No. 116, 1969.

15. MURPHY, P.E. "Apartment Location: The Balance Between Developers and Community," in FORWARD, C.N. (ed.) *Residential and Neighbourhood Studies in Victoria*. Victoria: University of Victoria, Department of Geography, Western Geographical Series, Vol. 5, 1973, pp. 149-177.

16. LAI, C-Y. "Socio-Economic Structures and Viability of Chinatown," in FORWARD, C.N., *op. cit.*, reference 15, pp. 101-129.

17. FORWARD, C.N. "The Immortality of a Fashionable Residential District: The Uplands," in FORWARD, C.N., *op. cit.*, reference 15, Figure 1,1, p. 2.

18. MURPHY, P.E. *A Neighbourhood Study of Victoria, B.C.* Victoria: City of Victoria, 1974.

19. GOULD, C. *Wartime Housing in Victoria, B.C.: Resident Reaction to Standardized Housing Design*. Victoria: University of Victoria, Department of Geography, unpublished M.A. thesis, 1977.

20. ROBERTSON, R.W. "Anatomy of a Renewal Scheme," in FORWARD, C.N., *op. cit.*, reference 15, pp. 40-100; and PORTEOUS, J.D., *op. cit.*, reference 11, pp. 304-306.

21. FORWARD, C.N., *op. cit.*, reference 17, pp. 1-39.

22. Undergraduate research studies (unpublished) of this phenomenon include, TAYLOR, R. "The Residential Geography of Victoria as Perceived by the Real Estate Industry" (1973), and JUNE, L. "The Real Estate Industry and Its Influence on Neighbourhood Images," (1977), Department of Geography, University of Victoria.

23. Undergraduate research studies of this topic include KEHL, B. "An Examination of Social Ranking, Job Promotions, and Intra-urban Residential Mobility," (1977), Department of Geography, University of Victoria.

24. JONES, K.A. *The Intraurban Mobility of the Elderly: A Study of a Suburban Silver Threads Centre, Victoria, B.C.*. Victoria: University of Victoria, Department of Geography, unpublished M.A. thesis, 1975.

25. MURPHY, P.E., *et. al. Housing for the Elderly.* Victoria: St. Joseph's Church, 1974.

26. PORTEOUS, J.D. "The Burnside Teenage Gang: Territoriality, Social Space, and Community Planning," in FORWARD, C.N., *op. cit.*, reference 15, pp. 130-148.

PLATE 28 Views of Modern Mining (by I.H. Norie). *N. Bateman Photos* ▶

17 THE ESSENCE OF VANCOUVER ISLAND

I.H. Norie

Photo Captions Page 344

4

4

LIST OF PHOTOGRAPHS

Plate

1   The beautiful and rugged coastline of Vancouver Island's west coast with the village of Ucluelet in the foreground. *B.C. Government Photo*

2   Friendly Cove, one of the many isolated lighthouses along the rugged western coastline of Vancouver Island. *B.C. Government Photo*

3   Kyoquot, a typical coastal fishing village nestled in a protective inlet. *B.C. Government Photo*

4   The west coast shorelines are beautiful but inhospitable. *B.C. Government Photo*

5   A typical "float camp" along the west coast of the Island, home to loggers and fishermen. *B.C. Government Photo*

6   Northern Island landscape with Utah mine development in foreground. *Nick Bateman Photo*

7   Campbell River, sportsman's paradise and the supply centre for the Northern Island. *Daily Colonist Photo by Petri*

8   Nanaimo, former coal town, now the Island's Hub city for industry and commerce. *I.H. Norie Photo*

9   Beauty and tranquility of Ladysmith Harbour with the central Island mountains in the background. *I.H. Norie Photo*

10   Home for many logging families, a now seldom used float camp on an inland lake. *B.C. Government Photo*

11   Cowichan Lake Village, centre of logging activity for the past 60 years. *Victoria Press, J. Ryan Photo*

12   The city of Duncan, urban centre of the Cowichan Valley. *I.H. Norie Photo*

13   Tranquility and rural atmosphere of the Saanich Peninsula before development. *I.H. Norie Photo*

14   Victoria's Inner Harbour, with Metchosin and Sooke Hills in the background. *I.H. Norie Photo*

344

EPILOGUE

Vancouver Island is a distinctive region of British Columbia made up of many contrasting elements that somehow mesh with each other to produce a certain degree of functional unity. The key to the Island's unity is the pervading influence of the forest industry. Wilderness and city cooperate in the great task of harvesting trees, on the one hand, and processing them into marketable wood and paper products, on the other, for shipment to consumers throughout the world. The transportation system performs effective linkages between the rural, primary resource extraction realm and the urban, manufacturing and servicing realm, as well as providing external connections with the North American mainland and points overseas. Although the Island has functional unity, its many contrasts lend it a character that makes it an interesting and satisfying place to residents and visitors alike.

Its resource wealth, favourable climate and scenic qualities combine to endow Vancouver Island with advantages over many other parts of the country. Although its economic dependence on the forest industry is pronounced, it enjoys the diversifying effect of government activities, both provincial and federal. Development throughout British Columbia inevitably fosters provincial civil service growth of benefit to Victoria and its situation on the Pacific enhances its national importance for military, coast guard, hydrographic and fisheries bases. Probably its basic hedge against future adversity is its inherent attraction as a place to live or visit. Many people retire to Vancouver Island, bringing their sometimes considerable estates with them. On a small scale, this movement resembles the flocking of people to the sunbelt of the southern United States. Vancouver Island certainly is no Florida, but in the northern, snowbelt land of Canada even Vancouver Island looks good.

Despite this favourable future assessment, there are signs of possible trouble unless management policies and practices are improved to use the Island's resources more wisely. The dangers of environmental damage through water and air pollution, overcutting of trees, or excessive scarring of the landscape by logging, mining or construction have been pointed out in various contexts. Many of the Island's attractions and potential for economic diversification depend on the unimpaired preservation of its favourable natural environment. The growth industry of tourism for example, relies heavily on the Island's natural attractions, as do many recreational and sporting activities, such as hiking, boating and fishing. The maintenance of environmental quality and the careful management of the Island's resources will go a long way toward the assurance of continued prosperity.

345

THE CONTRIBUTORS

Michael C.R. Edgell, B.A., Ph.D., Associate Professor, Department
of Geography, University of Victoria. Dr. Edgell received
undergraduate and graduate training and degrees from the
University of Birmingham and University College, London.
From 1965 to the present he has taught at the University of
Victoria and Monash University, Australia. His teaching
and research interests include biogeography, environmental
perception, and forest resource utilization, especially around
urban centres.

Charles N. Forward, B.A., M.A., Ph.D., Professor and Chairman, Department of Geography, University of Victoria. For a period of eight
years before going to Victoria in 1959, Dr. Forward was engaged
in research with the Geographical Branch, Ottawa. His degrees
are from the University of British Columbia and Clark University and his major research interests are urban geography and
port functions. Dr. Forward served as President of the Canadian
Association of Geographers in 1977-78.

Harold D. Foster, B.Sc., Ph.D., Associate Professor, Department of
Geography, University of Victoria. Dr. Foster received his
university education at University College, London where
he was awarded his B.Sc. in 1964 and Ph.D. in 1968. A geo-
morphologist and hydrologist by training, his main research
interests are natural hazards, renewable energy policy and
water resources management. He is the editor of the *Western Geographical Series.*

Charles H. Howatson, B.A., M.A., Associate Professor, Department
of Geography, University of Victoria. Mr. Howatson took
his undergraduate training in geology and M.A. (1947) in
geography at U.B.C. and attended Syracuse and the University of Washington for post-graduate training. His major
fields of interest are in geology, land use problems and air
photo interpretation.

David Chuen-Yan Lai, B.A., M.A., Ph.D., Associate Professor, Department of Geography, University of Victoria. Dr. Lai received his Ph.D. from the London School of Economics and Political Science, University of London. His research interests include overseas Chinese in Canada, industrialization and urbanization of Hong Kong and China.

Malcolm A. Micklewright, B.A., Ph.D., Associate Professor, Department of Geography, University of Victoria. Dr. Micklewright received his Ph.D. in 1970 at the University of Washington. He was born in Winnipeg, Manitoba where he received his primary and secondary education. Post-secondary education was at the University of Washington. He is currently teaching regional analysis and regional planning at the University of Victoria in the Geography Department. His research interests are mainly in inter-country comparisons of regional development strategies.

Peter E. Murphy, B.Sc., M.A., Ph.D., Associate Professor, Department of Geography, University of Victoria. Dr. Murphy was born in England. After completing his B.Sc. (Econ.) at the London School of Economics he attended the Ohio State University where he obtained his M.A. and Ph.D. degrees. The focus of his graduate training was consumer behavior and this has evolved into a specific interest in the tourism industry since his arrival in Victoria in 1970. Dr. Murphy's current research interests are urban planning and tourism development.

Ian H. Norie, Department of Geography, University of Victoria. A native-born Canadian, Ian Norie was initially trained in electronics, survey and photogrammetric engineering, and cartography. During the period 1957 to 1969 he was promoted to various technical positions within the Ministry of the Environment, Province of British Columbia where he reached the position of Assistant Supervisor. Since that date he has worked at the University of Victoria where he is now the Senior Academic Assistant in charge of administrative and technical services in the Department of Geography and production manager of the *Western Geographical Series*.

Robert E. Pfister, B.Sc., M.Sc., Ph.D., Assistant Professor, Department of Geography, University of Victoria. Dr. Pfister is a resource geographer with specialization in recreational resources. His interests include resource policy, land use economics, and water resource conservation along with a regional teaching/research commitment to Latin America. He obtained his doctorate from Oregon State University in 1976.

J. Douglas Porteous, B.A., M.A., Ph.D., Professor, Department of Geography, University of Victoria. Dr. Porteous received his B.A. and M.A. degrees from Oxford University, and his doctorate from the University of Hull. He then spent a year as a post-doctoral fellow at Massachusetts Institute of Technology and is an affiliate of the Harvard-M.I.T. Joint Center for Urban Studies. He has been a faculty member at the University of Victoria since 1969.

William M. Ross, B.Ed., M.A., Ph.D., Assistant Professor, Department of Geography, University of Victoria. Dr. Ross is a native British Columbian who has worked in the fishery industry. He attended both U.B.C. and the University of Toronto and completed his Ph.D. at the University of Washington. Dr. Ross teaches courses on resource management and is currently working amongst other topics on the legal and political problems of fishery management.

W.R. Derrick Sewell, B.Sc. Econ., M.A., Ph.D., Professor, Department of Geography, University of Victoria. Dr. Sewell is an expert on resources management policy who received his Ph.D. degree from the University of Washington. He has undertaken research on water, energy, fisheries, and recreational resources problems in North America, Europe, and other parts of the world. He is author or co-author of some 20 books and well over 100 articles on such matters. He is an advisor to the United Nations, the World Bank, and governments of several countries on problems of water and energy resource development.

348

Stanton Tuller, B.A., M.A., Ph.D., Associate Professor, Department of Geography, University of Victoria. Dr. Tuller received his B.A. degree from the University of Oregon in 1966 and both his M.A. and Ph.D. from the University of California in Los Angeles, the former in 1967 and the latter in 1971. Dr. Tuller's research and teaching interests have as their focus the applied aspect of micro-climatology.

Colin J.B. Wood, B.A., M.A., Ph.D., Assistant Professor, Department of Geography, University of Victoria. Dr. Wood received his Bachelor of Arts Degree in Geography and Anthropology at the University College of Wales, Aberystwyth in 1963. He came to Canada in 1964 and undertook graduate work at McMaster University, Hamilton, Ontario where he received his Master of Arts Degree in 1966 and his Doctoral Degree in 1971. Since 1969 he has been teaching Economic and Cultural Geography, specializing in the Resource Management field. He has completed and published research on topics such as settlement location, decision making and innovation diffusion, and is currently working on the analysis of resource management conflicts.